The WRESTLECRAP Book of Lists!

The WRESTLECRAP
Book of Lists!

R.D. Reynolds &
Blade Braxton

ECW PRESS
ecwpress.com

Published by ECW PRESS
2120 Queen Street East, Suite 200, Toronto, Ontario, Canada M4E 1E2

LIBRARY AND ARCHIVES CANADA CATALOGUING IN PUBLICATION DATA

Reynolds, R.D., 1969-
The WrestleCrap book of lists! / R.D. Reynolds and Blade Braxton.

ISBN: 978-1-55022-762-8

1. Wrestling—Miscellanea. 2. Wrestlers — Miscellanea. I. Braxton, Blade.
II. Title.

GV1195.R493 2007   796.812   C2006-906829-1

Cover design: Randy & Crystal Baer
Typesetting: Mary Bowness
Printing: Thomson-Shore
Cover photos: Matt Balk
Authors photo: Troy Ferguson
Color Photo Section Credits: Zombie and Jay Lethal: Christine Coons; Kurt Angle: Troy Ferguson; Wildcat Willie: Mike Lano. All other photos: Matt Balk.

This book is set in Cronos

DISTRIBUTION

CANADA: Jaguar Book Group, 100 Armstrong Avenue, Georgetown, Ontario L7G 5S4

UNITED STATES: Independent Publishers Group, 814 North Franklin Street, Chicago, Illinois 60610

EUROPE: Turnaround Publisher Services, Unit 3, Olympia Trading Estate, Coburg Road, Wood Green, London N2Z 6T2

PRINTED AND BOUND IN THE UNITED STATES

ECW PRESS
ecwpress.com

This book is dedicated to Earthquake John Tenta, Allen "Ted" Baer and Paul Ferguson. We miss you dearly, but we know you are up there laughing down at us.

Both authors would like to thank:

The WrestleCrap crew: Dr. Keith Lipinski, Madison Carter, Alfonzo Tyson, Derek Burgan, Jed Shaffer, Harry Simon and Sean Carless (www.thewrestling fan.net), Adam Boshnyak and Bill Brown; the staff of Figure Four Weekly (f4wonline.com), namely Bryan Alvarez and Vince Verhei; Dave Meltzer of the Wrestling Observer (wrestlingobserver.com); the entire staff of ECW Press; and last but certainly not least, Greg Ogorek at Global Internet (globalin-ternet.net), the best Web host in the known universe.

We would especially like to thank every loyal WrestleCrapper holding this book, or any we've spoken to in person or on the Internet. You guys rule.

R.D. Reynolds would like to thank: My wife, Crystal (Mrs. Deal), and my son Rylan (R.D., Jr.), for putting up with the countless hours I was away, working on this book; my family, especially my mom, my dad (whom I miss dearly) and my brother, for believing in me; my friends Eric Kuehling, Casey (Trash Losagain) Stephon, "Diamond" Dan Garza, Jeff Cohen; Emma McKay; Mark Manford; Terry and Sally Corman, as well as everyone at Firehouse Image Center; Matt at X-Entertainment.com. Glory be to God for giving me the strength to make it through this book.

Blade Braxton would like to thank: The good Lord above; my family: my mom and dad — Pam and the late Paul Ferguson (Miss you, Dad); Amy, Austin and Elaina Wright; John, Lucille and Dennis Guthrie; Corliss and Bill Wheatley; my friends: Corey Merrill, Tony Kyles, Chris Mason, Gloria Starkey, Geoff Poston, Kris Thomas, Troy Mott, Steve Schneider, Floyd McMillin, and Kevin Garner. Extra special thanks to my alter ego, Troy Ferguson. If "he" didn't endure years of taking major amounts of crap from family/girl-friends/various people for watching wrestling, "Blade Braxton" wouldn't have been able to write this book. And of course, my good pal R.D., who welcomed me aboard this crazy train in the first place. Anybody else I forgot — hey, there's always next time.

Contents

Introduction
Pro Wrestling is Dumb

Pro wrestling is dumb.

An odd way, you are no doubt thinking, for us to begin. It's like we're spitting in the face of our target audience. After all, you probably didn't pick up something called *The WrestleCrap Book of Lists!* believing you were going to learn how to fix your golf slice or program in C++. No, you have this book in your hands because you, dear reader, are a fan of professional wrestling.

With such an opening, then, you may be led to believe the folks who penned this tome are not even true professional wrestling fans. Maybe we're just a couple of schmucks who want to drag wrestling through the mud and make both it and its fans look bad.

Actually, nothing could be further from the truth. We love wrestling and are, in fact, huge fans of the business. Actually, we'd go one step further than that — we have been obsessed with the business for virtually our entire lives. We would not want to see the sum of the money we have spent on our hobby: for tickets to live events, videotapes, DVDs, video games, action figures, magazines, books and inflatable chairs.

Yes, inflatable chairs, which were purchased, mind you, because they were splashed with a WWE logo.

It takes a special kind of person to reach into one's wallet and spend $19.99 on an inflatable chair. And, unquestionably, some would say we *are* special — special in a way that might suggest we probably should have ridden the short bus to school. And maybe we should have . . . but we don't care. We are hopelessly obsessed with professional wrestling. Not only have we spent all that money over the years, but we've spent something far more valuable on our obsession: time. Each of us has only so many days on this earth, so many hours in which to soak up all the wonders of the world. We, the authors of this book, choose to live it camped in front of a television set, screaming at grown men dressed as kings and midgets with shillelaghs, and having pretend fights. And why? Because it's so much fun. Seriously . . . has there ever been another form of entertainment quite like professional wrestling? It really is the best of all conceivable means of entertainment. Consider every form of amusement life has to offer. What other medium mixes and melds so many different elements in a single package? Wrestling gives you everything: action, comedy, suspense and heartbreak. And it's all held together by an athletic performance that can be categorized, at its peak, as an art form. And while pundits may scoff at hardcore fans rating matches with a star system as if they were movie critics, it makes perfect sense. Because wrestling is entertainment — it should be critiqued as such. That's why some people are so fanatical they become geeks: the kind of person who spends the better part of his or her life debating whether Ric Flair vs. Ricky Steamboat was actually a better match than Razor Ramon vs. Shawn Michaels. And of course it was . . . while the atmosphere of Ramon-Michaels was off the charts, this was largely because it took place at *WrestleMania*. It isn't even open to debate that the sheer technical acumen on display in the Flair-Steamboat encounter was far superior. Ramon-Michaels had the benefit (and some critics would say crutch) of the ladder stipulation, and while it unquestionably set the standard for what would become the hardcore revolution of the mid-1990s, it lacked the psychology and pacing of the NWA title match. Spots in Ramon-Michaels could understandably be seen as contrived, while Flair-Steamboat had no such weakness; it was two men exchanging holds, changing with the ebb and flow of the audience, two masters modifying the match on the fly to keep the audience on the edge of their seats. So while Ramon-Michaels may have been more *exciting,* it was not a *better* match than Flair-Steamboat. Oh, and we should note that the Flair-Steamboat match in discussion is the *Wrestle War: Music City Showdown* bout (on May 7, 1989, from Nashville), which slightly eclipses the April 2, 1989, three-falls encounter at *Clash of the Champions VI: Ragin' Cajun* from the New Orleans Superdome. While both are no doubt five-star classics, the latter match was longer, featuring a brilliant double-chicken-wing submission finish in the second fall, the pacing and psychology of the former was superior, and the post-match angle with Terry Funk attacking Flair, thus setting up the next program, was fantastic.

Now, where were we?

Right . . . explaining why we opened the book with "Pro wrestling is dumb."

You see, this stupidity opens the door for not only obsessed fans, but more importantly, for some downright bizarre folks in front of the fans and behind the scenes. It leads not only to insanity in the ring, but back-stage as well. With so many weirdos competing for such a small spotlight, comedy ensues.

Sometimes that lunacy is displayed right before us, on our TV screens. Other times, it is shrouded behind the curtain. But it's all there, and the time has come to categorize and criticize and mock and lampoon and —

hell — just have some fun with it.

This book is not meant to be read in one sitting, though you are more than welcome to do so. It's designed so that you can sit down, read a list or two, have a laugh, then continue on your merry way. And while this is a book of lists, it is more than that.

Consider it a wrestling encyclopedia for those with ADD.

There are things in this book you may have never heard of — characters long since forgotten, storylines you cannot imagine ever taking place and merchandise that will have you scratching your head. But it's all here, and it has all taken place within the confines of this great business.

So while we stand by our opening sentence, perhaps we should expand upon it a bit.

Pro wrestling is dumb . . . but that, dear reader, is what makes it great.

A Question of Character

What does it take to be successful in pro wrestling? One word: *character*. Not the ability to do the right thing or any of that other hackneyed garbage, but rather the creation of a character that folks want to see. When you think back on wrestling's colorful history, the first thing that comes to mind isn't the matches themselves — it's the characters who made them so much fun to watch.

Perhaps the most important part of a wrestler's persona isn't his in-ring ability or what he says, but rather his name. For example, would "Stone Cold" Steve Austin have become the biggest star in the business had he gone by the moniker Chilly McFreeze (which was, believe it or not, a suggestion from the WWF creative team)? And there are also names that are amazingly worse, names no one could have ever thought made any sense at all. Such as these handles . . .

THE 8 STUPIDEST RING NAMES IN WRESTLING HISTORY

8. **Test:** A lot of people have questioned over the years why Andrew Martin hasn't made a bigger impact in the business. Upon initial glance, he has it all: at a legit six-foot-six and over 250 pounds of solid muscle, he seemed guaranteed to become a huge star. However, things didn't

pan out for the big guy, and while injuries certainly played a role in his stunted development, his name certainly didn't help. After all, he was Test. Not *The* Test, not *A* Test, just Test. Is that someone you'd fear? That you'd want to cheer for? Here's a real test: can you imagine anyone ever saying, "My favorite wrestler is Test!" That just sounds stupid.

7. **Bo Dupp:** Here's another name we simply don't get. The story was that Bo was part of a tag team with his "brother" Jack Dupp. *Jack Dupp.* That we get. It's like "jacked up." It's stupid, but at least it sort of makes sense. But what the hell is Bo Dupp? Is he "bowed up" like an archer? Does he wrap presents in his spare time? We've pondered the mystery of Bo Dupp for years. And while we've yet to figure it out, we have come to this conclusion: if you have to spend that much time just trying to decipher a name, it's not a good sign.

6. **Key:** Yes, there was a wrestler named Key. No, he was not a locksmith. That would have made sense. Okay, maybe not, but it would have made a hell of a lot more sense than having a drug dealer named Key. Poor Vic Grimes didn't just have a bad name working against him, but a horrible outfit to boot, as he just showed up out of the blue one week dressed all in white. He actually looked less like a drug dealer than an ice-cream man. We've never bought drugs (we'd never do something so illegal or immoral), but if we did, it wouldn't be from a guy named Key who looks like he'd be more comfortable selling us an Eskimo Pie.

5. **Dingo Warrior:** Okay, we could buy this one if this face-painted wildman was representing Australia (though "dingo" still sounds like

a kiss of death for a wrestling name, regardless of origin). Anyway, it wasn't long before the man behind the face paint decided this moniker was not quite what he needed to be considered a major star, and thus dropped the Dingo in favor of Ultimate. He would later decide that he liked the Warrior aspect of the name so much he legally changed his name to Warrior Warrior. If there was a list in this book of wrestling's worst real names — hell, make that the world's worst real names — Warrior Warrior would be at the top.

4. Hugh Morrus: Reader, we ask you to pause for a moment and read that name aloud. Go ahead, do it. We won't laugh at you. Ha! We lied. The wrestler in question was, indeed, named Hugh Morrus. He was the Laughing Man. Would this make you want to buy a ticket? Would it make you want to cheer for this man? Maybe if he was a comedian. Which he wasn't. He was a wrestler, remember? We defy anyone to explain how this could possibly be taken for anything more than a dumb — and, ironically, not particularly humorous — joke. The saddest part is that he actually had an even worse name prior to becoming Hugh . . .

3. Man Of Question: When your name is not even a name, but a phrase, you're really screwed. No wonder he went with Hugh Morrus.

2. Henry O. Godwinn: What's so dumb about that, you ask? Well, look at his initials. H-O-G. *Hog!* See, he was from a family of farmers! Wee doggies, break out the moonshine, Ethyl! We seriously cannot imagine a dumber ring name than that.

1. Phinneas I. Godwinn: Or maybe we can. Sigh.

In addition to having names that don't completely suck, the most successful wrestling personalities have nicknames that kick ass as well. For instance, Bret Hart is The Hitman. Shawn Michaels = Heartbreak Kid. And of course, everyone knows "Your Olympic Hero" is Kurt Angle. Sometimes, though, things just don't pan out, even for the biggest superstars in the industry. Like in the case of . . .

THE 7 WRESTLING NICKNAMES THAT SOMEHOW JUST DIDN'T CATCH ON

7. Creepy Little Bastard: You have to feel for poor Jay Reso. While the guy undoubtedly has charisma and wrestling ability out the wazoo, he's been stuck with some pretty bad luck. Following the breakup of his tag team with "brother" Edge, it took him a while to gain traction as a solo act. When he finally did, settling upon a kind of sleazy, smarmy bad-guy persona, it seemed the sky was the limit, with fans ratcheting up their hate. But his run came to a screeching halt when it was decided the fans needed something to chant at him. And thus, Christian, the Creepy Little Bastard, was born. WWE went the whole nine yards, from making T-shirts with the slogan to having announcers mention his new handle approximately every four seconds anytime he was on-screen. On top of that, the top star in the company at the time, Steve Austin, appeared mid-ring and commanded that the fans chant "CLB! CLB!" in his presence. And how did those seat fillers respond? If you guessed, "With utter and complete silence," step right up and claim your prize. When Stone Cold can't make something work, it's probably time to just pack it in.

6: The Bionic Redneck: Speaking of everyone's favorite rattlesnake, Steve Austin was actually blessed with a ton of great nicknames. We are certain Austin must have come up with all of them on his own, since, prior to his rise as Stone Cold, the WWF marketing team . . . Well,

PHOTO: ECW

And that's the bottom line, 'cuz Chilly McFreeze said so!

Chilly McFreeze, remember? This is because they are idiots. Austin, though, he was a clever guy. Not only did he originate Stone Cold, but he also struck gold with the Texas Rattlesnake. Alas, even a guy that crafty is bound to hit the skids every so often, as he did with the handle the Bionic Redneck. What the hell does that even mean? Sure, he had just gotten back from neck surgery, but somehow the words *bionic* and *redneck* should never go together, kinda like *poison ivy* and *sphincter*. Oh, and pointing out that Steve Austin was the same name Lee Majors used in *The Six Million Dollar Man* doesn't make you cool. It makes you a dork just like us. But maybe if they had drilled a hole in the back of his head that you could look through like a telescope . . .

5. **White Thunder:** Who would ever have guessed that Scott Steiner was a huge Darrel Dawkins fan? (Okay, okay — with that joke and the *Bionic Man* action figure bit above, we've successfully fulfilled our 1970s reference quota for the book.) While Dawkins was known as Chocolate Thunder, Steiner apparently also looked to the skies and determined that it was his destiny to be known as White Thunder. Following a heel turn and the most extreme of extreme makeovers known to man, in which he went from being a guy with a collegiate wrestler gimmick to being the most jacked-up nymphomaniac the world has ever seen, Steiner was in need of an edgy handle. He would eventually try out a whole slew of nicknames, including Superstar and the Big Bad Booty Daddy. While we have no earthly idea what it means to be a booty daddy, let alone a big bad one, we do know that he quickly dumped the White Thunder epithet following a slew of complaint calls made to WCW's parent company, AOL Time Warner, for its alleged white supremacist allusion.

4. Big Nasty: When Paul Wight made the jump from WCW to the WWF in 1999, the company wasn't quite sure what to call him. After all, "Paul Wight" isn't the most threatening-sounding moniker, and even guys seven feet tall and 500 pounds need a decent name. So after weeks of speculation, Wight made his debut as the Big Nasty. No joke, every single time we heard this we thought it was a tie-in with McDonald's. See, their sandwich was actually called the Big Tasty, but one bite and you'd see our version, while admittedly not as market-able, was probably closer to the truth. We can only theorize that Wight, with his history of weight-control issues, would have thought the same thing, and therefore it's probably for the best that he was quickly redubbed the Big Show.

3. The Charismatic Enigma: Jeff Hardy is, uhh, unique. In fact, you could say he is mysterious — an enigma, if you feel like grabbing a thesaurus. And to his legions of female fans, he is obviously charismatic. Hey . . . you could say he was the Charismatic Enigma! You could say that, and if you did, you might just wind up in a stupid book of stupid wrestling lists, with your idea for naming the guy making the "dumbest nick-names" list. Congrats, TNA — you've finally made the big time!

2. Booger Red: The Undertaker is another one of those guys who has been around forever, and thus has been reincarnated countless times. When you're near the top of cards for the better part of fifteen years, this type of thing happens. So it makes perfect sense that the man once known as Mark Calloway would accumulate a veritable laundry list of monikers, such as the Dead Man, the Phenom, and the American Badass. Oh yeah, and our personal favorite, Booger Red. Sadly, this handle was short-lived and never fully explained, but we can only speculate it was given to him after someone caught him going "knuckle deep."

1. **The Colossus of Boggo Road:** Since most folks have zero clue what — or where — the hell Boggo Road is (and we sure the heck didn't prior to doing some research), we'll explain. Turns out it is an infamous Australian prison, one in which WWE wrestler Nathan Jones spent a good deal of time before deciding to get into wrestling. During his time in the big house, Jones discovered weight lifting and

PHOTO: MATT BALK

Despite countless requests for it, the Nathan Jones action figure did not come with lactating nipples.

spent his eight-year sentence attempting to transform himself into the second coming of the Incredible Hulk. To achieve this noble and most bizarre goal, Mr. Jones allegedly started to take all kinds of steroids, until his breasts actually began to swell and lactate. Yes, lactate, as in milk was pumping out his tatas. While you might find that disgusting (and really, who could blame you?), we find it more disturbing that with this knowledge, WWE creative couldn't come up with a better nickname for the guy. Something like Cow Juice Jones, Jublee Jones or our favorite, Big Vitamin D. Then again, maybe we're not giving WWE marketing enough credit, and misheard the "Colossus of Boggo Road" when it was actually the "Cow-Lossus of Boggo Road." Upon further review, we'd bet our milk money that was the case. And we'd hope that said milk didn't actually spew forth from Nathan's chesticles.

While a wrestler's name is obviously something fans hear before he even enters the arena, much lesser aspects of a wrestler's persona can either help build up or tear down a character. For instance, where he hails from. Forget Parts Unknown: good luck finding . . .

WRESTLING'S 7 WORST HOMETOWNS

7. **"A Little Town in France":** In the early 1990s, veteran Billy Jack Haynes donned a mask to become Blackblood, an executioner of sorts. And yes, he did come to the ring with a giant ax, thanks for asking. You might wonder where such a vicious, cruel man would call home. And after hearing his ring introduction, you'd still be wondering. See, he was billed as from "a little town in France." Scary, no? Umm . . . no.

Once we heard that was where this supposedly vile competitor put his head down to rest at night, all we could surmise is that his mighty blade was used for cutting up wheels of cheese.

6. **"Japan":** Speaking of vague places to live, it seemed that prior to 1995 every wrestler who had slanty eyes and the inability to pronounce the letter "r" made his residence in "Japan." Didn't really matter where he was really from, be it Japan (Tiger Chung Lee), Hawaii (Mr. Fuji) or Canada ("Kato" Paul Diamond). It would appear that sometime in the late 1990s, wrestling promoters discovered either an almanac or a map, and wrestlers from the Orient actually began to hail from recently discovered cities like . . . how do you pronounce this? "Toe-Key-O"? Oh come on, no one would believe that is a real name for a city.

5. **"The Outer Reaches of Your Mind":** Pop quiz: name the first two wrestlers to main-event *Monday Night Raw*. Bzzt! While we might believe you could name one half of that historic bout (the Undertaker), we are confident you would never come up with Taker's opponent for the evening, a self-professed lunatic by the name Damien Demento, who, should you remember him at all, no doubt resides somewhere in the outer reaches of your mind. Hmmm. Maybe it wasn't such a bad hometown after all.

4. **"The Woods":** If there's one thing we've discovered while working on this book, it's that wrestling needs more lumberjacks. And they should all live in the Woods. Such was the case when Matt Borne was christened "Big Josh" and brought before fans in the early 1990s, complete

with dancing bears. Now that's an entrance. If everyone in wrestling had dancing bears, it would be a better world. Even if they did all hail from some mythological "Woods."

3. **"The Last House on the Left":** It's a bit ironic that before ECW picked up major traction as wrestling's renegade promotion in the mid-1990s, it was more or less a traditional territory, employing somewhat normal wrestlers with somewhat normal names, such as J.T. Smith and Hack Myers. Myers, in fact, had what might be, in hindsight, the most normal home address in wrestling history — he hailed from "the last house on the left." We never found out the street, city or for that matter ZIP code. Therefore, we ask you, dear reader, to help us out. Please put down this tome and head down your street and knock on the door of the last house on the left. If we all work together, we might actually find Myers, who has been missing from the major-league wrestling scene since 1996.

2. **"The Kennel Club":** Stop me if you've heard this one. Wrestler signs for "loser leaves town" match. Wrestler loses. Wrestler "leaves town." Mysterious masked wrestler who looks exactly like wrestler who lost "loser leaves town" match, save for the fact that he is wearing a mask, debuts. It's happened hundreds of times. Give WCW credit that when it was Brian Pillman's turn on the lazy Susan of wrestling booking, they claimed he was a "Yellow Dog." Not only that, but he apparently lived in a dog pound called "the Kennel Club." Perhaps WCW wanted us to believe poor Pillman, having lost his income from professional wrestling due to that one match, had fallen on hard times and was forced to eat out of a bowl and sleep next to

a shih tzu. Laugh if you will, but this is also the same company that gave us . . .

1. **"WCW Special Forces":** Pity the poor 1990s tag team the Patriots, as their introduction to fans revealed they hailed from "WCW Special Forces." Whether this meant they lived in some bizarre, Ted Turner-sponsored housing development in Atlanta or were an elite commando unit, we are unsure. If it was the latter, however, we were somehow to be protected by a guy dubbed Firebreaker Chip, who represented this crack squad wearing nothing more than wrestling trunks, boots and a fireman's helmet (he apparently fought fires shirtless). May God have mercy on our souls.

Speaking of the very popular wrestling hometown of "Parts Unknown" . . . we don't know exactly where it is on the map, but it has the largest per-capita demographic of masked goofballs. Many of whom share the same name. Goofballs we like to refer to as . . .

PARTS UNKNOWN'S 5 MOST GENERIC RESIDENTS

5. **The Gladiator:** Russell Crowe these men aren't. The masked buffoons who dared to walk around with this sword-swinging name may have been better off being called Glad-I-Ate, to go with their pot bellies. Perhaps the most famous Gladiator was the one jousting in the WWF in the mid-'80s. Portrayed by perennial jobber Ricky Hunter, he displayed the irony that most of these scary-name masked guys displayed. Ricky was a "gladiator" who was short, pale, pudgy and over fifty years old. Gladiator, thy game is over.

4. The Nightmare: Oooh, spooky!!! Don't close your eyes, and definitely don't fall asleep. You wouldn't want to fall victim to a Nightmare from Parts Unknown. Actually, on second thought, keep your eyes closed. The scariest thing about these Parts Unknown Nightmares is usually their wardrobe. While the most famous Nightmare may be the sloppy one who battled with Dick Murdoch in the mid-South, the worst-looking of the bunch had to be the tag team known as — what else? — the Nightmares, who battled in the GWF tag team tournament. These two obese clowns looked like they robbed two garbagemen picking up the trash behind the Dallas Sportatorium, taking their stained and soiled bright orange uniforms in the process. Thankfully, one thing all these Nightmares have in common with real nightmares is they don't last long, and once you've awakened and the horror is over, you soon forget all about them.

3. Mr. X: Coming in at No. 3 is the dreaded Mr. X. In our neck of the woods, the letter X is usually used for something that has a dramatic impact. For instance, legendary African-American leader Malcolm X. Or the wonderful world of X-rated films. And who hasn't jumped for joy when they win a game of tic-tac-toe by placing the winning X in the bottom right-hand corner? Those are all great X's. Not so great, though, is the family of X's that roam the streets of Parts Unknown. For the last fifty years, Mr. X's have popped up, whether in the old WWWF, World Class or the modern WWF. The most famous Mr. X would have to be the scrawny one who roamed the WWF in the mid-'80s, a guy who lost every single match until he moved out of Parts Unknown and became better known as referee Danny Davis. From time to time you may run into some who actually thought more about their future than the average X did. After a little college education, they became known as Dr. X's. We're not quite sure what they are doctors of, but these masked jokers, who get their asses kicked on a nightly basis, better be able to prescribe a damn good painkiller. Or at least some quality antidepressants to deal with losing 200 matches a year.

2. The Executioner: Sometimes being a mere Gladiator isn't enough. Why just duel with someone when you can actually execute them? No potential death sentence was botched on a bigger stage than the one handed down to Tito Santana by an Executioner at the first *WrestleMania*. Sentenced to job by the unarmed, chubby masked man, Tito had ideas of his own, performing euthanasia on his rotund nemesis, in the form of a figure-four submission victory. The mere thought of these pathetic Parts Unknown Executioners is enough to make all inmates sitting on death row believe they have a long life ahead of them.

1. The Assassin: We've mentioned Gladiators and Executioners, but here are the much deadlier Assassins. No need for blunt or sharp metal objects to take a foe down, these guys are just hanging out on some grassy knoll in Parts Unknown, ready to strike. But there is no lone gunman here; there are more Assassins than there are JFK-Lee Harvey Oswald conspiracy theories. There are . . .
  - the Assassins
  - the Russian Assassins
  - the Pink Assassin
  - the Giant Assassin
  - the Flying Assassin

- the Super Assassins
- the Masked Assassin
- the Black Assassin
- the Dark Assassin
- the Sexy Assassins

Man, that's a lot of death dealers right there.

Often, bookers are just too damn lazy to come up with characters that are novel, fresh and, most importantly, multifaceted. So why not just lean on racial stereotypes? That's always good wholesome fun, as illustrated by our . . .

8 MOST STEREOTYPICAL WRESTLERS

8. The Full Blooded Italians/Salvatore Sincere: To be fair, these paisans were more of a comedy goof troupe — a parody, if you will — than a full-on racist blast. After all, when your crew contains the likes of Tracy Smothers, a redneck from Tennessee, and your don is fellow hick Tommy Rich, it's hard to take the stereotype seriously. It was much the same case when Tom Brandi portrayed Salvatore Sincere in the WWF during 1996. Talka like dis alla you wanna, but these guys were definitely not Italian, and the fans knew it.

7. The Samoans: Take your pick. Seriously, nearly every Samoan in wrestling history, from Afa and Sika to King Tonga to Tonga Kid to Umaga and almost every other one in between, has been pegged as a barefoot, skirt-wearing savage who swings from tree to tree, eating raw fish and cracking coconuts against his rock-hard skull. A light has finally appeared to break, though, as Samoa Joe has not only ditched the ceremonial outfit, but also — get this — he speaks! He even wears boots. A giant step for Samoans everywhere.

6. **Akeem:** Try to follow this one. The One Man Gang was a huge heel for the WWF in 1988, but he had started to wear out his welcome. It was decided he needed a makeover to increase fan interest in his character. This makeover would consist of his "returning to his African roots" — a bit odd since he was formerly a big white guy from Chicago. Anyway, the newly christened Akeem the African Dream emerged during a ceremony in what appeared to be a K-Mart parking lot, which would perhaps explain the hideous yellow and blue ensemble that made him look like a giant Easter egg.

5. **Kerwin White:** This would be Akeem in reverse. Chavo Guerrero was frustrated with what he perceived as a lack of love for his Latino background, so he decided to go the other direction and discover his middle-class American roots. Gone was his Latino entrance theme, replaced by a tune that could have been sung by Frank Sinatra (if he was, you know, still alive and so desperate as to sing wrestling themes). As Kerwin starched his shirts and drove a golf cart to the ring (complete with caddy), comedy ensued. Or maybe it didn't.

4. **The Mexicools:** With the succes of Rey Mysterio in WWE, it should come as no shock that the company would soon import more Hispanic talent. After all, the Hispanic demographic is one of the fastest growing, a fertile area to grow even more money trees for the McMahon family. What would come as a shock, though, was the way the trio of the Mexicools was presented to that audience: as guys

PHOTO: MATT BALK

Doesn't Super Crazy (top left) look thrilled to be part of this angle? Pump up the bass!

who would mow your lawn. No, seriously — they even rode a lawn mower to the ring! While this was horribly stereotypical, we do have to give the creative team a couple points for removing the John Deere logo on the side and replacing it with one that read "Juan Deere." If you're going to be offensive, at least try to be funny about it.

3. Kamala: As much as we love the big man from "deepest, darkest Africa" (now, there's a hometown), when compiling a list of racist wrestlers you kind of owe it to your readers to include an African cannibal. In this instance, though, it wasn't a promoter who came up with the idea; it was the man behind the moon and stars himself, Jim Harris from Mississippi. Since he's okay with it, maybe we should be too. Besides, there's something to be said for the image of Kamala and his handler, Kim Chee, chopping up carrots and potatoes and whipping up some Hulk Hogan stew. That's just stupid wrestling comedy, the way we likes it. Which isn't something we could say for . . .

2. Harlem Heat: Booker T has been one of wrestling's top stars for years, and with good reason. The five-time, five-time, five-time, five-time, five-time WCW champion is a great worker, a wonderful talker and flat out one of the most entertaining performers in the business today. What's amazing isn't so much that he became one of wrestling's biggest stars, but that he decided to stay in wrestling after his initial foray into WCW with his brother Stevie Ray. During their first appearances, Harlem Heat was actually brought to the ring in chains by a white sharecropper. Yes, in chains, as though they were slaves! Not offensive enough? Consider this, then: they were actually known at the time as Kane and Kole. You know, because he was black, like coal. Yep, those cats running Turner's wrestling shows back then may have been just a bit behind the times.

1. Saba Simba: While Kamala may have been the brainchild of the performer who portrayed him, Saba Simba was anything but. Tony Atlas was a star for Vince McMahon's WWF (as well as several other promotions) from the late 1970s through most of the 1980s. When he reemerged in the WWF in 1990, however, he had, according to the company, "rediscovered his African roots." Yes, just like Akeem, but at least this time the guy was, you know, black. Perhaps by returning to their roots they meant the roots of a marijuana plant, because he came out wearing a giant ceremonial headdress and danced about in the ring as though his feet were on fire. Oh, and he carried a big shield. And a spear! Can't forget that. We'd like to, but we can't. In fact, we can't forget just how horribly racist this gimmick was, and that seals the deal on it being the most racist gimmick in wrestling.

Vince McMahon loves to say that his Superstars are larger than life, often comparing them to movie stars or superheroes. In fact, there have been a lot of superhero wrestlers over the years, and get this — they pretty much all sucked. So what the hell, let's have a list of . . .

THE 4 WORST SUPERHERO WRESTLERS

4. **Batman:** From the "This Could Never Happen in Today's Litigious Society" file, in the late 1960s, Tony Silipini donned the cowl of the Caped Crusader. The timing, of course, isn't coincidental, as during this time ABC was airing the campy *Batman* television series. You remember that show, right? The one that featured a rogues gallery including the likes of Vincent Price as Egghead, Milton Berle as Louie the Lilac and, last but not least, Joan Collins as the Siren? Yeah, that was one great show. Too bad none of those villains ever crossed over to the squared circle. I bet a wrestler named "Egghead" would sell out arenas the world over.

3. **Super Stacy:** As you might have noticed, we have a tendency to make fun of people from time to time in this book, but we rarely call anyone flat-out stupid. Well, to whoever came up with this idea, let us state for the record that you are flat-out stupid. To wit: you have the hottest girl in the company in Stacy Keibler. And unlike all the other so-called Divas on the roster, she doesn't get over with fake balloony boobs, but instead her long legs and her face look to have been painted by angels. So what does the creative team decide to do? Make her a superhero sidekick to the Hurricane and put her in a mask. A mask, you would correctly assume, that covered her face. The only thing super about this idea was how super stupid it was.

2. **Arachniman:** You're probably looking at those ten letters and thinking, "Arachniman? Don't you mean Spider-Man?" Why, yes. Err, no. No, no, no. When Brad Armstrong decided he would become a wrestling superhero who shot webs at people, we're certain he'd probably never even heard of Stan Lee's creation. Sure, he dressed just like him, but the colors of Arachniman's costume were yellow and purple. Everyone knows Spider-Man's duds are red and blue. Totally different. Unfortunately for Brad and his employers at WCW, Marvel Comics didn't think that having an outfit of a different hue was quite unique enough and promptly eighty-sixed the gimmick by threat of a lawsuit.

1. **Rosie:** To be fair, it is debatable whether Rosie should even be included on this list. Yet another Hurricane protégé (man, that guy had enough of those to have his own Justice League), but his superhuman powers were questionable. While Hurricane's entrance video featured him

PHOTO: MATT BALK

I really am the S.H.I.T.!

flying around the globe, we never witnessed Rosie performing such feats. And his homemade costume can best be described as "nerd-tastic." At the end of the day, Rosie was pretty much what he claimed to be: a superhero in training. Oh wait, a Super Hero In Training. SHIT! That's super indeed!

Of course, those folks had no real superpowers to speak of, so they couldn't be taken seriously as superheroes. But there is one man in wrestling who did, in fact, have powers beyond those of mortal men. And he was no mortal man: he was a Warrior. Don't believe us? Then we offer up . . .

THE 5 PIECES OF CRAP EVIDENCE THAT THE ULTIMATE WARRIOR HAD SUPERHUMAN, OTHERWORLDLY POWERS

5. **Ability to Be Called Upon for Duty by a Very Familiar Apparatus:** Need the first clue that Warrior could be your personal Superfriend? Then consider this undeniable fact: when he appeared in WCW, a beacon would shine on high. This was not just any old spotlight, but a spotlight with the Warrior logo right smack dab in the middle, just like the famous Bat Signal. And just in case anyone thought Warrior was the half-naked, shoestrings-tied-on-the-biceps, pro-wrestling version of the Dark Knight Detective, he began to conclude his interviews in a manner he never had before, stating that he would appear next week, "Same Warrior time, same Warrior channel."

4. **Ability to Make Image Appear in Certain Reflective Surfaces:** During this same period, Warrior unleashed another secret trait. His primary foe, Hulk Hogan, was at his breaking point following Warrior's unending mind games. What caused Hogan to go completely over the edge was seeing Warrior in his dressing-room mirror laughing at him. Hogan spun around . . . and there was no Warrior! Hogan turned back around, and there was the Warrior in the mirror again, laughing and laughing at him. We're not quite sure how this ability would operate in the apprehension of criminals, but you have to admit it's something we have been unable to do (not that we haven't tried).

And you know, upon further reflection (no pun intended), it seems more of a vampire trait than something in the superhero realm.

3. **Ability to Transform a Five-Word, Seven-Syllable Sentence into the Next *War and Peace*:** If you ever plan on surfing to Warrior's Web site, a word of warning: give yourself plenty of time. Warrior may not have a lot to say, but it takes him a lot to say it, the classic case of asking a guy what time it is and getting a detailed description of how to build a clock. We're just thankful we've never been caught behind the guy in a drive-thru. Imagine trying to explain to your boss why your trip to Taco Bell took four hours. In addition to his mastery of the written word, he has apparently also been given an open license by Funk & Wagnalls to create his own words, such as *destrucity*. We can't wait for the 2007 edition of the dictionary so we can find out what the hell that word actually means.

2. **Ability to Turn Invisible:** While there is debate as to whether Warrior's reflective-surface appearance/disappearance is as a super-power, there can be no doubt about this one. Much like Sue Storm of the Fantastic Four, Warrior has the ability to vanish at a moment's notice. While this might sound like wrestling hyperbole or hobo folklore, it is fact. If you don't believe us, call up Vince McMahon and ask him. Warrior vanished before Vince's eyes no fewer than three times: once following *SummerSlam '91* (following a pay dispute), once prior to *Survivor Series '92* (following a pay dispute) and once in 1996 (following . . . well, nothing — he just disappeared). It wasn't until his WCW run, though, that he unveiled this power to the public. His invisibility was always preceded by huge billows

of smoke, and almost always followed by a wrestler being injured. These wrestlers, such as Perry Saturn and Davey Boy Smith, claimed that Warrior's vanishing act included trap doors — trap doors they landed on that seriously wrenched their backs. Although Smith actually had a months-long stay in the hospital following one such incident, we find it impossible to believe that a hero the caliber of Warrior would resort to such hackneyed magic tricks.

1. **Ability to Offend Gays, Lesbians and Pretty Much Anyone Else in a Single Bound:** Following his retirement from the squared circle in 1999, Warrior did something no one who listened to even one of his wrestling promos could have ever believed possible: he became a public speaker. And if there was any question as to his political leanings, they became very clear during a speech at the University of Connecticut, in which he seemingly went completely loco, explaining to a homosexual in the crowd, "Queering don't make the world work." He followed that up by telling an Iranian student that she needed to "go get a towel." We can only theorize that the ability to turn invisible caused Warrior to go clinically, legally insane, just as it did Claude Rains in the 1933 Universal classic *The Invisible Man.* Unlike Rains' character, however, Warrior was not murdered by his enemies. At least not yet. And considering the number of enemies he's built up over the years, that might be his greatest superpower.

Warrior may have been wacky enough to think he was from out of this world, but he never actually *claimed* such a thing. Others, though, did — such as . . .

THE TOP 6 WRESTLERS FROM OUTER SPACE

6. The Galaxians: As we all know, the character of Jim Cornette was instructed, led and funded by Mama Cornette. But Mama was not only a brilliant wrestling mastermind, she was also one of the first females to dabble in space travel. Before little Jimmy was blessed with guiding the legendary Midnight Express, he was stuck with these two jokers she discovered, the Galaxians. Claiming to be from the outer galaxy, these intergalactic clowns and their losing ways soon showed the world they were mere *Battlestar Galactica* Cylon posers in a *Star Wars* Stormtrooper wrestling world.

5. Spaceman Frank Hickey: Since the dawn of man, we have feared that if life forms from another planet ever showed up on earth, they could be a mentally and physically superior species that could overthrow us. For the sake of all mankind, we can only pray the invaders would resemble the 1950s and '60s space traveler the Spaceman, Frank Hickey. Physically, he was dominated by many a wrestler, relegating him to jobber status. As far as his mental capacity, with the entire female population at his fingertips, he picks Mae Young as his wrestling companion. Mae freakin' Young?! One can only wonder if Frank was rendered blind by his silly-looking space helmet, or perhaps he simply left his saggy-puppy-detector ray at home when he set out on his journey to earth.

4. ECW Alien: When the new ECW television show debuted on the Sci-Fi Channel in the summer of 2006, rumor was that WWE was going to bring an honest-to-goodness Martian in to get destroyed in the ring. The alien was even spotted roaming around backstage. However, Sci-Fi was uncomfortable with the thought of one of its longtime representatives getting crushed in front of millions of viewers, so the green extraterrestrial was cut from the show, presumably never to be seen again. But, as you should know by now, Vince won't let a bad gimmick go to waste, so six days later on *Raw*, who should Vince come face-to-face with in the back? None other than the green ECW alien. Vince promptly yelled and cursed at the otherworldly invader, sending him on his unmerry way. Sadly, the alien never got the chance to offer Vince a membership in another exclusive fraternity: the Alien Probe My Ass Club.

3. Lazer-Tron: In 1987, NWA head honcho Jim Crockett decided to cash in on kiddie pop culture by introducing a wrestler based on a popular high-tech toy of the time. Unfortunately it was not a wrestling bear named Teddy Ruxpin, but rather the dorky-looking Lazer-Tron. Inspired by the Lazer Tag light-shooting game, he came to the ring decked out in an official Lazer Tag outfit and a token Parts Unknown mask. Evildoers beware: Lazer-Tron was also armed and dangerous, as he packed some heat — his Lazer Tag gun. You know, say what you want about Triple H's rubber sledgehammer or Mick Foley's plastic barbwire, but here's a doofus trying to intimidate with a gun that shoots a harmless, invisible laser ray. Did we mention Lazer-Tron also had red antennae sticking out of his head? It was a good look. When Hector Guerrero was in the ring, portraying a ray-gun-wielding alien ant from outer space, he had to think to himself, "It can't get much worse than this." Boy, was he ever wrong. But that's a turkey of a story for another list . . .

2. Max Moon: If ever there was a wrestler deserving of the tired "He comes from Uranus" joke, it has to be this rainbow-colored-suit-wearing buffoon. Hell, his cheeky-sounding name even reeks of anal alliteration. Poor Paul Diamond, the unlucky soul who was forced into the role of the WWF's resident cosmic superhero after Vince's original choice, Konnan, blasted off from the federation. At one point, the WWF was trying to outfit him with a jetpack that would propel Max into the ring, but problems with mechanics and fuel led to him staying grounded. Too bad the WWF just didn't feed Max an extra side of some spicy refried beans before a show. Lord knows, Max Moon blew enough ass as it was; perhaps a little boost of natural gas would've propeled this crappy gimmick to the equally gassy Jupiter.

1. **Tully Blanchard's Fists:** Finally we reach our No. 1, who on the surface appears to be a normal earthling. However, you could be wrong. In the mid-'80s, while threatening his longtime rival Dusty Rhodes during interviews on TBS's *World Championship Wrestling*, Blanchard stated that he was going to knock out the American Dream with the help of Mars and Venus. No, Tully was not the second coming of God, on the verge of sending two planets crashing down on Rhodes' Texas farmhouse and ending civilization as we know it. It turns out that Mars and Venus were pet names for Tully's right and left hands. Confused by Tully's bizarre out-of-this-world statements, we contacted world-renowned astronomer Dr. Mill K. Waye for an expert opinion. "Obviously Mr. Blanchard's hands are not really celestial bodies in orbit of the sun," explained Dr. Waye. "In the mid-'80s, he was managed by Baby Doll, an Amazon-like woman who was once know as Andrea, the Lady Giant. When getting intimate with his lady love, her size dwarfed the relatively small Mr. Blanchard, causing him to easily confuse her with our solar system. It was the foreplay he did with his hands that led him to believe

his tiny fists were actually planets rotating in the gravitational pull of Baby Doll's galaxy-sized boobs." Thankfully for all wrestling fans, he dumped Baby Doll before we had to hear any talk of Tully's Comet entering any of her black holes.

But what if aliens did attack? Time to call on the military. Let's just hope the folks who come to our defense are better than those portrayed in wrestling, namely . . .

THE 9 WORST MILITARY WRESTLERS OF ALL TIME

9. Cobra: The mere mention of the word *cobra* brings to mind images of the snake's scary-looking fangs, not to mention the dread of its paralyzing venom. Some viewers tuning into WCW in 1995 found themselves numb and drifting into unconsciousness, as if they had just fallen victim to a cobra bite. However, no snake antidote was necessary; they were just feeling the effects of a boring and dreadful match involving Cobra — the wrestler. Bringing a convoluted origin story with him, Cobra claimed to be back to seek revenge on military evildoer Sgt. Craig Pittman, who left him to die on the battlefield during some classified tour of duty. Amazingly, Pittman was actually booed for doing this. Cobra was never seen without his trademark Morse-code-like entrance music blaring in the background. While reviewing old video footage, doing research for this book, we were finally able to decipher what Cobra's entrance music was saying. Apparently, it was a military command from a high-ranking WCW official — "S.O.S., S.O.S. . . . stay offscreen, stay offscreen!"

8. M.I.A.: What do you do with a group of mid-carders who are going absolutely nowhere in your federation? Release them and save some money, perhaps? No, silly — this was WCW. Here, you put them in hokey-looking military outfits, grab the nearest, silicon-filled blond bimbo and throw them against the wall to see if they stick. Thus, the Misfits in Action were born. Answering the call to duty were Gen. Hugh G. Rection, Major Stash, Lieutenant Loco, Sergeant Awol, Corporal Cajun, and the group's secret weapon, the buxom Major Gunns. To help her team get the upper hand in battle, Gunns routinely hopped in the ring, ripping her camouflage top off to reveal her huge chesticles popping out of a bra two sizes too small. Make no mistake, she was great to stare at, and she certainly helped the M.I.A. get over with the crowd, but if we're in the middle of a war thousands of miles from home, we wouldn't want a woman who is just gonna tease us by tearing off her top. We'd want a woman who would love us long time, like . . .

7. G.I. Ho: Now, here's a woman after our hearts . . . or some other blood-filled muscle. This female grappler from Women's Erotic Wrestling let it be known to all that love is a battlefield, and that battlefield was gonna help her pay the bills. Always a hit at drunken parties with rear admirals, or admirals who liked some rear, G.I. Ho spent most of her ring time not on her back, but frequently standing up celebrating victory, achieving a few title reigns in her career. Outside the ring, though, you'd best be careful messing around with her, soldier. She is a high-risk candidate for a nasty discharge. And not an honorable one.

6. G.I. Bro: Talk about your wartime flashbacks. Surely Booker T felt like he was suffering from shell shock when he was told in 2000 that he'd be returning to a gimmick from his past, that of the grunt known as G.I. Bro. So, on the threshold of being one of the top stars in WCW, Booker threw everything aside for one more chance to play army dress-up. His face painted green, he made silly-looking entrances into the ring on rip cords and even became a member of the M.I.A. briefly. Thankfully, his second tour of duty as G.I. Bro was a short one, and he was quickly back to plain old Booker T. Nowadays, every time we hear him say, "Can you dig it, sucka," we don't know whether he's trying to get people pumped up with a snappy catchphrase or having a flashback to the day he instructed one of his jarhead buddies to dig a deep trench to forever bury every bit of the evidence of his stint as G.I. Bro.

5. Ranger Ross: In 1989, with Sergeant Slaughter defending the country in the AWA, and Hacksaw Jim Duggan waving Old Glory in the rings of the WWF, WCW was left in the cold without a patriotic do-gooder of its own. Enter Ranger Ross. Unfortunately for WCW, this ranger would have his hands full protecting picnic baskets from Yogi Bear at Jellystone Park, let alone taking on the global threat of the dastardly J-Tex Corporation. Ranger quickly fell off the wrestling radar and was barely heard from again during the 1990s. Well, except for that time he performed the highly patriotic act of robbing a bank and was sentenced to jail. What a Boo Boo.

4. Corporal Kirchner: When Sergeant Slaughter departed the WWF in 1985, it left a huge void in the company's camouflage-pants-wearing, flag-toting wrestler department. With the Iron Sheik and Nikolai Volkoff still raising hell, Vince decided he needed a red-blooded replacement immediately. Lacking a few good men — or even one good man — Vince enlisted the aid of a rather hippie-looking jobber named R.T. Reynolds (and no, kids, he's not a relative). Shaving off his long hair and grungy beard, he grabbed the nearest flag and dove headfirst into combat. Despite some initial success at *WrestleMania 2*, where he quickly squashed the evil Russian Volkoff in a few minutes, Kirchner's mind soon went AWOL. He committed one of the no-no's you should never do — he got into a physical confrontation with Vince McMahon. Tired of the antics of the crazy corporal, McMahon gave him his walking papers.

At this point in the countdown, no doubt you're thinking to yourself, "Man, do these guys suck. Maybe they wouldn't have stunk so much had they gone to boot camp and been instructed by the greatest military wrestler of all-time, Sergeant Slaughter." It's a reasonable assumption, but upon further review of the graduates of Camp Slaughter, that would be a big nugatory. Sarge's students were so bad, not only did they send audiences to the concession stand in a mad dash, but they also take up our final three spots, as . . .

THE 3 WORST GRADUATES OF CAMP SLAUGHTER (THUS, THE THREE WORST MILITARY WRESTLERS OF ALL TIME)

3. **The Unknown Soldier:** In Philadelphia, Pa., stands the Tomb of the Unknown Soldier, dedicated to the thousands of unidentified soldiers who perished during the American Revolutionary War. In 1989, the Sarge unleashed a masked Unknown Soldier — he was still alive, though his career was dead from the start. Not the most patriotic of wrestlers, the Soldier never carried an American flag, probably due

to his bizarre seizure-like movements that resembled something out of the early stages of Parkinson's. And forget about him leading a U-S-A chant with the crowd. His unintelligible grunts and groans on the mic made fellow short bus rider Eugene look like the second coming of Jake "the Snake" Roberts. But for all the ways he differed from the real unknown soldiers, the Unknown Soldier did have one major thing in common with them. He too got to hang out in dark, quiet tombs — AWA wrestling arenas in the late 1980s.

2. **Pvt. Terry Daniels:** In 1984, when Sergeant Slaughter was engaged in a full-blown war with U.S.A. haters Nikolai Volkoff and the Iron Sheik, he figured it was time to call for reinforcements. Help arrived in the form of Pvt. Terry Daniels. One quick glance at Terry, however, and you may wonder if he really achieved the rank of private or if he was so-named because he *looked* like a "private part." With his pale complexion and thin, lanky build, Terry one-upped TNA's Johnsons by actually resembling an honest-to-god walking penis. Sadly, before the walking wanker and Sarge's battle with the Sheik and Volkoff reached its explosive climax, Sarge pulled out of the WWF, leaving the flaccid Daniels on his own. Already physically challenged, Daniels' career would go totally limp, and by the early '90s he was gone from the sport.

1. **"Rambo" Greg Gagne:** Recipe for disaster. Take one part skinny pale wrestler from Minnesota. Add the gimmick of the current hit movie. Mix them up and you get a combination more hazardous than a nursing home for the blind's exercise walk through a minefield. Inspired by Sly Stallone's hit movie *Rambo*, AWA booker Verne Gagne thought he'd have a surefire hit on his hands if he took his son Greg,

the complete physical opposite of the buff Stallone, and turned him into a war hero. At Camp Slaughter, the Sarge would put him through the ringer, making Greg do such rigorous activities as running through the forest and jumping in and out of a nearby lake, making as much water splash as an anorexic, 175-pound wrestler can. To complete his training, Gagne chopped trees and later threw the wood around for no good reason, like a Boy Scout having a temper tantrum during a nature walk. After a weekend getaway in the woods, Rambo Greg was apparently transformed into a rough 'n' tough grunt, ready to take on the entire continent of Asia. Fortunately for wrestling fans, the Rambo Gagne gimmick was not long for the world, and in a few short years, Greg would announce his retirement.

Okay, say the military can't protect us. That means there's only one thing you can count on to save our hides: ninjas! Again, though, let's hope they are superior to those seen in wrestling . . .

THE 8 LEAST FEARSOME NINJAS OF ALL TIME

8. **Ricky "the Dragon" Steamboat:** Sometimes there comes a wrestler so talented, it's obvious to every wrestling fan that a hokey, gimmicky character is unnecessary. Ricky Steamboat is a guy who could come to the wrestling ring wearing white tights, white boots and calling himself Generic Grappler #2, and he would still sell out arenas. But in the wacky world of the cartoon-like 1980s WWF, a gimmick was a must, and thus "the Dragon" was born. Fans at home got to bear witness to the origin of the Dragon, in the form of skits on WWF TV, in which he beat the crap out of a gang of four-foot-tall midget ninjas,

hitting them in the head with sticks and throwing them off bridges. That's fighting fair and honorable right there, yes sir. Shame on you, Ricky, you big ninja bully.

7. **Super Ninja:** In the fall of 1988, the Ultimate Warrior had commenced his rocket ride to the top of the WWF, which would ultimately lead him to the WWF World Heavyweight Championship. But before the Warrior could even begin to dream about being the top dog, he had to pass a grueling test. Wanting the Ultimate One's Intercontinental title for his own, Mr. Fuji enlisted the aid of an evil ninja master, hoping he would vanquish the spastic champion on a broadcast of *Saturday Night's Main Event*. Mr. Ninja's pedigree? A lifetime spent in Japanese dojos, honing his skills, maybe? Being such a straight-edge warrior he wouldn't even take a sip of saki, perhaps? Wrong, try a resumé that includes a lot of beer drinking, tobacco spitting and brawling up in the Pacific Northwest. Turns out Fuji's Oriental hitman was really Portland's veteran grappler, Rip Oliver. And sure enough, faster than you can say Billy Jack Haynes, the Warrior crushed his "super" adversary in under a minute. Speaking of "super" . . .

6. **Super Giant Ninja:** Man, what was up with Superman's mom, screwing every member of the Krypton dojo? This fellow here is a rather odd one to describe. The guy behind the hood was the seven-foot-tall Ron Studd, who was smack dab in the middle as his role of the Dungeon of Doom's Bigfoot monster, the Yeti. Don't fret, we'll talk more about him later. For now, though, just understand that the man who emerged from a block of ice to become what appeared to be a mummy would soon be decked out in the finest Power Rangers ninja

outfit Ted Turner's money could buy. Confused yet? You're not the only one, as throughout Super Giant Ninja's chameleon-like appearance changes, not one ounce of an explanation was given. A Bigfoot monster who's really a mummy, dressed up in a karate outfit. Talk about an identity crisis, that's an identity *apocalypse*.

5. Shinobi: Poor Al Snow. That's a phrase heard countless times throughout the journeyman grappler's career. Despite being one hell of a wrestler, for many years he went from one failed gimmick to the next. One of his first gimmicks in the WWF was that of Shinobi, the stereotypical evil ninja. Thankfully Al wasn't too mean to the wrestling fans, as he quickly hopped out of his dark ninja gear and into one of the 217 other gimmicks he had along the way. Ironically, after finally achieving success with his "Head" gimmick, Al returned to the ways of the Orient in 2003, when he was hired by Jonathan Coachman to terminate the Coach's nemesis, Tajiri. Al's new name — the Five Star Ninja. Since when did *sensais* start ranking ninjas like generals?

4. Superstar Billy Graham: As the WWWF champion, Superstar Billy Graham was the prototype of the bodybuilder-style wrestling physique that future generations of wrestlers would strive for. When he lost the world title to Bob Backlund in 1979, the Superstar went into a self-imposed exile so secluded that many thought he had passed away. He reemerged in 1982, his once-flowing golden locks chopped off and replaced with a goatee and freshly shaved head. Not even wearing his black gi, bought at a Halloween costume shop, could disguise the fact that Graham knew jack squat about karate. His kicks barely reached above the waist, and he used a lame karate chop as a finisher. Ladies and gentlemen, Kung Fool Billy Graham.

3. **Jamie-San:** Even in its dying days, WCW had one thing the WWF could never counter: a top-notch cruiserweight division. As the company burned to the ground around them, these smaller athletes put on great matches that the fans could really get into. But damn, did those guys get stuck with some dumb, dumb gimmicks. You'd think being a member of a boy-band team known as 3 Count would be bad enough, but we have more pity for the members of the Jung Dragons, who had a ninja on their side called Jamie-San (who was actually a fantastic worker by the name of James Gibson). Yes, kids, they were befriended by a ninja . . . a ninja named Jamie. That's almost as dumb as a ninja named . . .

2. **Kwang:** Do we even need to write more than that? *Kwang?* But that was the name of the evil ninja who traipsed around WWF rings in the mid-1990s, whose dojo was located in the middle of Puerto Rico. Yes, Kwang was an evil Puerto Rican ninja. But hey, he shouldn't feel too bad. Years earlier, another ninja plied his trade for the company: Kato, who hailed from Canada. Did no one in Stamford have any clue as to what a ninja actually was?

1. **Larry Zbyszko:** Nowhere on earth, at no time in history, has there ever been a man so deadly, so ruthless, so lethal. Straight out of the famous Gagne dojo in the most lawless part of upper-class Minnesota comes Larry Zbyszko: Evil Ninja Warrior. Legendary tales have been told about the day sensai Larry gained his warrior weapons. (Verne Gagne pur-

chased a ninja playset on his Visa at the Mall of America toy store.) Even more impressive was the demonstration of his nunchuck skills as he destroyed poor, defenseless coconuts. A master in the highly disciplined art of fruit-fatality, Larry decided to bring an apprentice along to wreak even more havoc. Anybody wanna guess his name? That's right, Mr. Larry Miyagi's ninja running buddy went by the seldom-used moniker of . . . Super Ninja!!! If you guessed that, step right up and collect your prize: a big bag of nothing. Which is what all this amounted to, as it was dropped and never spoken of again.

If you look at the most successful characters of recent years, such as "Stone Cold" Steve Austin and the Rock, there is a constant: the characters in the ring are by and large just ramped-up versions of the performers themselves. Austin will tell you himself that he really is a Texas redneck, and Dwayne Johnson has said for years that Rock is simply himself with the volume cranked to "eleven." Sometimes, though, it seems creative teams or even the performers themselves think that characters are to be created from other real-life personas, not their own. What other excuse can you give for . . .

THE 6 WACKIEST CHARACTERS BASED ON REAL-LIFE AND, UH, NOT SO REAL-LIFE PERSONALITIES

6. John Morrison: Let's say you're on the WWE booking committee. You want to give the prospect Johnny Nitro a fresh new gimmick, one that will propel him and ECW into the future. One wouldn't necessarily think turning him into a clone of long dead Doors singer Jim Morrison would be a good idea, but believe it or not, it actually worked. With his '60s-style long hair flowing in the wind, and cutting wacky Jack Handy Deep Thoughts-inspired monotone promos, John was successful in pulling off an intellectual egomaniac-like vibe, and captured his first ECW world championship in the process. Note to WWE: that does not mean we need to see Melina Joplin or Joey Hendrix make their debuts. To quote Jim Morrison, that would be "The End."

5. **Johnny B. Badd:** Marc Mero is a true professional, and one heck of an athlete. A former Golden Gloves champ, he was thrust into the WCW spotlight almost immediately upon his arrival. What would the bookers have in store for this young Caucasian prospect? His wrestling career certainly got off to a bizarre start, when WCW decided that Mero's race should be changed to African-American. Mero went into the tanning beds and wasn't allowed to come out until he looked like the stunt double for C. Thomas Howell in the movie *Soul Man*. The purpose of the ethnic transformation? Mero was to become Johnny B. Badd, the wrestling equivalent of Little Richard, prancing around the ring in a very feminine manner. So not only did he become black, he nearly became a woman as well. In fact, he once stated in an interview, "I am so pretty, I should have been born a girl." With that statement, out the window went all respectability, and in came a closet full of girly feathered boas and sequined robes that would make Liberace's closet look as tame as Hugh Hefner's. A gun that shot confetti into the crowd completed the ensemble. After pinning his male opponents, Badd would place a very unheterosexual kiss on his opponent's cheek. Okay, so it was a glittery sticker in the shape of his lips, but still. Any act insinuating a smooch with a male opponent pretty much guarantees you'll wind up in every book that has the word *WrestleCrap* in the title.

4. J-Love: In the early 2000s, no celebrity was hotter than Jennifer Lopez. It was impossible to listen to the radio, watch television or pick up a trashy tabloid without being subjected to mention of the possessor of the world's most famous deluxe-size derriere. The only safe haven from J-Lo-mania, it seemed, was pro wrestling. But just when you thought your ears were safe, XPW, wrestling's only porn-funded league, introduced the world to J-Love, the wrestling version of J-Lo. "My J-Love character basically came out during each show and sang 'America The Beautiful,'" explains Lizzy Valentine, the wrestler who portrayed J-Love, "but I sang it horrrrrible, kinda like J-Lo." In her wrestling escapades, what would the conceited manager/wrestler's biggest problem be during the course of her career? No, it wasn't wrestling dirt-sheets, hounding her about flings with Ben Affleck. It wouldn't be music critics lambasting her for her terrible singing, because believe it or not, her dog-howl-inspiring voice actually sounded better than the real J-Lo. No, J-Love's metaphorical *Gigli* would come in the enormous frame of our next entry . . .

3. Pogo the Clown: Only in the bizarre world of XPW, could there be a wrestler based on a serial killer. The character of Pogo the Clown was based on notorious killer John Wayne Gacy's clown alter ego of the same name. Proving that the sanity of the faithful XPW fans was questionable, Pogo was cheered by the crowd, not only for his vicious hardcore matches, but also for beating the crap out of J-Love. Refusing to be employed as the bitchy wannabe pop star's bodyguard, Pogo decided he'd much rather perform his deadly finishing move on her — the tastefully named "Buried in the Basement." Hey, Pogo, Bill Curtis from A&E's *American Justice* called. They want royalties for use of one of their grisly, mass-murderer catchphrases.

2. **Waylon Mercy:** One of the WWF's lone gimmick introductions of the mid-'90s that didn't have a part-time job, or didn't moonlight as an athlete in another sport, was Dan Spivey's awesome portrayal of Waylon Mercy. The tattooed, intellectually long-winded Mercy was reportedly inspired by Robert De Niro's deranged, bible-quoting lunatic in Martin Scorsese's remake of the classic thriller *Cape Fear*, a performance that impressed Vince McMahon. Ironically, in the case of the one gimmick that looked like it might have the legs to be a force in the WWF for a long time, it was in fact Waylon Mercy — or more specifically Dan Spivey, who portrayed the cold-blooded killer — who didn't have the legs to carry on, as he required hip surgery and retired shortly after his debut.

1. **Disco Inferno:** When one thinks of the all-time greatest accomplishments in wrestling history, the simple fact that Disco Inferno's career lasted more than three weeks has to be right up there. That's not a knock against the fine wrestler who portrayed him, Glen Gilberti, and it's not necessarily a rip on his *Saturday Night Fever*-inspired white polyester suit. It's the fact he had to do the gimmick minus the most crucial element of any '70s disco rip-off — some Bee Gees music to shake his booty to in the wrestling ring. Seeing a clone of Tony Manero dancing to some terrible in-house WCW neo-disco music, and not the strains of "Jive Talkin'," was probably enough to make Andy Gibb roll over and do the hustle in his grave.

Finally, let us talk about those who just flat out couldn't come up with a character. Instead of simply competing under their own names, they did something better: watched some tapes and copied someone else. Oh yeah, and they did it much, much worse than the original. Without further ado, we announce . . .

THE 8 NOMINEES FOR THE MOST BLATANT COPYCATS IN WRESTLING HISTORY (SPONSORED BY XEROX)

Nominee: The Old Age Outlaws: The team of the New Age Outlaws, Billy Gunn and Road Dogg Jesse James, were a huge part of the late-'90s WWF Attitude popularity boom. Members of D-Generation X, their lewd comments and outrageous behavior were straight out of a drunken frat party. With its head up its ass as usual, WCW thought it would be clever to spoof them by hiring a gang of old, retired and semi-crippled stars from the past. Out of the mothballs, and looking more like your decrepit grandpas than a gang of hip frat boys, came Arn Anderson, Paul "Mr. Wonderful" Orndorff, Larry Zbyszko and Terry Funk. For no rational reason, other than senility amongst the bookers, they were entered in a feud with the main-eventing nWo. The angle was quickly dropped, however, without explanation. Rumors that the faltering WCW had begun cutting costs to ease its rapid business losses — one of those cuts being the purchase of Depends adult undergarments for its aging stars — are unsubstantiated.

Nominee: Dan Spivey — U.S. Express: When Barry Windham and Mike Rotundo decided to leave the WWF in 1985 during the initial boom of the Rock 'n' Wrestling era, the WWF found itself minus its No. 1 babyface team. A few months later, Rotundo would return, ready to make another run at the tag belts. However, his Texas two-steppin' buddy did not follow. With the memory of the U.S. Express still fresh in the fans' minds, the WWF decided to throw the white satin U.S.A. jackets back on Rotundo and any reasonable Barry Windham look-alike they could find. The blond clone in question this day would be one Danny Spivey. While the sight of a different tall blond tagging with Rotundo might fool someone's ninety-year-old grandmother with glaucoma, two things stood out. One, Spivey was a power wrestler, while Windham relied on technical skill. Two, and perhaps more important in the flashy, image-conscious '80s, Windham looked like a country heartthrob whose posters would be plastered all over the walls of young girls' rooms, while Spivey resembled a serial killer who had about six young girls locked up in *his* room. So that's where Waylon Mercy was born!

Nominee: The Juice: It's arguable who the premiere wrestler of the *Monday Night War* era was. While many will point to the "Stone Cold" Steve Austin character so many fans could relate to, others were drawn to the phenomenon known as the Rock. Not because they could personally relate to the former Mr. Dwayne Johnson, but because there was no wrestler — past, present or future — who could compare to the pure comedy and hilarious catchphrases he delivered when he was on the mic. Hopelessly lost in the ratings, the head honchos at WCW apparently thought the fans went gaga over the Rock simply for those catchphrases. They handed Mexican *luchador* Juventud Guerrera the microphone and a handbook containing the Rock's best lines, and thus "the Juice" was born. It's unfortunate they didn't give him a handbook on how to speak the English language, as the Juice was barely understandable while ripping off the Rock on the mic. On second thought, that's actually a good thing, as a semi-intelligible "The Juice says" was at least good for a laugh — at Juvie's expense. The sourness of the Juice wouldn't last long, however, as he was arrested for running around naked in a hotel lobby, under the influence of PCP. Unfortunately for Guerrera, those cops definitely knew what the Juice was cookin'.

Nominee: Asya: As the "Ninth Wonder of the World," the WWF's female sensation Chyna set new standards for what a woman wrestler can do in the ring. She also set new standards for just how bulky and manly-looking a woman can be before she is not allowed on a TV screen. Ready to jump on the she-male bandwagon, the fine folks at WCW countered the WWF by introducing the world to Asya. Because, you see, Asia is bigger than China. Ha! Despite the Oriental landmark names and being two scary-looking, muscular women, they had little in common. Asya, who was never a full-time wrestler, was a flash in the pan on a sinking WCW ship. Chyna, on the other hand, rode the wave of the popular WWF until her ego ultimately wiped her out. Well, there is one other thing they had in common. The strange "Y" both had in the spelling of their names. Either wrestling writers can't spell a lick, or the "Y" was there to symbolize both "guys" . . . uh . . . "gals" . . . uh . . . "them" having some manly Y chromosomes in their genetic makeup.

Nominee: Sivi Afi: With the big wrestling boom of the '80s in full swing, two circumstances occured that definitely didn't strengthen Vince McMahon's rapidly growing talent roster: the departure of the very popular Sergeant Slaughter and, shortly after that, Jimmy "Superfly"

Snuka. While the Sarge was just your basic brawler, the loss of Snuka really hurt, because he was regarded as the most innovative high-flyer around. Still looking for someone to perform the amazing Superfly Splash finisher, McMahon found another man from the islands and christened him "Superfly" Sivi Afi, a "cousin" of Jimmy Snuka. His aerial attack was generic, and today he is best remembered for his lame, circus-like entrance, where he would do a tribal dance and the old swallowing-fire trick. WWF fans were not impressed, yearning for the bearded lady and the thin man to appear instead. Sadly, the Fabulous Moolah had just waxed her lip and Greg Gagne was still under contract to the AWA.

Nominee: Buzzkill: WCW's second attempt at a spoof of the New Age Outlaws would find one of the Road Dogg's relatives playing the doppelganger this time around. Brad Armstrong, a well-respected veteran grappler from the famous Armstrong wrestling family, was called on to take the role of Buzzkill, a near-perfect clone of his younger brother, Jesse James. He had the same funky-style entrance music. He muttered the same "Oh, you didn't know" catchphrase. Heck, Buzzy even had those long slick braids of hair like his sibling. Granted, the braids were Barbie-doll hair sewn into the hat he wore, which would repeatedly get knocked off his head, revealing Brad's buzzcut, but hey, it's the thought that counts. While the Road Dogg achieved a huge run with the WWF tag team belts, becoming known as one of the best tag team wrestlers of the time, Buzzkill just killed airtime on shows like *WCW Thunder*, acting like a goofed-up stoner. It's too bad those who came up with Buzzkill never encountered another kind of stoner — the kind that handed out rocky death sentences to guilty morons in medieval times.

PHOTO: MIKE LANO

To paraphrase the late, great Hawk: What a Flush!

Nominee: Heidenreich and Animal: One of the best things WWE has going for itself today is its incredible video library. As owner of the complete video archives of the AWA and WCW as well as ECW, World Class and countless others, Vince McMahon has the history of wrestling in his hands. From that huge record of yesterday come many fine WWE DVD releases, often a biographical disc on a star from the past, such as Dusty Rhodes or Jake "the Snake" Roberts. And you can usually count on a cameo appearance or a small run from the featured wrestler upon the release of the DVD to help drive the sales. That formula was a bit of a problem for WWE when it released a

DVD on the careers of Animal and Hawk, the Road Warriors. Hawk had passed away in 2003, and it seemed WWE just threw a bunch of names in the hat, with John Heidenreich being the draw as Animal's new partner. Looking like the welfare kid who has only enough money to buy a Darth Vader mask and not the rest of the costume, Heidenreich came down to the ring wearing not the standard LOD tights his partner Animal had on, but instead his same old red boots and tights, the only addition being a skull-like paint design on his face. Never thought we would say it, but we liked Heidenreich better as an anal-raping poet.

And the Winner Is . . . Kamala II: Kamala, the Ugandan Headhunter, was perhaps the greatest example of the cartoonish characters that stomped about wrestling rings in the mid- to late-1980s: a giant black man with stars and moons painted upon his rotund midsection. The savage gimmick has been done over and over, but never so absurdly as with Kamala II. Yes, Kamala II, as in Kamala: The Sequel, or Kamala: This Time It's Personal. And if we were Jim Harris, the man behind the original Kamala, we'd consider it a personal offense that the man who dubbed himself the new Kamala would be Stan Frazier, better known to fans as Uncle Elmer. Yes, a big, fat and decidedly Caucasian man was now portraying himself as the man from deepest, darkest Africa. We wouldn't blame Harris if he actually did throw Frazier in a big pot filled with carrots and potatoes.

In the end, while Stan Frazier's Kamala II is the winner, there were no real losers here today.

Save, of course, for all of us at home, wasting our lives away, watching these stupid characters . . .

Mirror, Mirror on the Wall...
What's the Crappiest Look of All?

You never get a second chance to make a good first impression. Don't kid yourself — that isn't just some clever marketing slogan the good folks at Johnson & Johnson came up with, it's a cliché old as dandruff itself. And here's the thing — it's true. Before a wrestler even enters a ring, before he cuts a promo, a large portion of his fate is sealed. If he/she/it doesn't look like a wrestler, no one will take him/her/it seriously. And as you're about to read, that happens more often than you'd think.

But what is a good look and what isn't? What if you are a young, up-and-coming grappler who wants to get people talking? Don't sweat it, kid; this section of the book is just for you. Looking for something that will get the fans' (and therefore a paying promoter's) attention? Then just pick one of . . .

THE 10 WRESTLER LOOKS THAT IMMEDIATELY NEED TO MAKE A COMEBACK

10. Adrian Adonis, the Gay Birthday Present Look: As a rough and tough, leather jacket-wearing New Yorker, Adrian Adonis was one of the most talented and underrated wrestlers of the early 1980s. Near the middle of the decade though, he had put on a lot of weight and, as punishment, Vince McMahon turned him into the WWF's first "gay" wrestler. Adonis became "Adorable" Adrian and was given a drastic makeover. With Adrian's old Harley Davidson gear disposed of, what did Vince think his new gay wrestler should wear? Gift bows. Lots of multi-colored self-adhesive gift bows. With the addition of numerous scarves, Adrian literally looked like a walking, talking birthday or Christmas package. Mind you, a package that might be checking out your package. So, for those wrestlers who want to act a little more eccentric, your one-way ticket to instantly becoming controversial is just a trip to a Hallmark store away.

9. **Kip James, the TNA Years Look:** You'd never think that a wrestler could top being a mullet-wearing, mustachioed pseudo-cowboy, but Kip James (formerly WWE's Billy Gunn) was able to do so much more. Ten years and a federation later, Kip dumped the cowboy hat and plastic pistol, in exchange for pigtails, drooping tank tops, and shorts so tight that not only could fans discern what religion he was, but whether he ranked among such backstage wiener legends as Alex Wright and Too Cold Scorpio. He didn't, but this should not stop you from dressing exactly like him, posthaste.

8. **Koko B. Ware's Giant Pants:** He may have been the Birdman to legions of fans in the late '80s, but during his later WWF years, Koko B. Ware came up with a new look, featuring pants at least six sizes too large. As if that weren't fantastic enough, they often sported checkerboard designs, which were especially noticeable when he wore yellow; he often resembled a taxicab. Now, there was a marketing opportunity

right there: "Taxicab Ware," sold exclusively at WWE events. That's a virtual license to print money.

7. **The Zodiac:** Ed Leslie was the man of a thousand (failed) gimmicks in WCW, and this one was the most bizarre. With his face blanketed in white greasepaint and his hair pointed upward like the spines of a porcupine, he looked more like an electrocuted mime than a pro wrestler. And he wrestled more like an electrocuted mime as well. There you go, pal — that's a *WrestleMania* headlining gimmick.

6. **Vince McMahon's Patented Pompadour and Pastel Jacket:** Popular urban legend attributes the popularity of pastel clothing to the television show *Miami Vice*. That series, which starred Don Johnson and some dude we can't even be bothered to hop over to IMDB.com to identify, featured cops wearing stylish loafers with no socks and powder-blue dinner jackets. While we understand how this myth came into being, it is our duty to rain on Crockett and Tubbs' parade. Sorry, guys, but you were not, in fact, the men who brought chalky-colored outfits into prominence; that honor would go to Vince McMahon, who opened every episode of *WWF Superstars* wearing — yeppers — a powder-blue sports jacket. And he had it way over the TV cops in the hair department, too, featuring a pompadour that would make Elvis proud. *Miami Vice?* Try *Miami Vince*, baby. If you want to make it in today's WWE, you could do far worse than patterning your look directly after its owner. In fact, you may not be able to do better.

5. **Vince McMahon's Patented Pompadour and Zubaz:** As fantastic as his 1980s ensemble was, McMahon topped himself as host of *Prime*

Time Wrestling during 1992. Not only was his hairdo perfectly coiffed, his clothing now consisted exclusively of oversize sweatshirts and zebra-striped workout pants. During this period, it appeared that the owner of WWE moonlighted as a butcher, killing defenseless cows and making trousers from them. There you go, guys — a great look and a bizarre, original gimmick to boot.

4. The Fabulous Ones' Bow Ties, Top Hats and Suspenders: Want to make a mark as a tag team? Then we suggest going the Fabulous Ones route, with a wardrobe consisting solely of tights, suspenders, top hats and bow ties. This look is guaranteed to drive the ladies wild. Hey, if Steve Keirn, who so closely resembled a swamp hermit that he was later dubbed Skinner the Alligator Man by the WWF, can make panties moisten while wearing it, odds are you can too.

PHOTO: ECW

The Fabulous Ones

3. Missing Link: With his green face and tufts of hair, Dewey Robertson's Missing Link character was the prototypical 1980s wrestling madman, one of the very few pro wrestlers to ever get a full-page photo in *Sports Illustrated*. As Robertson got older, he legitimately lost most of his hair, forcing him to actually paste fake hair atop his head to continue doing the character. A great suggestion for those suffering from male-pattern baldness.

2. Sherri Martel Cat Face, *SummerSlam '89*: We've had plenty of suggestions for the guys, but what about you gals? Look no further than perennial fashion fatale Sherri Martel, who determined that it would be most beneficial to do up her mug to look exactly like an outcast from *Cats*. Maybe she had just seen the show on Broadway. Maybe she imagined that a wrestling ring revival of *Cats* would cause her opponent to fall to the ground and quiver in fear — much like the real show — thus making for easy prey. Whatever the reason, this is one look that absolutely must make an immediate return.

1. **Scott Hall's 1970s Porn Star Look, circa 1987:** With his macho good looks and six-foot-six frame, it was no wonder Scott Hall was a promoter's dream during the early 1990s. It came as little shock that he became a huge star for the WWF in 1992 as Razor Ramon, Cuban bad guy, complete with slicked-back hair and toothpick hanging off his lips. This was a far cry from Hall's original look, which resembled a 1970s adult film star. With his bushy hair and magnificent pornstache, Hall could have easily doubled for a muscle-bound John Holmes. Or for that matter, the Brawny Man (the old one, not the wimpy new guy). In fact, we urge Hall to file a lawsuit against the makers of Brawny for so blatantly ripping him off, and then use the settlement money to help out some indie guy looking to catch a break.

While Hall had a fantastic 'do, let's face it, there's nothing better than a mullet. In fact, wrestling has been built upon the Camero cut for decades. It is with great honor that we hereby induct . . .

WRESTLING'S TOP 6 MULLETS

6. **Brian Pillman:** Due to his outrageous "Loose Cannon" behavior, the

late Brian Pillman is and will forever be remembered as a pioneer of the "worked shoot" promo in the mid-'90s. It is his appearance here on our list of the all-time worst mullets, however, that makes you amazed he wasn't shot. With his huge permed mullet flowing in the wind, in combination with his Cincinnati Bengal-striped tights, he looked like a wild crossbreed poodle/tiger that escaped from some mad scientist's zoo. No need to call in animal control, however. Pillman would lose the ultra-girly locks just in time for his wicked shootin' days in ECW and the WWF. Good thing, too. With that feminine mullet in tow, he might have forever been known as the "Loose Rectum."

5. **Trent Knight:** It almost seemed that along with a potbelly and mismatching tights, a trailer-park mullet was a job requirement in WCW in the late '80s. But what sets Trent Knight apart from his contemporaries like George South and Pat Rose to land him on this list? Well, it's not what he did with his mullet, it's what he didn't do. At the *Clash of Champions VII*, Knight, along with his partner Mike Justice, was set to take on the Great Muta in a martial arts exhibition. From out of nowhere came "Hotstuff" Eddie Gilbert, who attempted to launch a fireball in Muta's face. The Great One moved, however, and it was poor Mr. Knight who caught the blaze right in his face. Certain doom and a raging inferno for Knight and his hair, right? Wrong. Unlike his contemporaries, who glazed their ape drapes with two or three cans of Aqua Net, Knight's hair was au naturale, and thus escaped a potential reenactment of the Michael Jackson Pepsi commercial. Trent Knight — poster child for the natural mullet.

4. Eddie Guerrero: Eddie Guerrero will be remembered for his great matches, his fantastic feuds and, hell, just being one of the greatest performers of our era. Oh, and his mullet. While he had great hair throughout his career, if we had to pinpoint when it was at its best, we would zero in on his stint with ECW in 1995. What a sweet, sweet mullet that man had. It will be missed.

3. Paul Heyman: Paul Heyman will forever be known as an innovator, a true genius in the wrestling business. His greatest invention? The Heyman skullet — none on the top, all in the back. Once a proud owner of a fine-looking mullet in the 1990s, Paul has lost so much hair on the top of his head that his 'do now resembles something a corpse that passed away in the late 1800s might be sporting today.

2. Mike Awesome: Bringing with him over two decades of mullet domination is former ECW heavyweight champion Mike Awesome, looking like a bulked-up clone of Billy Ray Cyrus. One can only dream where Awesome's career would've ended up had Vince McMahon signed him away from Japan in the early '90s. Our vision? Billy Ray Awesome, master of the Achy-Breaky Heartpunch. Sadly, this never happened, and after a series of failed stints in WCW and WWF in 2000-2002, Mike eventually chopped off his longtime running buddy, effectively giving the Undisputed Mullet Champion of the World title to . . .

1. Ricky Morton: With his spiky blond mullet, Ricky Morton of the Rock 'n' Roll Express was the man who made girls squeal in the '80s. Present day, the only squealing heard around Morton is likely coming from the tires of police cars. Despite his woes, did Morton sell out and sell his hair to the local cosmetology school for a quick buck? Hell no. To this day he continues to carry the torch for mullet-wearers everywhere, reminding everyone that as long as you're looking business up front, you've got an excuse to throw one hell of a party in the back.

PHOTO: MATT BALK

Rock & Roll will never die! — nor will Ricky Morton's Mighty Mullet!

But not everyone looks good in a beaver paddle, especially if you have a lot of fur up top. And trust us, these guys had that, and so much more . . .

THE 10 GREATEST WRESTLING PERMS OF ALL TIME

10. **Hillbilly Jim:** You wouldn't think there would be a plethora of stylists in Mudlick, Kentucky, but the frizztastic mane of its favorite citizen, Hillbilly Jim, would suggest otherwise. In fact, we feel somehow wrong for not ranking him higher for this very reason. But Jim's Kentucky curls were often covered by a floppy country-bumpkin cap, diminishing their impact. When you add in a near ZZ Top-caliber beard that also drew away attention, we sadly can rank Jim no higher. Which is actually a compliment: he had two different kinds of face fur that made an impact.

9. **Dr. Tom Pritchard:** Much has been written over the years about veteran grappler Dr. Tom Pritchard being transformed into Zip of the fitness-guru stable known as the Bodydonnas. The idea of a tag team of Zip and Skip, two men who were heels because they preached physical fitness, was spectacularly dumb. But one thing never before noted is perhaps the greatest crime of all: to mirror his partner Skip's crew cut, Pritchard had to buzz off his stylish '80s perm. As anyone who has seen pre- or post-Zip pictures of the good doctor would tell you, this is a crime of felony proportions. We're talking robbing-a-blind-cripple-by-beating-him-over-the-head-with-a-bag-of-abandoned-kittens wrong here.

8. **Curt Hennig:** During Curt Hennig's WWF tenure, he was known as Mr. Perfect. We can only assume Vince McMahon's crew came up with the nickname after just one look at Hennig's perfectly coifed skull cover. His introductory vignettes, in which he would shoot 100 free throws in a row or bowl a perfect 300 . . . those weren't perfect.

But that hair in all its fluffy goodness, especially before he began to wet it down, most certainly was.

7. Bryan Clark: Just a cursory glance at Bryan Clark's head mop tells us one thing very clearly: his stint as nuclear-powered Adam Bomb (no joke, he was billed as hailing from Three Mile Island) gave his hair superpowers. There can be no other explanation for his pitch-black, immaculately groomed head. Sadly, upon leaving the WWF, this follicle fancy diminished, as he joined up with Brian Adams to become the limp-haired Kronik. Had those two pot smokers reverted to their early 1990s perm jobs, we have no doubt WCW would still be in business today.

6. Barry Horowitz: He may have been a jobber, but Barry Horowitz had world-champion hair, representing the Jewish community with a lid that any self-respecting rabbi would kill for. Pat yourself on the back, Barry — your Jew 'do deserves a spot near the top of this list.

5. Bruiser Brody: Of all the premature deaths in wrestling history, the murder of Frank Goodish may be the saddest. He was a great in-ring performer, one who many in the business emulate to this day. While others have tried to copy the madman gimmick Brody perfected, all have failed. These folks can swing their chains and bellow at the top of their lungs, but trust us — they'll never equal the greatness that was Bruiser Brody. Especially not his hair. Never before and never again has a madman ever sported such a stellar perm.

4. Rick Rude: To ladies and, come to think of it, gay men in the late 1980s, Rick Rude lived up to his moniker of "Simply Ravishing." While many claimed this was because he had arguably the greatest six-pack in the business, we respectfully disagree. Rude's ravishingness was 100 percent due to his wavy, ultra-permed 'do. Don't believe us? Consider this: once Rude lopped off his curly locks, his career never recovered. Sure, he still did a main event here and there, but he was never the same, as all his charisma seemed to have vanished immediately, as if he were a swivel-hipped version of Samson.

3. **"Model" Rick Martel:** Sadly, Rick Martel didn't learn from the Rick Rude/Samson analogy, as he too made the mistake of lopping off legendary locks. Martel, who was such a handsome guy he was dubbed the Model (and even wore a giant button that read "I am a Model" in case someone didn't connect the dots), had one of the finest perms wrestling had ever seen. Sadly, after just a few weeks of shaking his little tush (and '80s-mallrat-worthy hair) on the catwalk, he scissored his locks plum off. This new style was sadly more mannequin than model.

2. **Jimmy Garvin:** For once, a self-proclaimed nickname in wrestling wasn't mere hyperbole. Jimmy Garvin called himself Gorgeous, and trust us, he had the hair to prove it. His long brown locks were wavy past the point of perfection. In fact, he had a hairspray-toting valet (either Sunshine or Precious, depending on the time in his career) whose sole purpose was to ensure his hair was always in top form. That's dedication, baby.

1. **Lanny Poffo:** While all these men had fine perms, none can compare to the sheer greatness of the 'do Lanny Poffo sported during his run as Leapin' Lanny. I mean, come on . . . just look at this mane:

PHOTO COURTESY OF LANNYPOFFO.COM

Just say no to steroids — by saying yes to a fabulous perm!

But why was Lanny's perm better than all others? Because it enabled him to stay *drug-free*. Oh yes. Here's what Lanny himself had to say about it when informed that he would be receiving the coveted top spot in this list: "That perm looked good for about a month, then I'd have a blowout. It got overfried and started falling out — not as bad as the Hulkster, but not good. On the plus side, it did make me look bigger, and not being on the juice in a steroid era, I needed all the help I could get!" So to all those grapplers who claim they can't catch a break without the juice, well, just get a perm. It worked for Lanny Poffo; it can work for you!

Don't ask us why, but over the years, countless folks in wrestling have come to the conclusion that to really get over with the fans you need to have a Mohawk. Maybe these folks idolized Mr. T or something. And while we loved the adorable B.A. Barracus too, you wouldn't catch us dead with one of . . .

THE 5 WORST WRESTLING MOHAWKS

5. Kevin Nash: Long before his glory days as Big Sexy in the nWo, and even before his reign as WWF World Champion Diesel, Kevin Nash was a part of a huge disaster of a gimmick. No, believe it or not, we're not talking about his urine-Yellow Brick Road stint as the all-mighty Oz. A few months before he began hanging munchkins from trees, he was known as Steel, one half of the WCW Road Warrior rip-off tag team the Master Blasters. Despite trying to look like street-worn and filthy nomadic warriors from some desert wasteland, the Master Blasters ended up resembling two greasy guys who just finished their shift at Jiffy Lube. While his running buddy Blade (Al Green) had a normal enough haircut for a guy supposedly from a post-apocalyptic world, Nash had a mohawk that could best be described as a giant orange Brillo pad running down the middle of his skull. If only Nash could've used his Brillo-hawk to clean up the mess all his crappy early-90s WCW gimmicks left behind.

4. Hawk: In the late '70s and early '80s, big, sky-high, mohawks were all the rage amongst the punks and tough street thugs. However, one style we've never understood is the reverse mohawk. Spiked hair in a line on top of your head is one thing; it's quite another to mimic a fifty-five-year-old geezer sporting a horseshoe 'do.

3. Mad Maxine: Even the hardest of hardcore fans likely does not remember the sad saga of Mad Maxine. Brought into the WWF in 1985, the tall and intimidating newcomer was apparently in line to receive a big push as a nemesis for women's champion Wendi Richter. The Mel Gibson-movie-inspired, red-and-green-mohawked vixen's look was so impressive, she was added to the initial cast of the *Hulk Hogan's Rock 'n' Wrestling* cartoon. However, as soon as preliminary shots of the cartoon began to surface, showing her as one of the series' characters, she had vanished from the WWF completely. Apparently, because her skills were as green as her mohawk, she was sent packing back to her own personal Thunderdome.

2. Haiti Kid: When Roddy Piper was in the midst of his feud with Mr. T prior to *WrestleMania 2*, one of his most famous moments was an attempt to do a number on one of T's friends. The friend in question? WWF midget sensation the Haiti Kid. First, Piper reenacted the Lindbergh kidnapping, grabbing little Haiti against his will and taking him to the Piper's Pit set, where, with the help of his stooge, Cowboy Ace Bob Orton, they did a test run for Brutus Beefcake's future barber gimmick. They duct-taped the poor little bastard to a chair, then attempted to delock him using a tiny pair of dull scissors that couldn't have cut tissue paper. Undeterred by the shabby blades, Piper forged ahead with the cutting, and the Haiti Kid wound up with a mohawk so sloppy and uneven, its styling could only be repeated by a disgruntled, epileptic employee of Supercuts.

1. Shannon Moore: When Shannon Moore made his return to the WWE family via the new ECW, he wasn't the same light heavyweight we remembered carrying Matt Hardy's luggage a few years earlier. No sir, this was a new Shannon Moore, with a new punk-rock attitude, and he was now known as The Reject. Now, that's an interesting nickname. Just what was Shannon rejected from? Apparently, judging by his 'do, he was rejected from a job at the adult novelty toy store, because this mohawk looked like a bunch of spiky-tipped vibrators glued to the top of his cranium. Despite his best attempts at penetrating the ECW roster as the premiere punker, the rise of CM Punk as the main sleazy rogue sealed the doom for poor ol' Dildo Dome.

But, hey, you can't fault these guys; they were just trying to stand out amongst the crowd. And since wrestling is built upon a foundation of uniqueness, not everyone has a mullet or a perm. Indeed, as we noted above, some can't even do a mohawk properly. Yes, some folks didn't opt for a mullet, perm or mohawk; they just made up their own looks, which we've documented for your reading pleasure via our . . .

TOP 6 HONORABLE MENTION WRESTLING HAIRSTYLES

6. **Butch Reed's "Natural" Blond Hair:** Lots of black guys have dyed their hair blond in order to make a fashion splash. Among those of note, Koko B. Ware and part-time nWo member Dennis Rodman. Our number six entry, Butch Reed, was a little bit different, though. You see, despite being a black man, he claimed his hair was 100 percent naturally blond, hence his nickname, "the Natural." Unfortunately, before he had a chance to talk about his incredible hair story on *Ripley's Believe It Or Not*, Reed left the WWF, and tragically his "natural" blond

hair transformed into a bland and boring shade of black, a color it has remained ever since.

5. **Sid Vicious's Perm-Mullet:** We debated whether to include Sid's head fur on the mullet list or the perm list. For years, his hair seemed to be an unholy combination of both. To that end, we have dubbed it the "Perm-Mullet," or "Permet." The best thing about it was that no one has ever attempted to pull this one off outside of Sid, and with good reason: they could never duplicate Sid's hybrid skull cover.

4. **Sting's Rat Tail:** While the Stinger will forever be known for his face paint and spiky blond hair, we would like to salute him for a long-forgotten aspect of his persona: a short-lived rat tail he sported in the early 1990s. Screw perms and mullets — if ever there was a hair-style in need of resurrection, it is the rat tail. With face paint. One doesn't work without the other.

3. **Davey Boy Smith Braids:** After the dissolution of the British Bulldogs tag team, following a myriad of injuries to the Dynamite Kid, Davey Boy Smith was left to go it alone. In an attempt to distance himself from his career as one-half of a team, Smith grew out his hair and braided it, making himself look like the muscle-bound, limey version of Whoopi Goldberg.

2. **Bull Nakano's Beehive:** In the mid-1990s, the WWF attempted to revive its long-since banished women's division by importing Madusa Miceli from WCW. Miceli was one of the era's finest women grapplers, but there was a small issue: she had no competition. After much

pleading, Vince and Co. decided to give in to Miceli's wishes and began to import some of Japan's top workers, such as Aja Kong and Bull Nakano. While both were awesome, Nakano was our favorite because she sported a giant hair helmet that would have made Marge Simpson proud. Although many claimed she got her hair inspiration from, say, a porcupine, it was actually a classic beehive look straight out of the 1950s. Bravo to Bull for bringing it back.

1. Jeff Hardy's . . . Errm . . . Hair: While all the other head toppings on this list were singular in nature, Jeff Hardy bucks the trend by having

PHOTO: MATT BALK

What's black and white and red all over? Why, Jeff Hardy's hair, of course!

wacky hair all the time, perpetually painted in some bizarre color. Sometimes it's red. Sometimes it's blue. Sometimes it glows in the dark. Sometimes he paints half of it one color and the other half another. Sometimes it matches his soul patch, but most times it doesn't. Much like a box of chocolates, with Jeff's hair you just never know what you are going to get. We believe this is because he is, at heart, an artist. A clumsy artist who dumps paint on his head.

Sometimes, sadly, there are performers whose hair just isn't up to legendary, Ricky Morton/Lanny Poffo/Jeff Hardy status. Some heads look even worse than Shannon Moore's, if you can fathom such a thing. In fact, some folks have such constant bad hair days that they need to cover their craniums. And to that end, we proudly proclaim . . .

WRESTLING'S 7 GREATEST HEADGEAR APPARATUSES

7. Farooq Asad's "Helmet": Ron Simmons was famous long before he made his WWF debut in 1996, and with good reason. Not only was he the first African-American world champion in WCW history, he was an All-American at Florida State University under head coach Bobby Bowden. In short, he was a pretty well-known guy. That didn't stop the WWF from rechristening him Farooq Asad and claiming he was a descendent of Roman gladiators. Simmons rightly wanted to hide his face at such an idiotic persona, and attempted to do so wearing a powder-blue helmet that appeared to have been created by the Nerf corporation. While we doubt this would have stopped a sword swung at his skull, it did provide adequate protection from beer cups and popcorn boxes.

6. El Gigante's Headband: We've had a lot of laughs at our old pal Jorge Gonzales over the years: he was arguably the worst in-ring performer the world has ever seen. We believe we understand why he sucked so mightily. It wasn't that he was rushed into the ring (following a stint as a basketball player for the Atlanta Hawks), it was that he was a xenophobe. Confused? Bear with us for a moment. As one of Earth's largest human beings, he would obviously be a prime abduction candidate for any passersby from outside the Milky Way. Therefore, in an attempt to thwart Klingons and Wookies, he wrapped what appeared to be aluminum foil around his brow, to block their evil alien signals from entering his noggin. We can only assume this somehow altered his brainwaves, thus preventing him from learning any wrestling moves. Or maybe he just sucked.

5. **Warlord's Shiny Silver Mask:** The Warlord was near the top of the wrestling world when he and his Powers of Pain partner, the Barbarian, entered the WWF in 1988, fresh off a hot feud with the Road Warriors in the NWA. Alas, following a confusing dispute with WWF tag champs Demolition (in which the teams did a double switch of their heel/babyface alliances), the team was split up and both men went on to rather stale singles careers. The Warlord became a protégé of Slick, who lived up to his Doctor of Style nickname by giving the Warlord a new look. This makeover consisted of a trident (complete with "W" head) and a shiny silver mask, thus recreating the former Road Warrior clone as a hybrid Terminator/Phantom of the Opera. Sadly, he never sang. We're thinking he'd have been the man to end Hulk Hogan's title reign if only he had belted out a Schwarzenegger-style rendition of "Music of the Night."

4. **The Barbarian's Antlers:** While the Warlord went high-tech with his revamping, the Barbarian apparently went hunting. Following the split, he began to wear an animal pelt and antlers into arenas. Sadly, he never actually lowered his head and rammed an opponent's midsection. Had he done so, he would have been tops on this list for sure.

3. Scott Steiner's Chain Mail: Scott Steiner has undergone countless transformations in his wrestling career, from clean-cut University of Michigan good guy to jacked-up thug. While many were stunned to learn that Big Poppa Pump was, in fact, Scott Steiner (he looked that different), we were too busy looking on in awe of his new headgear to even be concerned. Few things in wrestling truly baffle hardened veteran marks like us anymore, but the fact that no wrestler prior to Scott Steiner had ever channeled the spirit of King Arthur did stun us. Steiner's introduction of chain mail into the mainstream wrestling scene will likely go down as his greatest contribution to the sport.

2. Bam Bam Bigelow's Tattooed Skull: It's become common practice, not only in wrestling but in society in general, that when your hair starts to vanish, you simply shave your head bald. Steve Austin did this, complementing his new image with a goatee that made him look like a real badass. As much as we love Stone Cold, we have to state for the record that shaving your head to hide premature baldness doesn't make you a bad ass, it just makes you smart. No, if Austin really wanted to ratchet up his tough-guy persona, he'd have done what Bam Bam Bigelow did — tattooed his skull. Shaving? Smart. Tattooing that skull with all manner of evil fireballs and shit? That's hardcore.

1. Big Van Vader's Helmet: While all the items on this list are fantastic, none can compare with the big daddy of them all. And that would be a giant metal helmet that Leon White wore during his days in rings not only in the U.S., but also throughout the world in the early 1990s. Now, this wasn't just any old metallic helmet, oh no. This puppy had eyeballs that lit up and spewed smoke . . . via remote control!

That's right, Vader didn't have to push any silly buttons on that bad boy, he could be fifty feet away and it would fire away with Fourth of July-style antics. Sorry, guys — but your antlers and chain mail and tattoos just can't compare.

Of course, the top of your head isn't the only place where hair can make or break an appearance. You can also have all kinds of zany facial fur surrounding your pie hole. We can come up with only . . .

3 MEN IN WRESTLING WHO ACTUALLY MADE THE MOUSTACHE COOL

PHOTO: WILL WHEELER

Yes, Magnum still has that killer stache in 2007.
Seriously, would YOU shave if you had it?

3. Magnum TA: When Terry Allen was a young star on the rise in the mid-1980s, he turned to the world of television for inspiration. He found that inspiration in the form of Tom Selleck, aka Magnum PI. In fact, Allen decided that Hawaii's top television private dick was exactly who he should be, and thus changed his name to Magnum TA. The most important aspect of the transformation was unquestionably the stylish new pushbroom Allen sported, one of only three in wrestling history that somehow looked cool. We are sure Magnum's 'stache got him tons of rats back in the day and for that, we salute him, even if he didn't bother to bring a Higgins character in as his manager.

2. Big Bully Busick: In our whirlwind society, fashions come and go. The moustache is currently on an "out" trend, but believe us — if people start sporting handlebars, it will be back in a major, major way. For those who would like to start such a movement, we advise you to hunt down tapes of Nick Busick, who terrorized rings as Big Bully Busick in the late 1980s in the WWF. That dude had the most killer of 'staches, looking like he just stepped out of a boxing match with Max Baer. Complementing his lip warmer was a derby atop his head, which we have no doubt he stole when Mr. Fuji wasn't looking.

1. Blackjack Mulligan: Many of you are likely crying foul that Hulk Hogan doesn't appear on this list. Spare us the hate mail. While Hogan's Fu Manchu may have been a classic look, it was nothing — *nothing* — compared to the perfection that were Blackjack Mulligan's whiskers. In fact, we'd be willing to wager that when Hogan saw that pitch-black nose tickler, his own 'stache turned white with fright. There is no 'stache in history that can compare with Mulligan's mighty soup strainer, which is why it tops our list.

But hey, there are more ways to achieve wrestling-legend status than just having a great 'do or stellar pushbroom. While most in charge of the business today would advise performers to sport a killer tan, countless men have been able to hit the top being somewhat lighter in pallor. Well, not countless, and come to think of it, they never hit the top. Whatever. We just want an excuse to name . . .

THE TOP 6 WRESTLING PERSONALITIES WHO MAY HAVE BEEN PART ALBINO

6. **Bob Backlund:** One of the greatest scientific wrestlers of all time, this former NCAA wrestling champion was able to parlay those skills into the second-longest title reign in WWF history, right behind Bruno Sammartino. Called "Opie" by many due to his wholesome appearance, Backlund was perhaps the most vanilla wrestling personality the world had ever seen, not only in his bland interview style, but also thanks to his ghostly physique. In fact, in a Hawaiian Tropic showdown between Mr. Backlund and Casper, we'd put our money on the ghost.

5. **Bobby Eaton:** Eaton is another in a string of wrestlers who were overloaded with in-ring ability while being shafted on skin pigment. And like Backlund, Eaton also wasn't much of a talker, allowing men such as Jim Cornette to do all his yapping for him. There were times throughout Eaton's career in which he appeared to at least have knowledge of the concept of a tanning salon, but it never lasted, and

soon enough Eaton was right back to his pasty origin. Which, when you have as much talent as Eaton had, didn't really detract from the whole package.

4. **Mike Von Erich:** There are a great many wrestling pundits who will tell you that Mike Von Erich should never have stepped foot in the squared circle. Just one look at his lanky frame would seem to confirm the fact that he'd never follow in the footsteps of brothers Kevin, David and Kerry, but apparently father Fritz felt that if he was a Von Erich, by God, he should be a wrestler. It didn't help that in addition to being a beanpole, he had skin tone that ranged between Elmer's Glue and that paste you used in second grade (you know, the one with the pirate on it). All of which begs the question: isn't Texas supposedly warm and sunny? Has country music been lying to us all these years? Shouldn't poor Mikey have gotten something of a tan, just by osmosis?

3. **King Kong Bundy:** The Human Avalanche was a mainstay on wrestling cards throughout the late 1970s and into the mid-1990s, and with good reason: at six-two and 440 pounds, he was a mountain of a man. Shaved clean from head to toe (well, let's assume that at least — we're not about to go looking for what was beneath his black singlet), Bundy was a frightening man, and to that end, it is perhaps to his benefit that his skin had all the tone of your typical laboratory rat. After all, if we saw Bundy lying on the beach, we'd honestly be thinking along the lines of "beached whale," rather than that little dog tugging at his trousers as he applied liberal doses of Coppertone.

2. Hercules Hernandez: In many ways, Ray Hernandez was a poster child for what a wrestler was supposed to be in the 1980s, with his long hair, screaming interviews and a physique so impressive that he was dubbed Hercules. And trust us, if you've never seen the guy, he was jacked to the gills, and thus worthy of being proclaimed the son of Jupiter. Sadly, this Herc failed one of the twelve tasks laid before him: getting a tan. We've seen fish bellies that looked to have soaked in more rays, which leads us to believe that apparently there wasn't a lot of sun on Mount Olympus.

1. The Pale Horse: Before you scratch your head too hard, allow us to save you a bloody scalp: the Pale Horse wasn't an obscure masked wrestler who did weekly jobs on *WWF Superstars* back in the day. No, the Pale Horse was just that — a horse who was, indeed, pale. Looked something like this, in fact:

The Pale Horse is currently serving time for failing to register as a Peeping Tom / sexual predator.

PHOTO COURTESY OF JEFF BAER HORSE FARM

See, the Pale Horse was the cohort of Seven, a Vince Russo creation in which Dustin Rhodes dressed up like Uncle Fester. According to the vignettes preceding Seven's debut, the pair would sneak up to children's windows and peek inside. Was Seven a pedophile? Was the Pale Horse a pedophile? The world will never know, as the gimmick was dropped following his very first in-ring appearance. And we never saw the Pale Horse again, as he was no doubt shipped off to the glue factory.

Okay, so maybe Seven and his Pale Horse weren't pedophiles. But others in the wrestling business certainly appeared to have some manner of sexual dysfunction, judging solely on what they wore to the ring. To wit . . .

THE 5 MOST OFFENSIVELY DRESSED WRESTLERS

5. Rick Steiner: If you're known as the "Dog-Faced Gremlin," odds are there's something not quite right in your love life. Sport a black leather jacket with spikes, and we're certain of it. And when this spikey leather jacket sports dual silver Mack Truck bulldogs on the shoulders? Yeah . . . there's some sexual chicanery bubbling under the surface we'd rather not know about.

4. American Males: The eighteen to thirty-four male demographic is crucial for networks; hence they want to air hip shows that feature cool and sexy characters that appeal to said demo. One show of the past that could be considered a blueprint formula for attracting this crowd was CBS's *The Dukes of Hazzard*. It had lots of high-speed car chases and plenty of redneck bar fights. But the single most remembered element of the show was unquestionably Daisy Duke, bouncing around in her cutoff jean shorts. Fifteen years later, the higher-ups at TBS decided to boost ratings on WCW programming by featuring two — count 'em, two — new characters clad in Daisy Duke-style cutoffs. One problem: the individuals with the Levi's creeping up their fannies were Marcus Bagwell and Scotti Riggs, the American Males. The homoerotic fun didn't stop there, however. When it came time to send the soiled Daisy Dukes to the laundromat, Bagwell and Riggs were quick to hop into the nearest male-stripper outfits — complete with suspenders. Somebody should've had Roscoe P. Coltrane arrest these guys on about

1,000 counts of indecent exposure to male wrestling fans.

3. **The Booty Man:** Hey, remember earlier when we talked about Ed Leslie's ridiculous Zodiac gimmick? Well, as much as that sucked, it was a million times better than his stint as the Booty Man, a forty-year-old man who shook his ass for your (dis)pleasure. He'd shake his ass before the match, after the match, during the match. As if that weren't horrifying enough, Booty had giant holes in the back of his tights, exposing his orange-tanned butt cheeks, to the delight of no one. Another fun fact: during this period, Booty Man was accompanied by his manager, Kimberly Page, aka the Booty Girl. In keeping with WCW's insane love of showing only three-quarter-naked men in the '90s, while Beef's "cakes" were bouncing out of his pants and all around the ring, Kimberly was clad in tame cheerleader outfits that could easily double as the centerfold attire for *Nuns Monthly* magazine. While Mr. Leslie is often the butt of jokes, this time he was basically just a butt.

2. **The Bashams:** While Demolition may have innocently introduced a nation to S&M wrestling gear, Doug and Danny Basham metaphorically broke down the door with the force of a five-foot strap-on. As their dominatrix manager, Linda Miles, whipped them with her cat-o'-nine-tails while they walked to the ring, the Bashams became the first tag team to compete with ball gags in their mouths. Let us repeat that, in case you blacked out while reading that sentence: *they competed with ball gags in their mouths.* That would have been bad enough, but Miles shrink-wrapped in black leather? That was something we didn't need to see (and would have sooner taken a shot in the eyes from one of her double dongs to avoid).

1. **Naked Mideon:** Human civilization as we know it today is based on our intelligent forefathers' coming up with a great idea or invention, and then having the smarts to see it through to fruition. Great ideas like building the wheel, flying the first airplane . . . and a certain Canadian publishing company printing three different wrestling books with the word *crap* in the title. You can think of all those monumental ideas, and then suddenly you are reminded of how dumb we Homo sapiens truly are. Consider this, our No. 1 entry. One day, some mentally warped WWF booker thought to himself, "Hey, I've got a good idea. Let's make Dennis Knight wrestle naked!" As we sat and watched Mideon wrestle, clad only in a fanny-pack G-string, testicles flopping out for the entire world to see, we began to think to ourselves that Darwin was wrong. Maybe we haven't evolved that much from our monkey ancestors.

While those guys were offensively dressed, others are simply bizarre. And oddly enough, it is not unusual for such outfits to be debuted on the biggest stage of the wrestling year — *WrestleMania*. While these are usually quite awesome, there have been occasions when that was not the case. Never was this more apparent than at *WrestleMania 22*, when the three biggest stars in the company were given very elaborate ring entrances. Unfortunately, they all completely sucked. And those outfits . . . well, they were . . .

THE 3 OUTFITS THAT SHOULD HAVE BEEN RESERVED FOR HALLOWEEN

3. **John Cena as Al Capone:** Straight from the speakeasy came John Cena, wearing pinstripes and toting a tommy gun. Thank God prohibition

wasn't actually in effect, we couldn't have made it through this sober.

PHOTO: MATT BALK

2. **Rey Mysterio as a Human Peacock:** At first we thought Rey was coming in as an Aztec warrior. But looking at the photo above, we can only assume that WWE had cut a deal in which they agreed to

feature a human version of the NBC mascot.

PHOTO: MATT BALK

1. Triple H as Gonad the Barbarian: King of Kings? Try 'Tard of 'Tards. The only kingdom Trips could oversee in that outfit is Crapmeria.

Those were goofy outfits, to be sure, but one thing you cannot deny is that all three men listed above were in top-notch shape. Because, let's face it, if there's one thing a pro wrestler cannot be in this day and age, it is obese. Sure, in the past it's been hip to be anything but square (and trust us, some of the top heels in the past were the polar opposite), but today? You better be fit and trim or you won't even get a look. For you rookies with a bit of pudge around the middle, don't fret — we've got you taken care of with . . .

THE 7 GREATEST WEIGHT-LOSS PLANS/DIET SUPPLEMENTS/PERSONAL TRAINERS/OTHER ASSORTED FITNESS WACKAMAROOS IN WRESTLING HISTORY

7. **The Bodydonnas:** In the early 1990s, Tammy Sytch and Chris Candido were tearing up the independent scene. Candido was a short, stocky, spectacular worker with a pedigree: he was the grandson of Chuck "Popeye" Richards. And right beside him was his high school sweetheart, Sytch, who was not only beautiful but understood wrestling like few other women in the game. They were a dynamite pair, signed to the WWF and expecting a big push. What they got were vignettes in which they talked about how fit they were. And you know, come to think of it, they were. So maybe taking advice from these two wouldn't be the worst idea ever. Still, we would pass on their fashion sense, which included lots of cyan, magenta and yellow spandex. We don't care if you have three percent body fat, that never looks good.

6. **Cat Bo:** Ernest "the Cat" Miller may not have been the greatest in-ring wrestler on the planet, but we will say this for the karate instructor turned grappler: he was damn entertaining. In addition to

having great comedic timing, Miller was also very fit, so if you were looking for someone to pattern your physique after, well, you could do worse than the six-foot-two, 235-pound Cat. And Miller was right there to help you with his revolutionary Cat Bo system. Sure, you've heard of Tae Bo, and maybe even watched a VHS or two with Billy Blanks shadow boxing, but that stuff's for wussies. If you want to be a real man, you'd hunt down a rare copy of *Cat Bo*, which Miller marketed to WCW fans in 2000. While we're not sure what, exactly, Cat Bo consisted of, any program that gets you fit enough to dance a dance that James Brown wishes he could dance is A-OK with us.

5. **Muffy:** Of all the women who have graced the WWE stage, few were as flat-out physically fit as Caryn Mower, trainer to the stars. Actually, not just the stars — *the* star, the super-mega-colossal star, the brightest star in the known universe: Stephanie McMahon herself. When Nipple H decided she was going to actually compete inside the squared circle, she was determined to get into the best shape of her life, and thus Mower's alter ego, Muffy, was born. Loud, shrill and as annoying as a K-Fed cover of "Pour Some Sugar on Me," Muffy would screech out insults to the fans. We have no doubt that her thought-provoking cries of "You're fat!" would have inspired a generation to forgo two liters of Mountain Dew in favor of a glass of V8, but it was not meant to be. For Stephers realized that if she needed a fitness trainer, this would mean she was not, in fact, a model of fitness. Even as an on-screen character, that wouldn't fly, so Muffy vanished after just two appearances. Pity.

4. **ICOPRO:** As we mentioned above, wrestling is all about being muscular and hairless and oily. Can't have the muscles without the oil,

you know. Can't have the muscles *with* the hair, either. Since Vince McMahon is obviously enamored of perfect male physiques, almost to the point that one has to wonder which team he's playing for, it made perfect sense that he'd want to conquer the world of body-building as well. He gave it his best shot with the World Bodybuilding Federation. To ensure that these men would not be accused of uti-lizing illegal steroids, he urged them to build their bodies with ICOPRO (which was also heavily advertised on WWF programming). Sadly, the supplement vanished with the WBF, but we're betting you could hunt down some ten-year-old cans of the crap on eBay. And whatever the price, it would be well worth it. After all, if it worked for "the Dutch Oven," Aaron Baker, it would work for you.

3. **Four Horsemen Vitamins:** While ICOPRO may have been the fuel that gassed up the engines in the WBF, it pales in comparison — *pales in comparison*, we sez — to whatever the hell pills Ric Flair and his cronies were popping in the late '80s. Even though they were heels, they were kind enough to offer their pharmaceuticals to fans via television and magazine ads in the old Apter mags. We can only assume that gulping these things down like Goldfish crackers would allow you, too, to be a jet-flying, limousine-riding, kiss-stealing, wheeling-dealing son of a gun, one who could make all the girls cry by giving them rides on Space Mountain all night long. Woo. Err, we mean woooooooooooo-oooooooooo!!! There, that's better. No doubt the fine folks at Pfizer reverse-engineered the stuff and launched Viagra years later.

2. **Simon System:** When Mike Bucci was given the persona of Simon Dean, fitness guru, he could have seen it as the kiss of death, a silly gimmick

no one could possibly take seriously. Instead, he created a system — the Simon System. Wait, scratch that. The *patented* Simon System. This conglomeration of workout tapes, dieting instructions and protein-shake mixes was everything even the fattest pig in the audience would need to become fit as a fiddle, just like Simon himself. Indeed, one segment on WWE television saw Simon offer a free sample of his system to Dave Batista. Even though Batista is obviously a very well-conditioned man, just one slurp of a patented Simon shake gave him even greater strength . . . strength enough to power-bomb poor Simon into oblivion. Upon further reflection, perhaps Dean's system works a little *too* well.

1. **Playboy Buddy Rose Blow Away Diet:** In the late 1980s, Buddy Rose had a problem. The man who once tipped the scales at a lean, mean 218 had somehow ballooned to Hindenburg proportions. Jumping rope, running on treadmills, lying around on the couch . . . none of it helped him to get back into Playboy shape. But all was not lost, as Rose was about to discover the greatest weight-loss supplement known to man: Blow Away. And best of all, he would offer it to wrestling fans at home. Commercials for the product showed Rose, wearing only a tank top and very tighty-whities, looking glum and forlorn. No matter how large his banana split, he just couldn't shake his doldrums. But change was literally in the air, thanks to Blow Away, a white powder that would transform his life. Unlike other white powders that transformed wrestlers' lives, this one wasn't taken nasally, but rather dumped all over the body. After the "factory formulated" powder set into every nook and cranny of Rose's ample frame, he turned on a fan and watched the weight literally blow away! And though photos seemed to indicate he was just as blimpy as ever, the announcer proclaimed that he had

lost upwards of fifty pounds, and even showed a literal glob of gloopy fat to prove it. If there's one thing we've learned over the years of watching this great sport, it's that wrestling announcers never lie. Thus, there really is no other choice for our top spot on the list.

PHOTO: MATT BALK

Buddy Rose at a lean, mean, 218 —
that blow away diet really worked!

With the help of those products, you can certainly shed the fat. But one thing you cannot combat is the inevitable: age. Everyone gets older. It's just a fact of life. You're born, you grow up, you get old, you die. Along the way, though, some of us age better than others. You look at a guy like Dick Clark, and he appears as fresh as a daisy. Every New Year's Eve, you'd need to watch the ball drop just to see what the hell year it was, because if you just looked at the guy's face, you'd think it was forever 1964. Others, however, don't age as well, with their mugs becoming withered, leathery and tired. And in one case, it was much worse. To wit . . .

THE TOP WRESTLER WHO, UPON AGING, MOST CLOSELY RESEMBLES A CIGAR-STORE INDIAN

PHOTO COURTESY CASEY STEPHON

1. Greg Valentine: Now, please don't get us wrong. In his day, Greg "the Hammer" Valentine was one of the all-time greats, a phenomenal worker. Just how good was Valentine? Consider this: he was half of a tremendous WWF tag team championship tandem known as the Dream Team. His partner was Brutus Beefcake. Think about that for a second. He was such a great wrestler that he made matches featuring Brutus freakin' Beefcake not only bearable, but actually fun to watch. That takes tremendous talent. Sadly, the years were not kind to the Hammer, whose mug became so weathered that he began to resemble a face upon Mount Rushmore. Still, if we ran into him on the street, we'd for sure mark out and ask for his autograph. And probably a Super Belicoso. Because we're jerks like that.

Tell Us a Story, Uncle Vince

One of the key items that makes wrestling so different from any other form of sports is its scripted stories. While at times it has positioned itself as more sport than entertainment, especially before the mid-1980s, a storyline element has always been one of the business's main draws.

At its best, a wrestling storyline can really hook the viewers . . . and more importantly, the viewers' pocketbooks. Often it doesn't matter if the end match is the greatest bout ever; if the story is strong enough, fans will react big-time. One need look no further than the legendary Hulk Hogan vs. Andre the Giant feud. Two men who had been friends for years, one who was champion, one who was "undefeated." Finally, the friendship is destroyed because the non-champion wants a title bout, and it leads to a legendary match that, if unaccompanied by any type of story, would have been viewed as legendarily horrible.

That's the good side of wrestling storytelling. But good stuff doesn't happen very often, so don't get used to it. Just as often, there are stories that make no sense and leave you scratching your head.

But let's face it, professional wrestling is built on a simple foundation: two guys don't like each other, and fans pay to see them settle their disputes inside the ring. While various plot devices have been used over the years to explain why two men would want to battle, there have been at least . . .

5 TIMES WHEN WE WOULDN'T HAVE BEEN CONTENT WITH PINNING OUR FOE'S SHOULDERS TO THE MAT

5. You've Been Banging My Wife: This one is a time-honored tradition in the business. It's happened to countless men over the years, be it Randy Savage with Ric Flair, Jake Roberts with Rick Rude, Dustin Rhodes with Val Venis, and so many other loyal husbands who have seen sexual accusations made against their so-called better halves. Let's put you in the role of one of these wronged men. Say you come into work one day, and Phil from marketing comes up and says, "Your wife blew me last night, and sweet vagina, was it good!" What would your first thought be? To punch the guy right in his filthy, bile-spewing mouth? Or to lock up with this man and prove that you are, in fact, the superior grappler? Amazingly, most professional wrestlers lean toward the latter. What a strange business.

4. You Killed My Pet, Then Ate Him: But poor Jake Roberts didn't just have his wife's good name tarnished, he suffered a lot more than that. In fact, you could make the case that what Earthquake John Tenta did to Roberts was much worse than Rick Rude's prancing around with pictures of Jake's wife's face spray-painted on his crotch. Quake was an evil, vicious man who had no fear . . . save one. You see, he feared snakes. In fact, he hated snakes. Hated, hated, *hated* them. And he made it very clear to Jake just how much he despised them. During a bout between the two, Quake tied Roberts into the ropes and put the bag containing Damien in the center of the ring. The big man then proceeded to repeatedly drop his 462-pound frame on Jake's pet. A sickened Roberts was finally released from the ropes, but not before his beloved Damien had slithered on into the afterlife. All this would have been bad enough, but Roberts was about to see something far worse, as Quake appeared on *Prime Time Wrestling* and debuted his latest culinary creation: Snakeburgers. These tasty treats were presumably made of the remains of Damien, and Quake and evil cohort Bobby Heenan gulped them down with glee. Roberts was furious, heartbroken, and there was only one recourse: to use his patented DDT finisher on Quake and thus vanquish his pet's killer in a contest of grappling skill. This being Jake Roberts, we thought he might be a bit more vicious than that.

3. **You Killed My Pet, Then Fed Him to Me:** Now, what Quake did was wrong, there's no doubt about it, but what if Roberts had been force-fed the charbroiled remains of his pet python? Such an event happened to Al Snow, who at one point in his career had taken to carting around a small chihuahua named Pepper. The evil Big Bossman would have none of that, and dognapped Pepper at his earliest convenience. Snow pleaded with Bossman to return the dog to him unharmed, and Bossman seemed agreeable, going so far as to invite Snow to dinner. It was a home-cooked meal of pepper steak, which Al found delightful . . . until he discovered that it was actually Pepper steak, made from his pet. Obviously, calling PETA would have been anyone's first step had such an event occurred in real life, but that's not what Al had in mind, oh no. Instead, he challenged Bossman to a wrestling contest inside a specially constructed cage. Dubbed the "Kennel from Hell," it featured dogs running around ringside, peeing and pooping

all over the place (and that's not a joke — the canines were literally urinating in plain view of the camera). After a long battle, Snow emerged victorious not by pummeling Bossman into unconsciousness, but by escaping the cage. Yes, he exacted his revenge by running away from his dog's killer/cooker. We're ready to call PETA and ask them to make sure Al Snow never has a pet again.

2. **You Dragged Away My Father's Casket with a Chain:** Just when you thought Big Bossman couldn't be any more unsavory, he began to mock the Big Show's father, who had been diagnosed with cancer. Things took a turn for the worse when the man actually died, and funeral services were held. Bossman crashed the party, running over the Big Show with his car, then hooking a chain onto his casket and dragging him away. How did Big Show respond to this? By pummeling Bossman to the point that he needed his own casket? Oh no — something far more brutal. He met Bossman in a wrestling encounter, an encounter in which many holds were exchanged. Remember, kids — holds are the ultimate revenge.

1. **You Claim I'm Impotent and That You're My Son's Father:** Prior to Eddie Guerrero's untimely passing, he was involved in some seriously bad angles. The most notable may have been the one in which he was holding a secret over Rey Mysterio's head, a secret about Rey's son Dominic that Rey was desperate to keep hidden. Eventually, Eddie came out before a national audience and stated that Dominic wasn't really Rey's son, but Eddie's. Apparently, when Rey and his wife were attempting to start a *familia*, Rey was shooting blanks and needed Eddie to fill in. Fill in his wife's vaginal cavity, that is. As you can

imagine, Rey was livid at such accusations. So furious that he attempted again and again to pin Eddie's shoulders to the mat for a three count. Finally, Eddie decided that it was time to legally claim Dominic as his own. You can just imagine Rey's reaction to *that*. Oh yes, when someone makes such slanderous remarks, remarks about your own son, then threatens to take him away from you, there is only one thing you can do: place the custody papers above the ring and contest them in a ladder match. If that's how Rey exacted justice, we have to wonder if maybe Dominic would have been better off with Eddie after all.

There have also been those times when something more or less defies the laws of . . . well, the law. Makes you glad some of these guys aren't your neighbors. Take, for instance . . .

THE 6 CRIMES FOR WHICH WE'D HOPE KANE AND UNDERTAKER WOULD BE ARRESTED IF THEY LIVED IN OUR TOWN

6. **Crucifixion:** Not sure if you'd actually be arrested for doing such a thing, but we'd like to think that in the good ol' U.S. of A., it would be illegal to take someone against their will, strap them to what appears to be a cross and hang them high into the air. That should be against some sort of decency law at least. Such was the case, though, throughout most of 1999 as Undertaker ran rampant through WWE with his Ministry of Darkness. Not only did he crucify folks to honor, ermm, his own glory, but on at least one occasion, he took a knife and sliced open his followers like an Atlantic herring. You know, maybe Dennis Knight wasn't that great in the ring, but dissecting him

seems a bit extreme.

5. **Kidnapping:** You'd think that crucifixion and filleting humans would be much higher on a list of charges than mere kidnapping, but in this case we'd argue the point: Undertaker's main victim was one Stephanie McMahon. His brother, Kane, also did some kidnapping in his day; he once threw Triple H in the trunk of his car and sped away. It's not so much that we oppose the idea of Hunter and Steph being taken away, more that they were brought back.

4. **Concreticide:** You probably just looked at that word and thought, "Waitaminute . . . concreticide isn't in the dictionary!" Heck, even Microsoft Word would agree with that assessment. But you know what? Maybe you can't use it in Scrabble, but there's really no other way to describe Undertaker's actions on June 27, 2004, at the Scope in Norfolk, Virginia. Undertaker's manager, Paul Bearer, was locked up in a glass case as per a pre-match stipulation. Idling next to said case is a cement truck. The stipulation is that unless Undertaker agrees to take a dive, Bearer will be encased in concrete. Apparently, this type of wagering is legal in the state of Virginia. Although his mentor of over a decade will perish should he prevail, Undertaker fights valiantly and wins the match. He then proceeds to personally pull the lever to bury his pal. Some career advice to aspiring pro wrestling managers: never agree to manage Undertaker.

3. **Arson:** Again, you might believe that smothering someone in Quikrete would be worse than setting property ablaze. That usually rings true, but in the case of Kane, well, see, he likes to set *people* on fire. During

a televised interview with commentator Jim Ross, Kane became so irate that he pulled out a blowtorch and used the poor guy as kindling. The fact that he failed to brush his grilled Oklahoman with JR's own BBQ sauce may have been Kane's greatest crime. At the very least he should have put an apple in Ross's mouth.

2. **Gonad Electroshock Therapy:** Following Kane's attack on his mother, the half-human, half-android Linda, Shane McMahon decided he'd had enough of the Big Red Machine's antics and would take matters into his own hands. Kane responded by taking Shane's testicles into his hands. That would be bad enough, but then the insane one-eyed monster jumper-cabled Shane's jewels to a car battery. So if you happen to break down on the side of the road and see Kane tooling by, just let him pass. His idea of a "jump start" likely isn't the same as yours.

1. **Murder:** We would be remiss if we didn't travel back in time and explain that Kane and Undertaker are actually brothers (well, in storyline at least). It is also our public duty to explain that Kane is purportedly disfigured due to the fact that Undertaker set him on fire — along with his parents, who were killed in the same blaze. Kane later dug up his parents' caskets and presented them to his brother. In a touching moment, he then lit his father's coffin on fire and choke-slammed his brother through his mom's. It should be noted that despite doing all these things on national television, neither Kane nor Undertaker served any jail time. Perhaps they just had good lawyers.

After looking at the list above, one fact becomes undeniable. When you get right down to it, there are only two things in life you can count on: taxes . . .

AND THE FACT THAT PROMOTIONS DON'T UNDERSTAND THE WORD "DEATH"

1. Al Wilson: The sad saga of an old man and a woman thirty years his

PHOTO: MATT BALK

Dawn Marie: She's got the looks that kill — literally.

junior, this one had been done to death already, no pun intended. We've all seen it a thousand times, the timeless tale of old man meets daughter's voluptuous friend, old man marries girl against family's wishes, girl learns that old man's new wife really is a lesbian and is using the old man to convince girl to serve up her tuna taco, girl kills old man on their wedding night via sexual overload, girl and daughter duke it out at the funeral home and, of course, the hackneyed climax: girls knock over old man's casket and fight atop his corpse. Talk about tired and overdone.

Sometimes lives end before they even begin. And while abortion is something most forms of entertainment tread very lightly on, that's not the case with wrestling. In fact, in wrestling, it's just more storyline fodder. It's happened twice in the span of five years, those pesky . . .

ABORTION STORYLINES

2. **Miss Hancock:** Though most folks these days know Stacy Keibler by her real name, the former Baltimore Ravens cheerleader was first introduced to wrestling fans as the sexy librarian (well, that was her look at least) Miss Hancock in WCW. She was romantically intertwined with Ric Flair's son David behind the scenes, which WCW writer Vince Russo thought would make an interesting dynamic for both characters on-air. The storyline progressed to the point that Hancock was pregnant, but in a swerve (and oh how Mr. Russo loved his swerves), David was not the father. The big question, of course, was who had laid the egg in Stacy's nest. Rumors were rampant that perhaps Ric or even Russo himself was the father, but we never found out, as

Hancock lost her baby during a mud match with Major Gunns. So while some might state it wasn't technically an abortion, viewers of that match might well argue otherwise.

1. **Lita:** A few pages back we gave you a list of crimes perpetrated by Kane. But what you might not know, and surely wouldn't gather by reading that list, is that he is also a loving husband and father (at least in storylines). Sure, he basically blackmailed Lita into becoming Mrs. Kane, but once he impregnated her with his big red sperm, he turned over a new leaf and did everything he could to be a worthy partner to his bride. Sadly, this wasn't enough to save Lita from losing her baby due to the shenanigans of Gene Snitsky, who threw Kane right into his pregnant wife's belly. Though he originally claimed it was "not my fault," he later rescinded the statement and took glee in the fact that he was wrestling's answer to a wire coat hanger. He would soon give up killing babies in favor of his new hobby: licking women's feet for sexual plea-sure . . . an act which would make him a babyface.

Sometimes, a main storyline in wrestling has concerned family. The McMahons have been playing that one up for years. But unlike Vince, his wife and the kids, there have also been stories created in which a wrestler was instantly a member of a family. Even though he wasn't. Take, for instance . . .

THE 5 WRESTLERS WHO WERE RELATIVES WHO WEREN'T (AND 4 WHO SHOULDN'T HAVE BEEN)

5. **Ricky Steamboat:** What's this? Ricky Steamboat in a *WrestleCrap* book? Again? For shame! Everyone knows Steamboat was one of the

greatest wrestlers of all time. But what you might not know is the backstory to his name. During his early months in the sport, promoters saw the potential in him, but also knew he couldn't be a babyface under his real name, Richard Blood. While Ricky was struggling to come up with a new handle, a promoter noticed that he bore an uncanny resemblance to a popular wrestler from the '60s named Sammy Steamboat. The promoter told his ring announcer that Blood's name was now Ricky Steamboat and he was Sammy's son. Unfortunately, no one told Ricky about this, and upon being introduced by his new name, he insisted he was not, in fact, Sammy Steamboat's son. "Shut up," the announcer reportedly whispered to the newly dubbed Steamboat, "and listen to that reaction." Hearing the crowd's cheers, Blood decided that yep, Steamboat was a good name after all.

4. **Andre the Giant's Son — The Giant:** Given that Paul Wight was nearly seven feet tall, the Big Show, as he is known today, was set to make a huge impact upon his WCW debut in 1995. He was slated to feud with none other than the company's biggest star, Hulk Hogan, over the WCW World Title. Feeling that merely premiering a giant, athletic man (don't laugh — the guy used to be really slender and threw awesome dropkicks!) wouldn't be enough, WCW decided to try to recapture what was arguably Hogan's greatest feud ever, his battle with Andre the Giant. Since Andre was, you know, dead, they couldn't really do this with the real deal, so they instead declared that Wight was Andre's son. Fans were outraged, and WCW amazingly showed the good taste to end the angle quickly. Of course, they later followed up this display of good taste with another angle

between the two, in which Hogan threw Wight off the roof of Detroit's Cobo Hall. Ah well, can't win 'em all.

PHOTO: ECW

Sadly, The Giant never wore a pink herringbone suit, thus negating the legitimacy of the angle.

3. Ian Mooney: A best-forgotten footnote in WWF history is the period in which nearly every announcer looked exactly like a Ken doll. There was Craig DeGeorge, Todd Pettengill and, of course, Sean and Ian Mooney. What's this? You don't remember Sean and Ian Mooney? For the uninitiated, Sean Mooney was a very bland announcer, but he was attractive. We guess. We don't swing that way. Anyhoo, he would appear on WWF B shows and do both play-by-play and interview segments. But what would happen if he was sick? Or his kid had a soccer game? Who would cover? Why, his twin brother, Ian Mooney. Who wasn't really his brother. Because it was just Sean, inexplicably introduced as Ian. Don't ask. It just makes our heads hurt.

2. **Jimmy Jack Funk:** In the mid-'80s, Terry Funk was rampaging through the World Wrestling Federation, much as he had through every company he had ever worked for. He was doing so well, that the company offered his older brother Dory a deal as well, and sure enough, the Funks began tearing up the tag team ranks. Eventually, Terry tired of the exhausting travel that came along with being a WWF superstar and gave his notice. Since the WWF had built the Funks up as one of its top teams, the organization was in a tricky situation. The solution? Import Pacific Northwest star Jesse Barr, put him under a Lone Ranger mask and dub him "Jimmy Jack Funk," long-lost cousin. The fans' reaction to this new arrival? To paraphrase a nursery rhyme: Jimmy Jack Funk, and I don't care. Despite this, Jimmy Jack remained on the WWF roster for years, long after Terry and Dory had departed. He never really did much, mind you, other than opening more cards than Hallmark.

1. **Lance Von Erich:** Pretty much everyone knows the Von Erich story, but if you don't, here's the *WrestleCrap* Cliff's Notes version. In the

mid-1980s, Texas was one of the hottest wrestling properties on earth. Leading the charge was the Von Erich clan, helmed by father Fritz. Now, Fritz loved his boys, but he loved wrestling even more and made no bones about the fact that he wanted all his sons to be in the business. Two were naturals: Kerry and David both looked the part and, especially early in their careers, lived up to billing. Despite a slender, lanky frame, Kevin was arguably the best in the ring. After that, Mike was way too slight to play the role, and Chris was so tiny that a role as a manager or commentator would have been more appropriate. Sadly, that didn't stop either of them from bulking up way more than they should have and getting into the ring.

Eventually, a lethal combination of fame and drugs had the family falling apart: David was dead and Mike was battling all sorts of addictions. Enter William Vaughn, whom Fritz debuted as cousin Lance. (Please note again, it's *Lance*, not *Vance*, the latter being the bogus cousin on *The Dukes of Hazzard*.) Due to his good looks and acceptable wrestling ability, fans bought into Lance for a while. In fact, Vaughn himself felt they liked him enough to ask Fritz for a raise. Fritz then informed Vaughn he wasn't really a Von Erich, so he wasn't about to make Von Erich money. Vaughn walked, choosing instead to work for a rival promotion. The move infuriated Fritz, who went on-air and proclaimed Lance nothing but a fraud. Having to forgo his newly revealed bogus name, Vaughn continued wrestling as the Fabulous Lance. While he didn't have much success, on the plus side he avoided the Von Erich curse. That is, unlike Fritz, Kerry, Mike or Chris, Lance actually, you know, lived.

We've looked at a lot of bad storylines, so let's shift gears and talk about a great one: the New World Order. The first incarnation of the nWo in 1996 could best be described as the evolution of the centuries-old format of simple good vs. evil in pro wrestling into the modern era. Where it was once considered taboo to cheer heelish behavior, it was now acceptable to root for a wrestler who had just attempted second-degree homicide inside the squared circle. The group was revolutionary in the beginning, with core members and legit superstars in Hulk Hogan, Scott Hall and Kevin Nash. But it soon sank into a de-evolutionary mode, where it seemed every Tom, Dick and Harry wrestling under the WCW banner — and even the concession-stand vendor — became an official card-carrying member of the New World Order, severely watering down the original idea of an elite group of stars taking over WCW. With that, we give you . . .

THE 10 WORST NWO MEMBERS OF ALL-TIME

10. **Vincent:** At one time, Mike Jones, best known as Ted DiBiase's bodyguard, Virgil, would've been considered a big enough star to have held his own as a member of the nWo. However, his push as the Roddy Piper-coached Million Dollar Champion quickly ran out of steam and Jones ended up floundering in the WWF midcard, doing such best-forgotten bits as dressing in drag as Virgilina. Let go by the WWF, he showed up in WCW in 1996 as the nWo's head of security, Vincent. Vincent's time with the group was noted for basically nothing. Perhaps his highlight was feuding with Stevie Ray over who would lead the midcard-filled nWo Black 'n' White, which had been abandoned by Hulk Hogan and subsequently dubbed the nWo B-Team. That's like feuding over who gets to eat a shit sandwich inside the kitchen and who has to eat directly from the Johnny-on-the-Job outside.

9. Nick Patrick: Despite the fact that Hogan, Nash and Hall were three of the biggest men in wrestling, size-wise and drawing-power-wise, they apparently thought they needed a little assistance to conquer the land of WCW. They would receive it in the form of corrupt referee Nick Patrick. In terms of making the nWo look like legit badasses, it was a major mistake. Hulk Hogan could slam Andre the Giant, but he needs a biased referee to count fast in order to defeat Sting? The whole evil-referee-helping-the-nWo angle had the feel of a high school team comprised of macho jocks turning to the nerd with a leg brace to help quarterback the team to the state championship. While Patrick didn't have a leg brace, his unnecessary inclusion in the nWo fold was one of the group's many handicaps.

8. Horace Hogan: With Hulk Hogan pretty much dictating the direction of both his career and the nWo, it was only a matter of time before he recruited his nephew, Horace, into the fold. While Horace possessed little more than size, the fact that he was related to the biggest star the sport has ever seen eventually led to his no longer jobbing on *WCW Saturday Night*, but stepping into the limelight. Like others on the list, Horace never made one memorable contribution during his nWo days. Wait, we take that back. He'd often stand behind Hogan, nodding and mean-mugging. Okay, that probably wasn't much either, but at *Halloween Havoc '98* he actually had one tiny moment of glory. That night, Horace stepped out from the shadows, and during the big Hogan-Ultimate Warrior rematch/disaster, he entered the ring and attempted to be the next Mr. October, doing his best Reggie Jackson impersonation by nailing the Warrior with a steel chair, allowing Uncle Hulk to pick up the win. Horace would hang around in the midcard as a member of the nWo B-Team, ultimately being released when — surprise — the Hulkster left WCW.

7. **Dusty Rhodes:** Just when it seemed that almost 99.9 percent of everyone who breathed oxygen and collected a WCW paycheck had been a member of the nWo, Dusty Rhodes made it officially 100 percent when he jumped onto the bandwagon by turning on WCW loyalist Larry Zbyszko during *Souled Out '98*. The logic behind Dusty's heel turn? Well, none. Maybe they wanted to promote a new line of nWo products for the big and fat portion of the crowd. We always wished it would've been the start of Dusty forming another rival nWo offshoot group — nWo offshoot group No. 47 — the nWo Tummy Splotches.

6. **The nWo Girls:** When the nWo was brought back from the dead in late 1999, WCW was getting pummeled by the WWF in the ratings war. To compete with all the scandalous WWF Divas, it was decided the nWo's initials would now stand for the New Whorehouse Order. It was skanks on parade during every edition of *Monday Nitro*, as no fewer than five chicks (April Hunter, Kim "Shikira" Kanner, Midajah O'Hearn, Tylene "Major Gunns" Buck and Pamela Paulshock) came bouncing down to ringside with all the wrestling knowledge of a lobotomized Jackie Gayda. Although by this point the nWo had two feet and an ass cheek in the ground, this core group of Jeff Jarrett, Scott Steiner and ten fake titties were a lot easier on the eyes than the man who was under the nWo banner just one year earlier . . .

PHOTO: ECW

Doesn't this just scream "nWo"?

5. The Disciple: Just when you thought it was impossible for Ed Leslie's ever-changing gimmicks to get any worse, in 1998 Hulk Hogan brought his old running buddy out of the mothballs for yet another disastrous gimmick in Ed's career — the leather-clad Disciple. It's funny, last time we looked up the word *disciple* in *Webster's*, it didn't state: "**dis·ci·ple** (di'-si-pel) n. 1. a white man who follows an orange man around while dressed like the centerfold for *Gay Biker Monthly*." The scene didn't look any more heterosexual when the Ultimate Warrior showed up again to resume his feud with Hogan. Proclaiming himself the leader of the OwN (nWo offshoot group No. 27), Warrior would fight Hulk over the right to possess Leslie's services the way the Bloods and Crips might fight over a bootylicious crack whore. In the end, the Warrior stole the Disciple away from Hogan's stable, culminating with a scene of the Warrior standing victorious over a bent-over Leslie. His role as the Disciple was the last run in the big leagues for Leslie, who would soon find himself bending over in another way — to pick up loose change off the ground.

4. **Kyle Petty:** It is one thing to see football or basketball stars like Dennis Rodman involved in WCW. After all, both of those sports involve athletes engaging in physical contact much like pro wrestling does. It is a whole other ballpark — or in this case, racetrack — to welcome a famous NASCAR driver into your stable of evildoers. But sure enough, in 1997, Hulk Hogan stated that not only was the nWo going to take over wrestling, but it was going to conquer the NASCAR circuit as well. To this day, we're still not quite clear why Hogan wanted to become the supreme ruler of the Daytona 500. Maybe it was all a part of a grand scheme to introduce a new line of nWo beer and whiskey to the untapped, non-wrestling-fan redneck demographic. Thankfully, before Hogan had a chance to cater to racing fans by crooning a horrid country-and-western album (we like to think it

would have been titled *Honky Tonk Hogan*), Kyle Petty and the nWo's car-racing days came to a quick, permanent pit stop. But not quick enough, as fans worldwide had already begun waving their yellow caution flags for the car wreck the once-mighty nWo had become.

3. **nWo Sting:** The majority of the nWo angle's heyday centered on WCW hero Sting trying to defeat evil ringleader Hulk Hogan and restore peace to WCW. To counter the long-time hero, the nWo brought in a fake Sting, who, unlike the real McCoy, did all kinds of dastardly deeds and tried to confuse wrestlers and fans into thinking the real Sting had turned evil and joined the nWo. Sounds like a remotely interesting concept, right? Well, initially it was, until two years had passed after his arrival and the fake Sting was no longer trying to impersonate Sting — he was simply deemed an official member of the group. Rechristened nWo Sting, the man behind the paint, Jeff Farmer (previously known as Cobra), would be seen hanging with the rest of the boys, bringing as much joy and satisfaction to wrestling fans as a "fake" orgasm, until the unthinkable happened — the real Sting became an nWo member by joining . . .

2. **The nWo Wolfpac:** By 1998, you might say that after the introduction of NASCAR drivers, middle-aged referees and crusty old geezers, the wheels were beginning to fall off the nWo wagon. You would be wrong. By the time the nWo Wolfpac was launched, the wheels had fallen off, the wagon had become engulfed in flames and it had crashed into a bus filled with nuns and Boy Scouts. But let us state that there was potential here for the group to be reinvented as a gang of street hoodlums. After all, Kevin Nash, on the stick, had a rather

sarcastic delivery, complemented by a pseudo-street-rapper vibe. Not realizing this was a trait only Nash could pull off successfully, WCW decided to make this a new and hipper nWo group. So out came Nash, Lex Luger, Konnan, and the man who said he would *never* join the nWo — Sting — all decked out in red and black nWo logos, flashing gang signs and spouting off gangsta-style catchphrases. Despite trying their best to look like they just came from a local Los Angeles meeting of the Bloods: Regional Chapter 187, a bunch of forty-year-old men wearing baggy clothing and trying to act cool came off as well as your overweight dad trying to impress a group of teenaged girls by karaokeing 50 Cent songs at a pool party. The Wolfpac was around long enough to sell the token merchandise and drive the group's legacy further into the ground, but they did do one memorable thing. They were responsible for the birth of perhaps the most hideous entity in nWo — and perhaps wrestling history:

1. **Lex Luger's Goatee:** Throughout his career, Lex Luger had one look. He was tanned, muscular and had long, wonderfully conditioned flowing blond hair. A clean-cut guy, he was the living embodiment of the buff bully who kicked sand in skinny guys' faces at the beach. But that look wasn't "fresh and dope" enough for a trendy Wolfpac member, so when the so-called nWo Red 'n' Black came on the scene, along with it came . . . Lex Luger's Goatee. Dear reader, this was not mere facial hair. No, it was a dark, *Spider-Man 3*–style alien entity that consumed Lex's entire face and took on a life of its own. With Goatee in tow, Lex embarked on a new era of hip-hop, rough-and-tough, bad-boy coolness that lasted about . . . two weeks. Like every white guy who has turned his hat around to be more "thuggish" and ended up

looking more like a douchebag of a tool, Lex saw the error of his stubbly ways and murdered Goatee with the help of an accomplice described as being small, white and yellow. Authorities have helped identify the suspect as a Bic disposable. In time, WCW followed suit and mercifully shaved the nWo Wolfpac off the booking sheet.

When you step back and think about it, acronyms like nWo have proven to be a huge part of wrestling. World Wrestling Entertainment is known as WWE. D-Generation X is always referred to as DX, and Triple H is never called by his full name, Hunter Hearst Helmsley. No wonder, that name sucks. With this in mind, it stands to reason that wrestling companies would always try to come up with groups, characters and even promotions that follow this formula. But it doesn't always work out, as is the case with . . .

WRESTLING'S 6 WORST ACRONYMS

6. VKM: As WWE is the big name in the wrestling biz, a lot of folks in smaller groups try to make their names by throwing out challenges to that organization, and in particular, its owner, one Vincent Kennedy McMahon. In 2006, the artists formerly known as Road Dogg and Billy Gunn decided they'd had enough of TNA and began to boast that they'd quit the promotion — while being on its TV shows every week. Just imagine this scenario played out in real life. You walk into McDonald's, telling everyone that you've quit, including the customers. Somehow we doubt the manager would allow you to keep working the drive-thru and intentionally give patrons apple pies when they've clearly ordered Filet o' Fishes. As you've probably noticed, logic often goes out the window in wrestling. Back where we were: the pair

PHOTO: MATT BALK

VKM: Vacant Kip Mind?

decided they would no longer be known as the James Gang (their TNA moniker), but were now to be called the Voodoo Kin Mafia, or VKM. See, they were using the same initials as Vincent Kennedy McMahon. It was like a crafty subliminal message. Nah, scratch that, it was a dumb message and none too subliminal. Plus Voodoo Kin

Mafia just sounds like a bunch of random words shoved together to make up VKM. It might as well have been Vivacious Kumquats Media or Vacant Karaoke Minds. Nah, those make more sense.

5. TIT: One of the reasons the WWF was able to best WCW in the infamous Monday Night Wars was its proliferation of beautiful women. One who is barely mentioned these days, but was featured on a regular basis back then, was Terri Runnels, who managed Goldust under the name Marlena. Following the split with her androgynous charge, she began to cycle through new clients as frequently as she changed her thongs. Eventually, she became embroiled in the tag team scene and created a tournament in which the winner would become her latest acquisition. The name of these playoffs would be the Terri Invitational Tournament. That's right, TIT. No doubt seven-year-old wrestling fans the globe over were giggling, then later asking their friends exactly what a "tit" was.

4. PMS: Following her dabbling in the tag ranks, Ms. Runnels decided she could conquer the wrestling world faster if she had more women helping her. And so a new coalition was formed, with herself as the leader and Miss Jacqueline and Ryan Shamrock (Ken's pseudo-sister) as her cronies. The group had a bad attitude toward men and dubbed themselves the Pretty Mean Sisters, otherwise known as PMS. Again, less an actual team name and more a Mad Libs gone wrong.

3. POWW: Say what you want about him, but David McLane has started no fewer than three women's wrestling promotions over the past twenty years. Sure, the wrestling wasn't great, but the groups were more about stupid slapstick comedy and showing scantily dressed women prancing about than wrestling, which is fine with us. In the beginning there was GLOW, the Gorgeous Ladies of Wrestling, and more recently there was WOW, Women of Wrestling. But sandwiched between those was yet another troupe: the Powerful Women of Wrestling, or POWW. Yes, they were known as POWW despite the fact that the initials to the company were actually PWOW. Maybe Brandi Mae was actually the Dyslexic Farmer's Daughter.

2. SEX: Okay, just look at the three letters to the left. Can there be any doubt — any at all — that a wrestling group with those initials could be the creation of any man but Vince Russo? Sports Entertainment Extreme, or SEX, was a group that threatened to take over a fledgling new wrestling company. And as hard as it might be to fathom, this company had an even worse acronym than SEX . . .

1. TNA: When Jeff and Jerry Jarrett decided to get back into the wrestling promotion business in 2002, they had many important decisions to make, not the least of which was what to name the company. Although they would compete under the ages-old National Wrestling Alliance banner, they believed NWA carried too much old-school baggage to be the company's brand name, especially since the idea was for the promotion to give fans a brand-new type of wrestling, one based on total nonstop action. Total nonstop action? Now, there's a name! And look at the initials: TNA! Why, people will be very curious as to what the hell we're up to! Such was the moronic thinking, and soon enough, NWA-TNA morphed into TNA. Want to have fun with the wife one night? Tell her that you and little Billy are going to watch some TNA. A little free advice to any future promoters: do not name your company in such a way that a) parents won't let their kids watch it, and b) it may cause domestic violence.

Oh yeah, and keep religion far, far away from wrestling. You'd think it would be common sense, just like it is common sense to keep church and state separate. While there is often debate on exactly how separate they should be, the fact is that here in America, pretty much everyone has the right to worship whatever god they want, so long as they aren't hanging up kidnapping victims on homemade crosses or cutting them open and extracting blood. Both of which, as we've already noted, have happened in pro wrestling's version of religion. You see, there's a reason wrestling doesn't air on Sunday mornings. Actually, there is more than one. We can think of ten, in fact . . .

THE TOP 10 EXAMPLES OF HOW WRESTLING AND RELIGION DON'T MIX

10. **Mordecai:** Promos hyping up the *Smackdown* arrival of Kevin Fertig had people talking. He was to be known as Mordecai, obviously a religious figure of some sort, dressed completely in white and carrying beads and trinkets. He even bleached his hair and whiskers white to show the world he was .56 percent more pure than Ivory soap. And just in case someone didn't catch the subtle innuendo, he'd pray before his matches and cut promos in which he called the audience a bunch of sinners. He would be the anti-Undertaker, and fans would be praying to see this literal battle of dark vs. light. Just one problem: his in-ring skills weren't quite up to snuff, and those behind the scenes didn't feel comfortable putting him in a main-event spot. Thus they cast him out (as in fired him). A short while later, though, he was

reborn as Kevin Thorn, a Nosferatu character complete with fangs. Apparently we missed the part in the Bible that detailed cast-out angels being reborn as vampires. Maybe that's in the yet-to-be-released *New — And Improved! — Testament.*

9. Dustin Rhodes Is Holier than Thou: When the great book of wrestling history is penned, there needs to be an entire chapter on Dustin Rhodes' Goldust character. It wasn't just some oddball persona, but a character who ventured into territory where wrestling had never dared tread. When Goldust first started stalking Razor Ramon — the storyline being that of a male wrestler infatuated with another man — it made a lot of people very uneasy. Apparently, it also made either the scriptwriters or Dustin himself a bit unnerved, as years later he would ditch the character in favor of being simply Dustin Rhodes. Not only had he changed his name, but his outlook on life; he was now a religious zealot who protested the excessive amounts of boobilage on display by WWF Divas such as Sunny and Sable. He began to wear shirts and armbands featuring a popular religious acronym: WWGD? Hey wait . . . that should be WWJD (What Would Jesus Do)! You mean this whole thing was a sham, a setup for his bizarre character to return, with the "G" standing for "Goldust"? Holy crap, that's lame.

8. Reverend D-Von: The Dudley Boyz (or Team 3-D, as they are now called) have long been one of wrestling's top tag teams. The brothers from a whore of a mother (and don't blame us, the original family also consisted of an Indian and an Asian) have remained popular over the years, regardless of the promotion in which they ply their trade.

In 2002, however, WWE decided their act had become stale, and split them up. Bubba Ray headed to *Raw* and D-Von was *Smackdown* bound. While Bubba was pretty much the same loud-mouthed fat man he'd always been, a modern-day Brian Knobbs almost, D-Von apparently did some soul-searching. Literally. He became Reverend D-Von, wearing the black suit, white collar, the whole nine yards. Even had the strains of a church organ accompany his jaunt to the ring. And if all that weren't enough, he had a deacon (Dave Batista in his first-ever WWE stint). While this went over like, well, a fart in church, we have to give the guy credit — anybody who's gutsy enough to hand fans a collection plate is okay with us.

7. **Brother Love:** Probably the most famous religious pro wrestling figure ever, Bruce Prichard played the role of Brother Love to the absolute hilt in the late 1980s, wearing an all-white suit and sporting bizarre red makeup we believe was to signify his Southern heritage. While he never actually preached the word of God (he preached the word of Love), his piped-in music, complete with choir, made it pretty clear he was a parody of televangelists such as Jim Bakker and Jimmy Swaggart, who had recently come under attack. He had a weekly interview segment on WWF television creatively dubbed "The Brother Love Show," in which he would stand at his pulpit and tell the fans' heroes how much he loved them (but also that he did not, in fact, *like* them). Every once in a while, he'd even perform miracles, such as helping a lame man walk or a blind man see. Prichard was so good in the role that he was able to parlay what should have been a two-month stay, tops, into a regular spot on WWF shows for years. In fact, at one point he even became a manager . . .

6. The Sisters of Love: . . . Of wrestling nuns, no less. They were dubbed the Sisters of Love and looked a lot like the Headbangers in drag (the "sisters" were actually Mosh and Thrasher, making their WWF debut). This was not quite as well-received, and to be frank, the level of satire had dropped from not-quite-clever to real-damn-dumb: one of the sisters' names was (and get ready to hold your tummy, there's a real belly laugh coming on) Mother Trucker. Was there ever any doubt this tandem would last less than a month?

5. Raven Crucifies Sandman: The original incarnation of ECW was a company that pushed limits like nothing that had ever come before. Sex, violence . . . ECW was anything but your father's wrestling. It almost made sense it'd be the first company to really kick down the doors of the church. Come to think of it, with this angle, ECW kicked down the doors, poured gasoline on the pews and ignited the place with a blowtorch. On one side, we had Raven, basically a martyr: even his signature taunt consisted of him standing mid-ring, arms spread as if on a crucifix. On the other, the Sandman, a beer-drinking, cigarette-smoking hero to the masses. When these two diametrically opposed forces collided, could there be any result other than Raven literally crucifying his foe, tying him to a cross and putting a crown of thorns on his head? And could the reaction, which included even the hardest of hardcore fans — fans who would chant "She's a crack whore" without batting an eye — vetoing the angle as being too offensive, have been any less in doubt?

4. Friar Ferguson: Another short-lived religious persona, Friar Ferguson was the brainchild of . . . well, we don't know. No one has ever admitted to it, and the man who was given the task of being a wrestling monk, Mike Shaw, has never outed the guilty party. While we don't have a photo of the good friar, he was exactly what you are picturing in your mind's eye: brown robe, bald head, sheepskin bag containing his holy water. Water, we should add, that he would splash onto fans at ringside, as he made his way down the aisle with the requisite chants blaring over the loudspeaker. Shaw would eventually (and when we say eventually, we mean inside of six weeks) be reborn as Bastion Booger, a character about as far removed from a friar as you can imagine, especially when you factor in the whole "cleanliness = godliness" equation.

3. **The Undertaker's Ministry of Darkness:** The Undertaker has always been a figure clouded in darkness. The original persona was something straight out of an Elvira B movie: an undead zombie who felt no pain. As the character has changed over the years, it probably comes as no shock that he became almost a devil worshipper, eventually creating a church for fellow wrongdoers. It was known as the Ministry of Darkness, and it was truly evil. Amongst its evil acts were kidnappings, crucifixions (which the WWF justified by stating that victims were actually strapped to an Undertaker symbol, not a cross) and cutting guys open to drink their blood. Good, wholesome family fun. But while everyone assumed that the Undertaker was the mastermind behind the whole scene, he soon began to talk of a "higher power" who was giving the Ministry its orders. After months of speculation, the higher power was revealed to be, yep, Vince McMahon. Which, of course, made no sense since he was the main guy the Ministry had been feuding against. Memo to Vince: the adage is "God works in mysterious ways," not "stupid ways."

2. **Shawn Michael's Tag Partner:** When the real-life Shawn Michaels turned over a new leaf and became a born-again Christian, it wasn't hard to understand why. After all, this guy had been a boozing, pill-popping, ladies' man who rubbed damn near everyone in the industry the wrong way at one point or another. But, as of this writing, it would appear that Michaels is true to his word. This did not stop his employer, however, from attempting to exploit Shawn's new outlook on life, as soon enough the evil Mr. McMahon character began to mock Shawn's religious beliefs on-screen, going so far as to claim that when he was beating on Shawn, God was nowhere to be found. Shawn claimed God was always by his side, which led Vince to book a tag match pitting Vince and son Shane against Shawn and his tag team partner, God. And sure enough, when the match came to be, God was indeed announced, heavenly music played, and a spotlight followed an invisible man down to the ring. Sadly, Shawn was pummeled by the McMahons. We view this as proof not that God doesn't exist, but that, much like the masses who failed to purchase the pay-per-view (it drew one of the year's lowest buyrates), He had better things to do on that particular Sunday than watch Vince McMahon wrestle. Can't blame Him for that.

1. **Brother Ernest Angel:** No doubt many of you are asking just who, exactly, is the man atop our list. It's not shocking you've not heard of Brother Ernest Angel; honestly, before we started doing our research for this list, we hadn't either. But he predates every religious character and angle listed in this book, and therefore we feel he is the cause of all of this. A manager in Memphis in 1988, Angel arrived just after the religious scandals involving Jimmy Swaggart, Jim Bakker and the

PTL Club were hitting the evening news. He even carried around the Good Book and would ask for donations, and proclaimed that those watching at home should place their hands on their television sets so as to feel the power. This infuriated the folks in the Bible Belt, to the point that the promotion actually had to have Angel come out on TV and admit he was not a preacher, his altar was actually a podium, and the Good Book he was hitting people with was not, in fact, the Bible. In other words, this guy had tons of heat . . . and yet you've never heard of him, and he didn't make a cent from the promotion. Indeed, God works in mysterious ways.

Speaking of God, if there's one thing we love, it's the holidays, especially Christmas. The tree, the carols, the unbridled commercialism of Black Friday . . . ain't no better time of the year than that between Thanksgiving and December 25. You'd think everyone would share the spirit of the season, but such is not the case. In fact, we're pretty sure everyone involved in wrestling hates it with a passion. Don't believe us? Then check out . . .

THE TOP 6 PIECES OF EVIDENCE THAT PROVE BEYOND A SHADOW OF A DOUBT THAT PRO WRESTLING HATES CHRISTMAS

6. Santa's Slay: We start off our trial with this lovely movie, aired on Spike TV and released on an unrated, uncut DVD in 2005. In the film, Santa is actually the son of Satan; he had lost a bet with an angel and had to be good for 1,000 years. Well, Santa's millennium of do-goodery has at long last come to an end, and he celebrates his liberation from his sentence in exactly the way you'd expect: by killing everyone in his path. Chris Kattan? Skewered. *The Nanny*, Fran

Drescher? Incinerated. Have to hand it to this St. Nick, he had his murderous rampage down to an art form. And he picked out the same people we probably would have if we had 365,000 days to think about it. But God wasn't about to take this lying down, and he sent the angel back down to earth to set forth another wager. Who knew God would view betting as an acceptable behavior for an angel? Anyway, all of this killing and wagering leads to a final showdown that involves curling. No, that's not a joke, and no, when we say curling we do not mean curling as in a beauty salon, but curling as in that wacky sport where you push a broom and try to land a stone inside a circle. Thrilling, no? "What does all this have to do with wrestling?" you ask. Well, the evil Santa would be none other than WCW phenom Bill Goldberg. And no wonder he hates Christmas — he's Jewish. Seeing all those other kids get video games and ponies while we got stuck with dreidels and gold-covered chocolate coins would piss us off too.

5. **Santa with Muscles:** But *Santa's Slay* isn't the only Christmas flick to feature a former world champion. And it's not even the worst one. We know, we know — reading the above description, you'd find that impossible to believe. But try this on for size: Hulk Hogan stars as Blake, an egomaniacal gazillionaire who is the richest man in ten states. For reasons far too dumb to detail here, Blake falls down a shaft, lands on his head, gets amnesia and believes himself to be Santa. Santa with muscles, you see. There's an evil elf named Lenny, fights with giant candy canes, spelunking, Garrett Morris, a showdown with Ed Leslie (who apparently had been hanging out with Mr. Miyagi, as he knew the crane technique), sword fighting, an orphanage filled with

annoying kids and, of course, the requisite giant explosion at the end. Strangely, missing from this "Christmas" film are trees, reindeer, eggnog, cheer, snow or anything connected with the holiday. We'd mention that good acting is missing as well; seeing as Hulk Hogan plays the lead, that probably goes without saying.

4. **The Christmas Creature:** Memphis has long been the home of the most cartoonish characters this side of Saturday morning, so it should be no surprise that come December, there's usually some wrestler or storyline to celebrate the season. 'Twas no different back in the mid-1990s, when a walking, wrestling Christmas tree was unveiled to wrestling fans. No joke — they had a wrestler (Glen Jacobs, who would later become famous as WWE's Kane) who was dressed up as a Christmas tree, complete with tinsel, ornaments and candy canes. Sadly, and inexplicably, without any lights. Yeah, it would have looked stupid having an extension cord dangling from the guy as he was running the ropes, but how much more ridiculous could it have been than having a guy dressed up as a Christmas tree?

3. **Xanta Claus:** Hey, we know what would be more ridiculous! How about a dude dressed up as jolly old St. Nicholas himself? Or better yet, what if, instead of boring old Santa Claus, he was actually Santa's evil brother, who lived at the South Pole and went down chimneys on Christmas eve to steal presents? Sound too good to be true? Wait. Sound too *dumb* to be true? Well, believe it, Jack, because it actually happened in the WWF in 1995. Even better, when Xanta attacked babyface Savio Vega, Vince McMahon cried out in horror as if someone had . . . well . . . told him Santa Claus wasn't real. So yes,

during a time when the WWF was primarily marketing to kids, not only was there a Santa character, but he was a heel. Can there be any doubt at this point that wrestling truly despises Christmas?

2. **Santa Gets Pummeled. Repeatedly:** What? You still need more convincing? Then consider this: every single time Santa has appeared in a major promotion in the last ten years, he has been beaten unmercifully. From ECW's 911 to "Stone Cold" Steve Austin, anytime Santa dares show his face in a wrestling ring, the result is the same: the poor old fat man gets beaten within an inch of his life. But that's better than what happened to him when he ran into the Ultimate Warrior, at which time . . .

1. **Santa Gets Raped:** Bet those were three words you thought you'd never see strung together. But such was the case in the Warrior's 1996 comic book. There was no text to explain what happened, so we can only offer up a description of the ink drawings within. Namely, that the Warrior KO'd Father Christmas, then depantsed him, stripping him down to only his underwear. He followed this up by chaining him to the wall and looking at him in a manner we can only describe as . . . disturbing. Presumably he came down St. Nick's chimney shortly thereafter. Or maybe he came up his chimney. Who knows. We'd rather not think about it.

The defense rests its case. And rest assured, no amount of letters from kids addressed to Kris Kringle at the country courthouse is going to change the verdict.

While many believe in God — or Santa, for that matter — others pledge their allegiance to entities that are not actually seen. Such as . . .

WRESTLING'S 5 MOST TALKED ABOUT — YET NEVER SEEN — PERSONALITIES

5. The Boss: The Global Wrestling Federation wasn't known for much; it was basically a company that attempted to revive the Dallas territory that was hot during the heyday of the Von Erichs in the early 1980s. And, as with every company that has tried since, it failed. One thing it did deliver, however: a long, arcing storyline in which the promotion's leading heel stable, the Cartel, committed acts of violence against the promotion's good guys, all under orders from a vile — yet never shown — gangster known as the Boss. Mystery surrounded this man, until finally, after over a year of storylines, he was revealed as GWF commissioner Max Andrews. The Cartel celebrated this announcement by promptly disbanding, and the company itself collapsed shortly after that.

4. Joey Numbers: Fans were outraged when longtime ECW star Tazz came into WWE and was basically treated as an afterthought. The reason, of course, was simple: Tazz was a legit five-foot-eight or so, and that was death to virtually any performer in the company, as Vince McMahon likes his superstars larger than life. Instead of being shown the door, however, Tazz was given a shot as a color commentator, which he made the most of; he would eventually be among the best in the business. One has to wonder how he wound up with such a cushy job, one in which he doesn't have his body beaten to pieces, one in which he doesn't travel 300 days a year. Perhaps it was thanks to Joey Numbers, a bookie/hitman/informant/Mafia crime boss whom Tazz has referred to constantly over the years. In fact, Numbers was once mentioned so frequently that it seemed inevitable he'd actually debut in the ring. With such a backstory (how many bookie/hitman/informant/Mafia crime bosses do you know?), there's little doubt he'd immediately be more over than 90 percent of the current WWE roster.

3. **The J-Tex Corporation:** A look at this 1990 WCW stable, which contained the likes of Terry Funk, the Great Muta and Gary Hart, would seem to indicate that J-Tex Corp. actually stood for Japan-Texas Corporation. But according to several interviews conducted during this time, J-Tex wasn't just a wacky group of wrestlers, but a wacky group of wrestlers funded by an honest-to-God (or honest-to-Kami or honest-to-Buddha) company that funded a professional wrestling stable, presumably as a tax write-off. One can only imagine the J-Tex board of directors discussing how their wrestlers should attempt to suffocate "Nature Boy" Ric Flair with a grocery bag. One can only imagine how long they discussed whether to use paper or plastic. Ah, to have been a fly on the wall at that board meeting. Speaking of which . . .

2. **Rick Steiner's Pet Fly:** You probably don't recall Rick Steiner's pet fly, but it was he who befriended Steiner during a very rough stretch when he was a member of the hated Varsity Club in 1988. Steiner would often speak in interviews about listening to his friend for words of comfort. Sadly, the world was deprived of ever meeting his mentor on-screen. One can only imagine the sage wisdom this insect imparted upon his young friend: "Okay, Rick, now when someone has you set

up for a German release suplex, what you want to do is shift your hips, swing behind him and grasp him around the waist for a suplex of your own. Oh, and always regurgitate on your food prior to eating it. It's much easier to chew that way."

1. **Jim Cornette's Mama:** Not a single Jim Cornette interview would conclude in the 1980s in which he did not mention his lovely mother, easily the most famous of all invisible wrestling personas. Mama Cornette, you see, funded all of her son's endeavors, be that hiring wrestlers such as the Midnight Express and Big Bubba Rogers, buying outlandish clothes or paying for phantom tennis lessons (an excuse for him to wield a tennis racket as a weapon at ringside). Fans, therefore, saw him as nothing but a "Mama's boy," a fact Cornette played to the hilt, becoming one of wrestling's all-time top heel managers. And, in turn, that's a testament to Jim Cornette, who came up with the idea. If you ever want to see why Cornette is considered one of wrestling's greatest minds, look no further than Mama Cornette. A character, mind you, you'll never be able to see.

Then there are those storylines that didn't just have imaginary characters, but imaginary endings. Or more precisely, no ending whatsoever. We call them . . .

WRESTLING'S TOP 7 UNCONCLUDED STORYLINES

7. **Dave Batista, Rapist:** When the topic of wrestling comes up among people in the mainstream entertainment business, the reviewer will usually state that wrestling is a "soap opera for guys." In 2006, the

PHOTO: MATT BALK

Would you invite an alleged rapist to your wedding? While the groom looks like he thinks this is a grand idea, we don't believe the bride — or the bridesmaids — are quite as convinced. . . .

writers of *Smackdown* decided they would actually make wrestling live up to that slogan, when they took the Batista-MNM feud for a naughty turn. Channeling the spirits of Luke and Laura, two characters from television's *General Hospital* who were part of a controversial rape storyline, MNM's manager, Melina, came to the ring and announced to the world that World Heavyweight Champion Batista had "sexually assaulted" her. What a bombshell revelation. Would the fan favorite Batista be able to prove his innocence? Would a police warrant to search Dave's house uncover his hidden stash of roofies? We never found out the truth. Less than a week after the accusation, Batista tore his bicep during a match, subsequently forfeited his title and was taken off television. In effect, the lesson appeared to be that all you needed to get off the hook for a crime was to somehow get injured. Note to real-life criminals: this scenario only works in wrestling. If you try to figuratively cover your ass in court by blowing out one of your arms, it will only pose problems for you later in the slammer, when you literally try to cover your ass with only one arm, while Bubba Jo and Jerome introduce you to the wet and wacky world of prison shower time.

6. **The Dark Lord of the Shits:** As the evil face-painted antithesis to the WCW's favorite son, Sting, Vampiro often found himself in dark storylines, providing wrestling fans with such family-friendly antics as setting Sting on fire and attempting to kill the Kiss Demon in a graveyard. But in the summer of 2001, a big reveal was made. Vampiro was not actually the mastermind behind these tombstone-tipping, pyromaniacal actions. It turned out Vampy was a mere minion to an even creepier figure. The wicked madman dishing out orders to Vampiro

was a hooded, Satanic figure whose name was rumored to be "the Lord." We know what you're thinking, and we must state that Lord Alfred Hayes did not jump ship to WCW and engage in any murdering of small animals or sacrificing of nubile virgins. This dark lord was actually portrayed by Christopher Daniels, making his first appearance on WCW television. His first — and, we might add, only — appearance as the Lord. Seems that while Vince Russo could have every single female on the roster be half-naked or pregnant out of wedlock in the storylines, a goofball who wore a black bathrobe and looked like a *Star Wars* nerd dressed up as the Emperor was deemed too controversial, as the network believed it bordered on devil worshipping. The Lord angle was scrapped, Vampiro went solo again and all prototypes of officially licensed WCW Ouija boards and wall pentagrams still in the design phase were ordered destroyed.

5. **The Kat's Right to Nudity:** In the spring of 2001, a war was waged. A war between a group of self-righteous, uptight squares and a lone woman, a woman who fought for the sole purpose of showing that she was the undisputed queen of the skanks. As the Steven Richards-led Right to Censor roamed WWF rings, trying their best to eliminate all the questionable content in wrestling, they would meet their biggest nemesis in the form of the Kat. She claimed that if they had the "right to censor," she had the "right to nudity." The Kat, who had already gone topless by exposing her cans at *Armageddon 1999*, was poised to drop trou when she had Jerry Lawler fight for her (dis)honor in a stipulation-filed match against Steven Richards at *No Way Out* 2001. If Richards won, the Kat would be forced to join the RTC. If Lawler came out on top, oh boy, hide the kids, the Kat would strip naked! To the dismay

of teenage male hormones everywhere, Richards prevailed, and the next night on *Raw*, he forced the Kat to wear a burlap sack as her new wardrobe design. The following day, due to a serious problem with her backstage attitude, the Kat received her walking papers from the WWF, thus ending the whole Right to Nudity storyline in mid-angle. One question: would she have remained with the RTC and revitalized the once-dead burlap-sack fashion craze? Okay, two: would she have rebelled and shown more bush than an all-day C-SPAN tribute to George W.? The answers, unlike the Kat, were never let out of the bag.

4. **Harley Davidson and the Giant Marlboro Man:** When the nWo hit its full stride, many of the once-reserved characters took drastic 180-degree turns. Hulk Hogan became diabolically evil. The once mild-mannered Eric Bischoff became what appeared to be the Mattel Toys living prototype for their new Harley Riding Poser Ken doll. Scott Hall became a demon-filled, raging alcoholic. Unwilling to be outdone by the Bad Guy's vices, the Giant, Paul Wight, decided he would become wrestling's first nicotine addict. Not satisfied by stinking up the ring with his workrate alone, the Giant decided to start smoking cigarettes while he was inside the ring during the nWo's promos. It's unfortunate that WCW dropped the angle so quickly. Imagine the drama that could have been added to the Giant's matches. In the midst of a nicotine fit, and facing off against an opponent like Sting, would the seven-foot grappler try to cover his prey for a three-count, or would he forsake the pin opportunity for a quick smoke break? Decreased stamina could've been a problem, but that would be countered by his new ability to cough up nasty brownish-green lung loogies and spit them in his opponent's eyes. Thankfully, before the Giant

made a face turn and started to wear nicotine patches, WCW extinguished the angle. It was the last time a fag would be seen on wrestling until Rico showed up in WWE six years later.

3. **Who Drove the Black Hummer?:** It was *the* mystery in 1999: who was behind the wheel of the mysterious black Hummer that crashed into Kevin Nash's limo? Who was responsible for this heinous vehicular homicide attempt? Nash's rival at the time, Randy "Macho Man" Savage? Perhaps it was the leader of nWo Hollywood, one Mr. Hulk Hogan? We would never find out who drove the black Hummer, because in the following segments, the Hummer inexplicably changed colors, thus changing the question to . . .

2. **Who Drove the White Hummer?:** At this point, we could've used Michael Jackson singing "Black or White" to help us solve the mystery. Lex Luger tried to convince everyone that Hogan was behind the Hummer assault, showing a photo of Hogan driving a white Hummer that was nothing like the black one initially used in the angle. The story was put on the backburner for a few months, only to be brought back in 2000, as prime suspect Hogan became the target of a Hummer driven by Billy Kidman and Eric Bischoff. Those looking for a logical conclusion to this mess would be left disappointed, because the Hummer angle became so mucked up and convoluted, WCW decided to pull the plug on it, before the mystery was unraveled. One rumored conclusion had Carmen Electra (yes, *that* Carmen Electra) as the driver. Which would have made, of course, no sense, but hey, it being WCW at the time, nothing did.

1. Baby Doll's Photos: Ah yes . . . the most infamous of all unsolved angles — the mysterious photos that Baby Doll possessed and utilized to blackmail Dusty Rhodes. The backstory: in 1998, as the valet of Larry Zbyszko, Baby Doll flaunted an envelope she claimed contained incriminating photos of Dusty Rhodes. A week later, she added fuel to the fire by showing Rhodes (but not the audience) the pictures, and he had a conniption fit worthy of a teething toddler. And it all led up to . . . nothing. The angle was dropped with no warning and no conclusion. Just what was on those notorious photos? Well, since WCW never offered an answer, leave it to us to finally solve the mystery. We've actually uncovered some of Baby Doll's photos, and here they are! Dusty Rhodes frolicking as a participant in a wet T-shirt contest!

PHOTO: TROY FERGUSON

To paraphrase what Dusty said during his stint as a WWE butcher, "You can beat my prices, but I will beat my meat."

(**Note from editor:** Sorry, this is the only photo we're allowed to print. ECW Press has a firm policy: no photos of manboobs are allowed in our publications.)

Oh, and speaking of Dusty, we'd be remiss if we didn't mention . . .

DUSTY RHODES' SINGLE BIGGEST DISAPPOINTMENT WITH THE BOOK YOU HAVE IN YOUR HANDS

1. He thought it was actually *The WrestleCrap Book of Lisps.*

And as we draw this chapter to a close, we cannot help but think there are storylines that have been hashed and rehashed, then served as leftovers, then chopped up and put into a stew. Point being: it seems every storyline we see today is one we saw years ago. Except that years ago, it had the benefit of being fresh — as well as being done much, much better. And before we take leave, we'd like to dedicate this final list to any promoter or booker out there who might happen to be reading. You'll note it's short — just two items. That's really not asking too much. You have carte blanche to redo all your other dumb storylines; just please, please, no more of these two again . . .

THE TWO STORYLINES WE NEVER, EVER WANT TO SEE AGAIN

2. The Heel Commissioner/Heel Referee: When Vince McMahon created the vile Mr. McMahon character in the late 1990s, he was, without question, one of the greatest heels the wrestling industry had ever seen. His interaction with Steve Austin was the very essence of professional wrestling storytelling: the mean boss forcing his redneck worker to do things his way. The redneck worker responded by kicking the boss's ass. It was fantastic stuff, and McMahon was off the charts as the lunatic megalomaniac. Like all things, though, it would get old. But to McMahon's credit, that took a couple of years.

Still, the act did get old and McMahon decided to leave TV for a while. But the character was to remain. And so we got heel commissioners and general managers out our ears, from Eric Bischoff to Jonathan Coachman to every other schmuck on the roster, it seemed. That would have been bad enough, but other promotions got in on the act, and soon WCW and later TNA would have their on-air companies run by bad-guy CEOs. With all those evil-doers in charge, soon we would be inundated with heel referees, men who were evil and thus hated the good guy in the bout, yet weren't ready to simply say that the good guy submitted when he was in a chin lock or just count three even when his shoulder was up at two. Because they were, we suppose, "fair" heel referees. The one common trait all these goofs had, and the one they all suffered from: before they even started, before they even committed their first nefarious act, their act was played. Because they could never top the first time it played out on the big stage. That first time, the role was played by a master.

1. **Montreal:** Of course, McMahon also had a huge advantage that none of these other folks had: reality was on his side. The reality of Montreal. We're not going to do a detailed recap of the whole incident again; it's been done a hundred times, most notably in our own *Death of WCW*. Long story short, Vince McMahon told Bret Hart how his match was going to end, then swerved him by doing a different ending. Bret was furious and public opinion was on his side, thus making him a hero and Vince a villain. But companies have tried for years to reenact this scenario, again and again and again. It never gets over, because there is no reality to it, and

without reality, it doesn't work. It will never work again, guys — so drop it.

Or we might pay off the Warrior to pretend you're Santa.

4

Employee of the Month:
The Dog-Faced Gremlin

While we've spent a good deal of this tome discussing the ins and outs of what makes wrestling work, what about the performers themselves? They labor long and hard preparing for battle inside the squared circle, and when they're not doing that, they're flying or driving to the next arena on the tour. It's truly a nonstop lifestyle that few of us could even fathom.

But what happens to these men and women outside the ring? What happens, for instance, when a wrestler's career ends and he is forced to put food on the table some other way?

Well, they become average Joes just like you or me, with jobs just like yours or mine. But you have to admit, it would be strange to encounter a retired grappler working as a stocker at Wal-Mart. Or, for that matter, one of these guys . . .

THE 6 WRESTLERS WITH JOBS YOU'D NEVER EXPECT

6. Rick Steiner, Realtor: Just imagine looking for a new home, when who meets you for the walkthrough but the Dog-Faced Gremlin himself, Rick Steiner! If you live in Georgia, you may not have to imagine. Not only is Steiner a realtor down south of the Mason-Dixon, but he has also been dabbling in politics. Instead of attempting to follow in Jesse Ventura's footsteps and win the governorship, Steiner believed his best bet to get into the political arena was to start small and win a seat on the county school board. It was a good plan, except for one small detail: apparently, he didn't know his own name. See, he attempted to run under his wrestling name, and not his real name of Robert Rechsteiner, a ploy rejected by his chosen Republican party. As a write-in candidate, Steiner was unable to make the grade. But hey, we hear he has a great split level over on the west side, if you're interested.

5. **Mick Foley, Sports Announcer:** In the world of professional football, many big-name players make the move to the broadcasting portion of the business when their playing days are over. In 2000, when Mick Foley decided his body had suffered enough punishment and that it was time to retire from active competition, it was only natural to assume the very well-spoken Foley would transition himself to the sports-commentating booth. And he did, but not for the WWF. Instead, Foley became the host for TNN 's show *Robot Wars: Extreme Warriors*. The show's premise? Remote-controlled robots with names such as Sir Killalot and Sergeant Bash would face off against each other in a gladiator-like duel to the death. Incredibly, watching two battery-operated Robbie the Robots trying to destroy each other in a demolition-derby-meets-Thunderdome showdown suddenly made watching *Star Trek* seem less nerdy. But before Foley ever got the chance to call an Optimus Prime vs. Sir Killalot fight to the finish, he left the show and returned to the ring. TNN responded to Foley's departure in perhaps the best way possible — by sending this robotic piece of crappy television to the scrap heap.

4. **Barry Darsow, Photocopier at Large:** One of the most amusing workers of all time had to be the man of a thousand gimmicks, Barry Darsow. While he is well-known for roles such as the Repo Man and Krusher Kruschev, he is best known for his role as Smash from the tag team Demolition, who despite holding the record as the longest-reigning WWF tag team champions in history, some critics dismissed as being copycats of the Road Warriors. Upon his retirement from wrestling in 2000, Barry decided to take his copying to the next level, when he took a job with MRS, a printing service based in Minnesota. While most photocopy businesses require their employees to dress in a suit and tie, imagine the goldmine MRS would've had had they required Darsow to come to work decked out in his Demolition bondage gear. Their new slogan — "MRS: We're kinkier than Kinko's!!"

PHOTO: MATT BALK

"Do you really want extra cheese? That'll cost ya!" Ladies and germs, the girl who gives us a "Fat Tony," Victoria.

3. **Victoria, Pizza Maker:** When you go out to eat at the local pizza parlor, odds are you're gonna see a fat Italian guy named Mario or Luigi tossing the dough up in the air, preparing a tasty supreme pizza for you. Take a trip to Fat Tony's Pizzeria in Louisville, though, and odds are you might find some hard Sicilian sausage inside . . . but not from the restaurant. It would be from the customers, as their pizzas might be served by one of the hottest WWE Divas of all time, Victoria. The thought of seeing Vicki playing in the dough, and dressed up like Chef Boyardee, is enough for us to not only forsake the Atkins Diet, but overload on carbs from massive amounts of pizza consumption — until we are deemed obese enough to audition for the role of pre-Subway Jared in his motion-picture bio.

2. **Dan Spivey, Fashion Model:** What's a wrestler to do when a career filled with injuries finally renders him unable to compete anymore? Dan Spivey, who suffered a career-ending hip injury while portraying his awesome Waylon Mercy character, did something crazier than his Waylon character would ever dream up in his most diabolical day-dream. Spivey decided he was gonna strut his stuff on the runway. Yes, folks, say hello to Dan Spivey, fashion model! Clad only in a pair of boxers, trying desperately to become the next Derek Zoolander, Spivey launched a Web site loaded with images of him wearing the hottest spring and fall fashions, trying to make a splash in the modeling industry. Sadly, the market for balding, six-foot-five models who look like mass murderers is relatively thin, and Spivey was forced to put on some pants and get a real job. His 85 percent naked body was never seen that nude again, as he closed the door on a very brief — pun intended — modeling career.

1. Nikolai Volkoff, Would-Be Politician: God bless America. Only in this country can a man who spent a quarter of a century telling us how much he hates it here be given a chance at political power. Such was the case for longtime commie evildoer Nikolai Volkoff, as he attempted to run for state delegate in Baltimore during the 2006 elections. His opponent wasted no time engaging in mudslinging, as he brought up the scripted no-good-Russian pro-wrestling past of Nikolai in an attempt to discredit Volkoff's campaign. How did Nikolai respond to show voters he was a legit politician, worthy of the people's vote? He turned to his old ally, the Iron Sheik, to help him. Surprisingly, the Sheik's campaign slogan — "Nikolai Volkoff: Do It the Old Country Way in '06" — turned out to be a bust, as Volkoff came out the humble loser when the votes were cast.

Of course, for many wrestlers, becoming a realtor isn't in the cards. They'd rather continue on as a performer in some manner, usually with the thought of Hollywood on their minds. But for every Rock who makes it big, there are a dozen Muhammad Hassans who vanish into thin air. This is usually because, well, they're just not very good.

But hey . . . maybe that's just us being jerks. You might find this impossible to believe, but there are folks out there on this big blue-and-green ball we call earth who feel that we are too critical of wrestling movies. Oh yeah, and of movies starring wrestlers. "Oh, lighten up, guys — these movies aren't that bad!" Apparently we're just big meanies who don't give these poor flicks a chance. Sure, maybe we once said that getting hit in the head with a lead pipe was a superior alternative to watching *Ready to Rumble*. And sure, there was that time when we called Hulk Hogan more wooden than a sequoia. Maybe you guys are right. In the interest of fairness, let's ask some other folks their opinions. Are we the jerks here? We'll allow you to make the call via . . .

THE 14 GREATEST WRESTLING/WRESTLER MOVIE REVIEW QUOTES

14. Regarding *See No Evil*, starring Kane: "As shallow as a toilet bowl and twice as rank as its usual contents." — Nich Schager, *Slant Magazine*

Man, that last guy was a prick (and we're not just saying that because he's stealing our thunder by using a crap analogy). I bet that others would have kind things to say about the movie that was originally dubbed *Eye Scream Man* (now, that would have been a title).

13. "It might be hard to imagine a career move that is a step down from directing porn videos, yet Gregory Dark has accomplished just that with his feature-film debut, *See No Evil*." — Colin Covert, *Minneapolis Star Tribune*

Then again, maybe not. But how about *Ready to Rumble*? Would it really be better to get walloped in the noggin with a lead pipe?

12. "Fans of ***- and feces-based humor will be rolling in the sticky, sticky aisles. Others may be only slightly amused." — Brent Simon, *Entertainment Today*

See, you might be slightly amused! That's high praise right there. Let's see if we can go two for two with the movie that previewed David Arquette's wrestling prowess.

11. "Yes, film fans, there is a new worst movie of all time." — Jay Boyar, *Orlando Sentinel*

All right, maybe not. How's about *Santa with Muscles*, the holiday classic starring Hulk Hogan?

10. "A 98-pound weakling of a comedy." — Joe Leydon, *Variety*

Sheesh, what a Scrooge that guy was. Let's try it again with the Hulkster as Jolly Ol' St. Nick.

9. "One of the most nonsensical movies I've ever seen, truly silly in no good way." — MaryAnn Johanson, *TheFlickFilosopher.com*

PHOTO: MATT BALK

"Utter Crapola? We'd consider that a ringing endorsement!"

Now granted, Hogan's been in some bad films, but other guys, like Roddy Piper, surely did better, right? Especially if you're in a film called *Hell Comes to Frogtown*.

8. "If you rent a film with this title, you deserve what you get. Utter crapola." — Jonathan R. Perry, *Tyler Morning Telegraph*

Okay, so maybe those old guys were in bad films. So let's try something newer, perhaps *The Marine* starring John Cena.

7. "*The Marine* proudly admits that it's junk. Who am I to disagree?" — Brian Orndorf, *Filmjerk.com*

That seems awfully harsh, like something we would say. Let's get a second opinion.

6. "It's as fast and loud as you'd expect, but where it catches you off-guard is in its breathtaking stupidity." — Jay Antani, *Box Office Magazine*

Yowtch. Okay, maybe *The Marine* did suck. But it had to have been better than the first-ever Vince McMahon-produced flick, *No Holds Barred*.

5. "Charmless, stupid and badly made." — Richard Harrington, *Washington Post*

Oh, it couldn't have been that bad. How about when Mr. Bollea portrayed an over-the-hill karate guru in *3 Ninjas: High Noon on Mega Mountain?* That one was okay, wasn't it?

4. "Don't get the wrong idea. *3 Ninjas* is not completely lacking in entertainment value, at least for four-year-olds. There's lots of crotch kicking, head banging, a nice adult picks his nose, and there's even a yo-yo with built-in blades to throw. Oh, and sweet Mom offers her boys a 'bacon, ham, bologna and cheese' sandwich, so the film has fine dietary advice, too. But what's most heartwarming here is watching actors with no talent (Mr. Hogan), minor talent (Mr. [Jim] Varney of the 'Ernest' films) and occasional talent (Ms. [Loni] Anderson) at their absolute, abortive worst." — Brandon Judell, *Entertainment Asylum*

Man, dissing the Hulkster is one thing, but Loni Anderson? Surely Hogan couldn't have brought her down to the depths of celluloid hell. We bet it was just the material he had to work with there. No doubt one of his other films would fare much better. Like, say, *Mr. Nanny*.

3. "Do whatever is necessary to avoid this movie. If your children mistakenly believe that this would be a good way to spend an afternoon, offer them anything to change their minds. And I do mean *anything*. *Mr. Nanny* isn't entertainment; it's an exercise in masochism." — James Beradinelli, *ReelViews*

Come on, now. Was it really that bad?

2. "The cinematic equivalent of garden shears in the eyeballs." — Scott Weinberg, *eFilmCritic.com*

Alrighty then. But hey, none of these things were so bad they made a film critic just want to quit his job, right?

1. "Somebody was asking the other day, do I ever get tired of going to the movies? Naw, I said, I love movies and so some days it's not really a job, it's more of a lucky break. But I wasn't feeling lucky the day I saw *Suburban Commando*, and you know what? By golly, by the time it was over, I was feeling kind of tired of going to the movies." — Roger Ebert, *Chicago Sun-Times*

Maybe we weren't so vicious after all.

But wrestling movies aren't just for the big screen. When wrestling hit it big in the late '90s, direct-to-video movie studios lined up to cash in on the craze. Heck, a few even hit prior to that point. But before you rush out to the local Family Video and try to hunt down a few, a word of warning: don't. These releases almost universally suck. But some suck past the point of sucking. If you dare rent a DTV wrestling picture, please do so with extreme caution. And keep in mind . . .

THE 5 MOVIES YOU ABSOLUTELY, POSITIVELY, MOST DESPERATELY WANT TO AVOID IF YOU SEE THEM AT THE VIDEO STORE. IN FACT, PLEASE BURN DOWN THE WHOLE DAMN STORE

5. *The Wrestler*: Unless the idea of Ed Asner (*The Mary Tyler Moore Show*'s Lou Grant) in a love scene is your idea of a good time, we'd suggest staying very, very clear of this film from way back in 1973. You can forgive *The Wrestler* for some of its faults due to the fact it was made over thirty years ago, but Ed Asner in the sauna ain't one of them. Still, if you're looking to see what professional wrestling was all about in 1973, you could do worse. In fact, about forty-five minutes into the movie, a training session breaks out in which various holds and maneuvers are explained in detail. In the end, though, the *The Wrestler* is basically a bio pic for Verne Gagne, who stars as Mike Bullard, aging champion whom everyone wants to see drop the belt. The irony, of course, is that Verne would continue to put himself in the spotlight in his own promotion, the AWA. For the next fifteen years. A case of life imitating "art," we suppose.

4. *American Angels*: Less a movie than an excuse to show oiled-up women "wrestling," this release was a vehicle for Magnificent Mimi Lesseos,

who was rumored to have financed the production herself. In the film Mimi is the champion, with everyone gunning for her. If WWE in recent years has taught us anything, it's that putting up the moolah gives you carte blanche to be the star. Lesseos was hot, no doubt about it, but there's a big world of Internet porn out there, so why someone would choose this as an outlet for sexual release is beyond us. The plot — and we use the word in the loosest possible sense — details the efforts of several women to become part of a women's wrestling troupe known as the American Angels. These women include an illegal immigrant, a stripper and a hooker. All wind up making the cut, so if you're an aspiring women's wrestler, apparently these careers are great primers for the big leagues. Who knew?

3. **Slammed:** Wrestling + hot women + stupid comedy. That's the formula for *Slammed*, and it sure sounds like it should work. But it doesn't. *Slammed* is the story of "back bar" wrestling, which takes place in bars. In the back of bars, we'd guess. We're not sure, because despite having followed professional wrestling for 127 man-years, we never heard such a term until this movie. The film actually has a fair number of real actors, if you consider bit players from *Charles in Charge, Home Improvement* and *Step by Step* stars. In the world of wrestling movies, we definitely would. Anyway, apparently this type of wrestling is shoot wrestling, meaning these folks are actually fighting. We've seen a few bar fights in our day. They never included moonsaults. And just when you think the movie can't get much more idiotic than that, we are treated to the sight of Hulk Hogan's old *No Holds Barred* nemesis Zeus spanking his monkey to a mail-order-bride catalog. Kids, that's not good entertainment. But hey, don't take our word for how bad this movie

is — take the producers' word: they left the film unreleased for four years before unleashing it on the world. Maybe they were just hoping the masters would decompose in that time. We can't blame them for that. However, we can blame them for everything else.

2. ***Thunder in Paradise***: Okay, technically this isn't a movie. Well, technically, none of 'em are, but we're already in for a penny. Nevertheless, this mighty franchise has seen recent release as the *Thunder in Paradise Collection* on DVD. It's basically a compilation of different episodes disguised as "movies," and we'd feel remiss if we didn't give fair warning. For the uninitiated, *Thunder in Paradise* was a television show Hulk Hogan starred in during the mid-1990s. He played Spence, the sometimes-eyepatched, sometimes-not-eyepatched captain of a boat called "Thunder." But "Thunder" wasn't simply another dingy, it was a high-tech collection of gadgets and gizmos that just happened to be buoyant. Call it *Knight Boat* (thank you, Homer Simpson) and you'd be on the right track. The show featured Hogan battling terrorists who looked a hell of a lot like wrestlers the Hulkster had faced in the ring. If your idea of a good time is watching guys like Ed Leslie, Jim Neidhart, Giant Gonzales and Brian Knobbs trying to act, and watching Charlotte Rae (TV's Edna Garrett from *Facts of Life*) prance around in a swimsuit, this is the flick for you. Oh, and by the way, you're an idiot.

1. ***Backyard Dogs***: And now here we are, at the very bottom of the bottom of the barrel. In fact, we'd go so far as to say *Backyard Dogs* is so awful that it somehow burrowed under the barrel, maybe to China. Instead of going into great detail about the plot, we ask you to just take everything outlined above in *Slammed* and replace the word bar with yard

and that's pretty much the whole movie. Again, it portrays its wrestling as a complete shoot, but that's only about 1/5000 of the troubles this waste of celluloid faces. See, although these competitions take place in front of a dozen or so kids in their backyards, this is apparently big business — you can retire from your earnings, according to the film. The title is the moniker of our heroic stars, a tag team who so dub themselves after the omen realized when one of them steps in dog crap. Really. A bat crashing through Bruce Wayne's window it was not. The finale takes place in a junkyard, a truly fitting end. It's just a shame it took them eighty-nine minutes to get there.

But, come to think of it, we believe there were some guys who could have easily made the jump to the movies. Maybe even good movies. If you look at in-ring personas and translate that to the big screen, there's likely money to be made. And we can think of no men who'd have an easier time switching over than . . .

THE TOP 4 HORROR-MOVIE-THEMED WRESTLERS

4. **Vampire Warrior:** Before he was known as Gangrel, the WWF's resident red-fluid-guzzling vampire, David Heath was a fixture on the independent wrestling scene. As the Vampire Warrior, he sported his actual, real-life fangs and the basic outline of his neck-biting character that would ultimately gain him cult fame a few years down the line. Others may have come along and claimed to be vampires, but how many guys had fangs? Plus, he got to bag Luna Vachon back when she was hot. Well, back when she wasn't quite so bad, anyway. Oh, and for those of you newer fans who've seen ECW's vampire, Kevin

Thorn, and decry his absence from this list, let us ask you: how scary is a vampire named Kevin?

3. **Leatherface:** It was well-documented that Mike "Corporal" Kirchner was a bit of a loose cannon, with a dash of madman thrown in. So, it seemed like a perfect fit when he was offered the role of *The Texas Chainsaw Massacre's* resident psycho, Leatherface. Only problem was, it appeared Mike was not too familiar with Leatherface's trademarked killing toy — a chainsaw. Therefore, he decided to do a little character modification of his own: his weapon of choice was a board with a bunch of nails sticking out of it. A board he proceeded to place on the neck of one of his unlucky opponents and step right on it. Maybe it's just us, Mike, but the title *The Japanese Ten-Penny Nail Massacre* just isn't as catchy as your namesake's film.

2. **Jason & Freddy:** Fifteen years before they would appear together on-screen in the crossover flick *Freddy vs. Jason*, the fine folks at USWA decided they would be a little ahead of their time and bring them together in the world of wrestling. One short trip to the local costume shop to pick up some official Freddy and Jason Halloween masks, and the feel-good, homicidal buddy tag team of the '80s was born. We'd talk about how these two were kinda bad, but realistically, with Freddy and Jason in the ring, what were you expecting? The British frickin' Bulldogs?

1. **ECW's Zombie:** When ECW's weekly television show was resurrected, one would assume the term "resurrected" was being used metaphorically. However, no sooner had WWE wiped the mud off its reani-

mated side project than something else would arise from the grave. Slowly stumbling down to the ring, growling at the top of his lungs, the Zombie was the first wrestler ever seen on ECW's new show on the Sci-Fi Channel. He entered the ring, promptly grabbed the mic and proceeded to cut a promo that could best be described as sounding like a ball-gagged Lou Albano finally taking a dump after a long battle with constipation. With the fecal-audio decibels rising, longtime ECW hero the Sandman came down to the ring, accompanied by his trusty Singapore cane. Sandy and Singy quickly sent the Zombie back to his grave (or swamp or wherever the hell zombies come from) for a second time. It was assumed the Zombie was a heel, but in retrospect, maybe he was just a good, honest, undead soul trying to keep another dead and rotted carcass — in this case ECW — from returning to the world of the living. Didn't anyone in this company ever see *Pet Sematary*? No matter how good something was when alive, when you try to bring it back to the surface, it always stinks.

You might question the absence of a certain worm-eating, Darth Maul-looking crazy man from that there list. And we admit: there can be little doubt indeed that Boogeyman is unquestionably the greatest horror wrestling character of all time. Indeed, the saddest moment in wrestling in the past twenty-five years had to be the notice on WWE.com that Boogeyman had been released from his contract. Then he was hired back. We can only assume he could not find suitable employment elsewhere. After all, what's a Boogeyman to do? We tell you in . . .

THE TOP 6 JOBS BOOGEYMAN COULD DO WHEN HE'S DONE WRESTLING

6. Dancer: For those who've seen the Boogeyman's entrance to the wrestling ring, this potential employment opportunity needs no further explanation. But for those unfortunate souls who've missed out on this grand spectacle, let us elaborate. The Boogeyman is a dancer without peer. Just imagine Fred Astaire and you have a pretty good idea. If Fred had his face painted red and was missing his front two teeth. And he was black. And he had ants in his pants. And he was hooked up to an electrical outlet whilst standing in a pool of water. Oh, yeah. That Boogey can boogie.

5. Antler Model: An oft-forgotten aspect of Boogeyman's past is his Ohio Valley Wrestling tenure. OVW is basically WWE's farm system; they send new hires there to get training for the big time. The Boogeyman was there, and decided to compete while wearing antlers. Seriously, antlers like you'd find on, say, an antelope. It was a good look, one that had sadly been missing in professional wrestling since the heyday of the Barbarian in the WWF in the early 1990s.

4. Midget Scarecrow: Has your home ever been besieged by midgets, imps, pixies, dwarves, pygmies or other such height-challenged creatures? Then call Boogeyman! During his initial appearance on *Smackdown*, he ran into a group of little people and scared them out of their tiny pants — one was so mortified that he leapt into the comforting arms of *Smackdown* GM Theodore Long. If midgets are what ails ya, the Boogeyman is the cure.

PHOTO: MATT BALK

He's the Boogeyman — and he's wormtastic!

3. Worm Wrangler: But let's say midgets are not, in fact, what ails ya. Let's say there's something even smaller, slimier and more lacking in vertebrae. Something like, say, worms. If that's the issue, no one on the planet is more qualified than our Man o' Boogey. Not only will he take care of them for you, he will do it in the manner you deem best, whether that be dropping them from a ceiling or eating them. Your call. The dude doesn't care.

2. **Timepiece Demolition Service:** Tick-tock, tick-tock, is there anything more annoying than a clock? Who wants to be constantly reminded that your time on earth is running out? Not Boogeyman, who seemingly concluded that this world would be a better place if every single clock on the planet was demolished. In fact, let's start a fund so we can put a bounty on the head of Flavor Flav. Maybe Boogeyman can get him before we have to endure another season of *Flavor of Love.*

1. **Oral Surgeon:** If you blinked, you might have missed Boogeyman showcasing what would likely be the most profitable career he could partake in post-wrestling: oral surgeon. In this instance, though, Dr. Man would not be taking care of molars and bicuspids, but instead using his oral features as a surgical instrument. He did this when Jillian Hall had what appeared to be a mole/birthmark/tumor/novelty slab of vomit on her cheek. Boogey, seeing the potential health hazards, took it upon himself to remove it by first licking, and then chomping, the unsightly disfigurement right off her face. One week later, Jillian was completely healed. One can only imagine the advances in the field of health care with Dr. Boogey Man, MD. Would have made for a hell of a reality show.

That's it! Reality television! You either love it or realize that it completely sucks. And let's face facts — most reality shows are "real" in name only. Seriously — how real will you act when there is a freakin' camera five feet in front of your face? Don't you think that knowing millions of people are watching you might change how you act just a little bit? Still, while most of these stupid shows attempt to at least pretend they are based in fact, there's one that even the dumbest couch potato has to know is 99 percent utter bullshit: *Hogan Knows Best*. And while we have to admit to being humored by the "real-life drama" of Hogan, his saint of a daughter, carnie of a son and bitch of a wife, we can't imagine that VH1 might not do better elsewhere. Like, for instance . . .

THE 6 WRESTLERS WHO MUST HAVE A REALITY SHOW

6. **Scott Steiner:** What could be more fun than thirty minutes a week with a camera covering the every exploit of Big Poppa Pump himself? A quick glance at his past reveals a man who is, to say the least, very mentally unbalanced, ready to snap at a moment's notice. For instance, he once attempted to run over a construction worker when he was informed that an exit ramp was closed. Then there was the time he attacked an EMT who was backstage at a WCW show. Good times. One can only imagine the sheer fury Scotty might display at, say, McDonald's, if they were to inform him they were out of McNuggets. Why, we can just hear the tirade now: "McNuggets! Where are my McNuggets? The Big Bad Booty Daddy needs his fucking McNuggets!!" Then he'd throttle the acne-ridden sixteen-year-old behind the counter, pausing only to point at his arm, kiss his bicep and proceed with the manslaughter until his McNugget craving has been fulfilled. Could that *Joe Millionaire* weenie do that? We think not.

5. **Ric Flair:** Has there ever been a more entertaining performer in pro wrestling than the Nature Boy? We emphatically answer that ques-

tion with a "nay." When you combine that charisma with some of his outside-the-ring issues, we're thinking his reality show would be a ratings jackpot. Whether Flair would be attempting to entice ladies to take a ride on Space Mountain or spending the day on the run from the IRS (the government agency, not Mike Rotundo in a bad tie and even worse spectacles), we're knowing this is surefire comedy gold. And if the producers have any sense at all, they'll be sure to equip his car with at least a dozen cameras, to capture any future road-rage incidents. Seeing Flair hop out of his Beamer, pull some schmuck out of a 1987 Yugo and begin to chop the hell out of his chest all the whilst yelling "Wooooo!"? That would garner the ratings of six Super Bowls plus the *M*A*S*H* finale.

4. **Billy Jack Haynes:** Older WWF fans will remember Billy Jack Haynes as Oregon's greatest practitioner of the full nelson. While that distinction alone would qualify him to be the greatest wrestler in the known universe to most fans (well, at least those in his immediate family), there's much more to Billy Jack than that. For instance, you might not be aware of the fact that for years Haynes was allegedly a drug runner for a Portland marijuana ring. Just imagine the fun viewers at home would have as Billy Jack makes his daily drug runs to various pimps and crack hos, all the while wearing his patented giant black hat with green headband. We smell a new fashion trend.

3. **Warrior:** As you can probably tell from what we've already said, the artist formerly known as Jim Hellwig is a strange, strange entity. Let's face it, anyone who'd legally change his name to Warrior Warrior probably ain't all there.

Whether he's writing 80,000-word diatribes about the virtues of "destrucity" on his Web site or telling gays that "queering don't make the world work" at the local community college, one thing is guaranteed: the dude is damn fascinating to watch. In fact, we bet that even an everyday life occurrence such as a trip to the dentist would make for captivating television.

"Okay, Jim, what we need to do today is—"

"Warrior."

"Excuse me?"

"My name is Warrior, not Jim."

"Ah, all right, Warrior . . . we've discovered two cavities, and we're going to need to fill those today."

"Cavities? A cavity is little more than a vacancy caused by the decay of a tooth. So too is the human race as we know it. While others would theorize that such instances in daily existence are little more than a random string of events, those more learned know it to be far greater than the sum of its existential parts. To wit, there are three fundamental philosophical pillars that one must comprehend and obey so that one might exhibit the confidence in order to not only exist, but to go beyond the day-to-day mundane tasks that most view as an existence. Those who fail to accept this as fact will fail to achieve complete enlightenment. This is not debatable, but is a fact, a given in the mathematical formula that turns the earth on its axis."

"Ummm . . . okay. Silver all right for the fillings?"

2. **New Jack:** The only problem with a television show chronicling the life of Jerome Young, better known to fans as New Jack, might be

finding a network that would be able to air it without censorship. And not just because the man cannot complete a sentence without at least one instance of the word "fuck" occurring. As a former bounty hunter with a reported four justifiable homicides (that we know about), the man is obviously a bit volatile, to say the least. Imagine the fun if Jack were at a wrestling show and he asked for a Sprite and was given a 7-Up. We can just picture him going totally insane, pummeling security guards and being forcibly restrained by a dozen or so police officers. What's that? That really happened? Good God, this idea is a license to print money.

1. **The Iron Sheik:** Insane. Completely, utterly and wonderfully insane. That's the only way we can describe the Iron Sheik, who in recent years has gone from forgotten Cold War wrestling villain to the nutty Iranian grandpa we all wish we had. The most notable example of Sheiky Baby's total loss of lucidity was on display in a 2005 interview when he was quizzed about his *WrestleMania III* memories, which turned into a tirade about how B. Brian Blair was a "punk little gay," a "faggot son of a bitch" just like Michael Jackson. He also explained in great detail how Wendi Richter vetoed his sexual advances, despite the fact that he gave her some of his medicine. (That's a crazy folk term for dope.) There could be only one explanation why this woman would give him the Heisman: she was a lesbian, just like Rosie O'Donnell and "Ellen Degenerate." Don't ask us, the man was on a roll. In fact, now that we think about it, we're ready to pitch our concept to VH1: *Flavor of Sheik*, a reality contest in which lesbians and gay men attempt to win Khosrow's affections. We have no doubt that should this ever hit the air, Nielsen would have to invent a whole new ratings system.

But sometimes wrestlers prefer to focus on the sports side of sports entertainment. Remember when Brock Lesnar left wrestling to become a football player? Oh, right, that flopped. Well, remember when Brock Lesnar left football to become a mixed martial arts competitor? Jury's still out on that one, but we'd wager he'll be back. Or maybe he'll just go into boxing. He wouldn't be the first wrestler to do that. In fact, we can think of . . .

6 WRESTLERS WHO DECIDED TO GIVE BOXING A SHOT

6. Derrick Dukes: Now, that's a name for a boxer: Derrick Dukes! Odds are, though, despite the tailor-made name, you've never heard of Derrick Dukes the boxer. Or his predecessor, Derrick Dukes the wrestler. So a bit of history: Dukes was primarily a tag team performer in the dying days of the AWA, most notably as one half of the Top Guns with Ricky Rice. Rice left the promotion, leaving Dukes on his own, doing basically nothing of note other than dropping a "Loser Gets Painted Yellow" match to Colonel DeBeers. Deciding that being doused in Dutch Boy was a highway to a danger zone he wanted no part of, Dukes left wrestling, became a boxer and eventually secured a high-profile encounter against NFL star Mark Gastineau. As in the squared circle, Dukes did the job to the former Jet in short order. It would later be discovered, however, that Dukes was paid off to take a dive. Somehow, we doubt Goose would have approved of that.

5. Paul Roma: What is the only thing more sad than a wrestler spending the better part of a decade on the undercard, barely being noticed? How about said wrestler thinking that the solution to his mediocre enhancement-talent ways was a mediocre career in boxing? In 1992, that is exactly what Paul Roma thought. He gave up his days of jobbing in the WWF and laced up the gloves. However, a future in fisticuffs was not to be, as Roma quickly showed he wasn't about to part with his jobber ways; he was TKO'd in his boxing debut by the "immortal" Jerry Arentzen, possessor of a career record of two wins, eighteen losses and one draw. It wasn't long before Roma decided he wanted his ass-kickings to be predetermined and less painful, and thus joined WCW, where he was immediately made a member of the elite Four Horsemen. Yes, really.

4. **Brian Adams:** Poor Brian Adams. The early 2000s certainly weren't kind to him. First WCW goes under; then, after finally being picked up by the WWF, he and his Kronik partner, Bryan Clark, are both shown the door after their debut match. What, you ask, could the former Crush do to solve his unemployment? What else? Take up the craft of boxing! After all, he was a spry *thirty-eight* at the time. But he wasn't going it alone, as none other than Randy "Macho Man" Savage was gonna be one of his cornermen. The two made various media appearances, including a guest spot on Fox Sports' *Best Damn Sports Show*, praising Adams' impressive skills and hyping his boxing debut, which was slated to occur on a Top Rank Boxing–promoted pay-per-view. However, par for the course for the never-staying-too-long-in-one-spot Mr. Adams, he injured his shoulder shortly before his scheduled bout and promptly announced his retirement from boxing. Despite never taking one punch in the ring, Adams could have been certified punch-drunk when he took up his next post-boxing career job — that of bodyguard on Randy Savage's musical concert tour.

3. Bart Gunn: While the previous two guys decided for themselves they wanted a career change, Mr. Gunn accidentally kicked ass en route to his first-ever legitimate boxing match. After quickly knocking out and embarrassing the trio of "Dr. Death" Steve Williams, the Godfather and Bradshaw to win the WWF's Brawl for All title, he was lined up to face a real professional — former Toughman champion Eric "Butterbean" Esch. The fight was set for the big stage of *WrestleMania XV.* And we use the term *fight* loosely. In a mere thirty-eight seconds, Butterbean landed one hell of a haymaker, knocking Bart Gunn's head off and effectively killing his career. Shed no tears for Gunn, however. He is now the annual leading candidate to play the Headless Horseman in weekend matinees of *The Legend of Sleepy Hollow* every fall for the rest of his life.

2. Joanie Laurer: If there's one thing you can count on in life, it's the fact that the artist formerly known as Chyna will always be on some Z-list celebrity reality show and make a fool of herself, which guarantees good comedy. Such was the case in the main event of the May 22, 2002, airing of Fox's *Celebrity Boxing,* as Joanie took on Joey Buttafuoco. Remember him? That was the guy who got his weiner cut off, right? No, wait. *That* was John Wayne Bobbit, who, ironically enough, was to be Buttafuoco's original opponent. Buttafuoco was the grease monkey who had the affair with underaged Amy Fisher, who grabbed a gun and popped a cap upside Joey's wife's jaw. Such an act makes you famous in America. Famous to the level, we should add, that he was on a celebrity boxing show ten years later, competing against Bobbit's stand-in, Joanie Laurer. Unfortunately for Joanie, her attempt at clinging to fame via pugilism was cut short via a three-round deci-

PHOTO: MATT BALK

Here's Chyna with the only man who ever really wanted to see (or touch) her box, X-Pac.

sion win for Buttafuoco. All was not lost, however, as less than two years later she was a judge at the World's Most Beautiful Transsexual Contest in Las Vegas. And no, we're not making that up.

1. **Antonio Inoki:** When Japan's most famous wrestler, Antonio Inoki, entered the ring to square off against perhaps the greatest heavyweight boxer of all time, Muhammad Ali, in a boxer vs. wrestler showdown in

1976, fans were certain they would see something for the ages. What they got was a contest that simply aged them. A brief Japanese lesson here: the word Inoki does not, in fact, translate as *laying on back like porn star*. Those watching this bout would be excused for the misinterpretation, however, as Antonio showed the whole world his best Linda Lovelace impersonation. Refusing to stand toe-to-toe with Ali, Inoki was content to lie on his back on the mat the entire time, kicking at an equally reluctant Ali's legs. After the full fifteen rounds, the bout was declared a draw. Speaking of things also drawn, no word on the total number of chalk lines drawn around those poor, unfortunate viewers who were painfully bored to death during this hideous snoozer.

But, hey, it's not just those watching that match who had a bad day. Face it — there are times in everyone's life when things just don't go right. Your car breaks down, your wife buys a cat, your wife's cat dies, your wife blames you for feeding the cat Tootsie Rolls (who knew they were bad for a cat's intestines?), your wife leaves you, then your wife sues for custody of the other cat (like you'd even want the damn thing to begin with). You know the drill. Life got you down? Then contact one of . . .

WRESTLING'S TOP 3 INSPIRATIONAL PERSONALITIES

3. Smilin' Diamond Dallas Page: Dallas Page is an inspirational guy for a lot of reasons. For one, he started his career in his mid-thirties, a time when many are either winding down or out of the business completely. He certainly didn't have the look of a pro wrestler: he resembled a rode-hard, put-away-wet bouncer at your local nudie bar. Which, ironically (or not), is exactly what he was prior to making his name in the old AWA as a manager. By the time he reached WCW in the early 1990s, it seemed that if Page were to be anything in the business, he would be a manager, not a wrestler. He proved everyone wrong, however, snaring three WCW world titles. He was also one of the few stars WCW ever created, and a lot of that was due to his own hard work both in and out of the ring. That's all well and good, but those things have nothing to do with why he made the list. No, he was inspirational to us because he liked to smile. In fact, following a failed stint in WWE as a stalker, he simply began showing up on TV and smiling. If that weren't enough, he soon decided he needed to be a motivational speaker and became Positively Page. Sometimes he'd talk to other wrestlers in need of a boost. Other times, he'd hang out in a gym and look at girls' leotard-covered snatches. Eventually, he created a workout program called Yoga for Regular Guys, which combined his smile and taint fetish. As the man himself would say, "That's not a bad thing . . . that's a good thing."

2. **Gary Spivey:** You know him. You may think you don't, but trust us, you do. That psychic guy that's on at 3 a.m., the one with the giant Brillo pad on his head? That's Gary Spivey. And believe it or not, he has a wrestling connection. See, in 1995, Paul Orndorff was going through an identity crisis. He'd been losing match after match, and didn't know if he was even worthy of his "Mr. Wonderful" nickname. His career had never been lower (not even when he was a fourth-string "Dude with Attitude" back in the 1990 WCW). Just when things looked most bleak, through the door walked none other than Gary Spivey. Orndorff's exclamation was priceless: "Gary Spivey? Of the Psychic Companions Network? What are you doing here?" Now, sure,

we'd all say such a thing if ol' SOS head suddenly appeared in our living rooms, but we'd probably follow it up with something like, "Now get the hell out of here before I call the cops!" Orndorff, though, looked at him as though Jesus himself had come to his rescue. Spivey explained to Paul that he was still "Mr. Wonderful," and that all these failures were simply in his head. He convinced Orndorff to look at himself in the mirror and love himself again. After what seemed like minutes of this rah-rahing, Orndorff agreed that he was still wonderful after all. This newfound enthusiasm lasted approximately six weeks, as Orndorff retired from injuries shortly after Gary's visit. We bet Miss Cleo would have seen it coming. Up yours, Spaceball!

1. **Sean O'Haire, Devil's Advocate:** Sean O'Haire seemed like a can't-miss prospect since his first days in pro wrestling. At six-six and 270 rock-hard pounds, he was the kind of guy Vince McMahon absolutely loves. But following WCW's closing in 2001, O'Haire just never got much of a chance in WWE. There was a brief period, though, where it seemed Sean would get a chance not only as a wrestler, but also as a motivational speaker of sorts. Now keep in mind we wrote "of sorts." In early 2003, he began to appear in vignettes in which he encouraged the fans to, among other things, cheat on their wives, cheat on their taxes and do drugs. He explained that everyone did these things, but were afraid to admit it, his catchphrase being, "I'm not telling you anything you don't already know." With this advice in tow, he showed up on *Smackdown* and convinced performers to do all kinds of wacky stuff, like cheering Dawn Marie on to flashing the audience. Getting a really hot chick to give everyone a free peep? How much more inspirational can one man be?

Finally, let's take a look at those instances where things just collapse into one gigantic mess. Usually a mess that involves the police. Wrestlers seem to be magnets for issues with the law, so it's not uncommon for a blotter to appear with a superstar's name on it. From the old days of Ken Patera lobbing a boulder through a McDonald's window to Rob Van Dam and Sabu getting busted for dope, the song remains the same. And now we present . . .

6 MEN WHO SHOULD HAVE PRIMPED FOR THEIR MUGSHOTS

6. Booker Huffman (Booker T): Okay, maybe this is one instance in which our wrestling buddy didn't need to primp. After all, one has to wonder what, exactly, young Booker Huffman did to make himself so pleased at getting a Polaroid in the pokey (he robbed a Wendy's, if you must know). Think about it: he was being arrested and carted off to jail (he served nineteen months of a five-year term). Why on earth would he be pleased as punch? Was he jonesing for three squares a day in the slammer cafeteria? Did he actually look forward to bending over and picking up the soap? We'll likely never know the reason. Seriously — have you ever seen a man more content?

5. Andre Roussimoff (Andre the Giant): What could the Eighth Wonder of the World have done to improve his looks following his arrest for roughing up a cameraman in August 1989, you ask? We'd suggest combing his hair, then perhaps confiscating a bowie knife and attempting to saw off the mutton chops adorning his jowls. But above all . . . change your shirt, buster. Sure, it looked great in *The Princess Bride*, but it's not really the kind of thing you should be modeling in everyday life.

4. Monty Sopp (Billy Gunn/Kip James): And here we have Monty Sopp

PHOTO: MUGSHOTS.COM

doing what he does best: looking confused. Photographed after being arrested for disorderly conduct, his perplexed pucker seems to say, "Why am I here? What is that you are pointing at me? What is it going to do? Did you know I used to be known as Mr. Ass? What did that even mean? Why did my theme song, entitled 'Ass Man,' go, 'I like to pick 'em, I like to stick 'em'? Why would I want to pick an ass? Or stick an ass? Am I gay? Should I be gay? I mean, I was gay in a wrestling angle where I was going to marry my life partner, Chuck, but that was just a silly storyline. Wasn't it? Maybe I really am gay. That's okay, isn't it? Have you seen my latest hairdo? The one where I put it up in pigtails? That looks pretty cool, doesn't it? Have I told you how much I hate Triple H? I mean, I really, really hate the guy, and you know why, right? Hey wait a second . . . why am I here? Oh wait, I'm starting all over again . . ."

3. Paul Wight (the Big Show — arrested for assault in 1999): Umm, excuse us? Mr. Wight? Would it be too much to ask for you to be

conscious for your mugshot? We'd appreciate it, sport.

2. **Richard Fleihr (Ric Flair):** For a man who has for decades prided himself on "styling and profiling," the Nature Boy was neither during his
trip to the sheriff's department in North Carolina's Mecklenburg

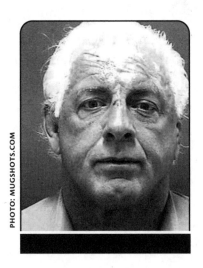

County in November 2005. Not only does Flair appear to be approximately 327 years old, his face also seems carved out of stone, like he was a missing head on Mount Rushmore. That or the officer in charge of the photo said, "See this quarter? How closely do you think you could approximate George Washington? That's it — perfect!" Aside from blatantly impersonating U.S. currency, he was also charged with road rage (he was eventually cleared).

1. **Lawrence Pfohl (Lex Luger):** It would be a fair assessment to state that the new millennium has been anything but kind to Lex Luger. Though he was a huge wrestling star in the '80s and '90s, Luger has been persona non grata in the business since the collapse of WCW in 2001. His personal life has been an unending series of arrests and tragedy, most notably the death of his girlfriend, Liz Hulette (known to wrestling fans worldwide as Miss Elizabeth), in 2003. While our heart goes out to him during this most trying time, one has to admit this photo is anything but flattering.

PHOTO: MUGSHOTS.COM

If only he were arrested again so he could have a chance at a better, more flattering shot.

PHOTO: MUGSHOTS.COM

Ah, thanks, Lex. We knew you wouldn't let us down.

Those Poor, Poor Promoters

Throughout this book we've chronicled how difficult it is to be a wrestler. You're constantly on the road, which makes maintaining any type of family life a near impossibility. Your body experiences tremendous wear and tear. And whatever idiotic storyline or character you're given, well . . . such is your fate. You want the dime, you do the crime. And if you don't do it, rest assured, some other schmuck will.

But enough boo-hooing about those guys in the ring. You know who really has it hard in wrestling? Promoters. They work tirelessly behind the scenes and what thanks do they get for it? Nuthin'!

Sure, you might argue that Vince McMahon is an honest-to-God billionaire, but other than the ability to go to sleep atop large piles of money and to just throw himself into the middle of whatever the hottest angle is on his shows, what does he have to show for it? Money and fame may be okay for some people, but for hardworking, honest folk like wrestling promoters, well . . . they need more.

Like, for instance, the ability to lash out at their chosen enemies. That's better than money any day of the week. At least, that's what we've been led to believe, given that promoters often create storylines that have nothing to do with generating fan interest, but plenty to do with grinding an ax. Don't believe us? Then check out . . .

6 STORYLINES CREATED FROM REAL LIFE . . . JUST TO SPITE SOMEONE

6. **Russo Hates Standards and Practices:** When Vince Russo came to WCW, he had high hopes, and so did his new employer. He was, after all, the driving force behind WWE becoming not only the No. 1 wrestling promotion, but the No. 1 television show in all of cabledom. Sure, he wasn't actually in the ring. And come to think of it, he didn't ever appear as an on-screen character, either. But, hey, he was the guy who penned all the storylines that caught fans' attention. There was just one problem: his scripts combined sophomoric humor, loads of violence and oodles of sex. And that was a major issue, as WCW was under much tighter regulations than WWE. Those in charge at Turner frowned on men-on-women violence and weren't big fans of near-naked chesticles during prime time. This lead to mucho infighting between Russo and the higher-ups at TNT, as Russo felt the organization's Standards and Practices Department was sabotaging his efforts to bring WCW back to the top of the wrestling mountain. Russo's solution? Create a tag team known as Standards and Practices to express his displeasure. Of course, this infuriated Russo's superiors, who already viewed him as little more than a pain-in-the-ass con man. It wasn't long before he was shown the door. But not before Russo had the chance to unleash one more of his creations on the wrestling world . . .

5. **Russo Hates Jim Ross:** Russo had his fair share of detractors in WWE as well. One of these naysayers was Jim Ross. Good ol' JR often found Russo's writing insulting, as he had learned more traditional wrestling

sensibilities under the tutelage of men such as Bill Watts. Upon his arrival in WCW, Russo decided to let the world know just how much Ross's second-guessing bothered him. He created Oklahoma, a very thinly veiled parody of Ross portrayed by Russo's writing partner Ed Ferrara. This high-class mockery included such comedy as making fun of Ross's Bell's palsy. The pair did this bit as a one-off in the WWF, but it was quickly dropped, as it made no real sense and, more importantly, no one in the stands cared. But once the pair got to WCW, they had free rein and went full on with the character. Besides, it's not like those fans who paid money to attend shows mattered, right?

4. **There Goes the Neighborhood:** In the ultimate show of power, Vince McMahon once created a wrestler to showcase on national television as a means of telling his new neighbors how much he despised their uppity attitude. You may have even heard of him — his name is Hunter Hearst Helmsley. Now waitaminute, you are no doubt saying . . . the almighty Triple H was created out of spite? He sure was. The backstory here is the epitome of pettiness: McMahon had tried to purchase a house in Greenwich, and his new neighbors were none too pleased when they found out their new neighbor made his money through such lowbrow entertainment. And so Hunter Hearst Helmsley, snooty American blue blood, was born. He'd stick his nose high into the air and mock the middle class. And, as if you even need to ask, he most certainly did hail from Greenwich, Connecticut.

3. **PTC, RTC, WTF?** In 2000, L. Brent Bozell's Parents Television Council was causing all kinds of troubles for WWE. The group stated very clearly and, most annoyingly for WWE, very loudly to all who would

PHOTO: TROY FERGUSON

Every parent, television and council's nightmare —
the Godfather and his Ho Train.

listen that WWE's flagship *Raw* was all manner of evil, showcasing
pimps and hos and other family-unfriendly characters. While many
within wrestling considered this nothing more than the ravings of a
right-wing lunatic, his group did much damage to WWE. They were
able to get the ear of advertisers, many of whom decided to forgo
their WWE sponsorships, despite the fact that *Raw* was far and away
the highest rated program in all of cable television. Vince's answer?
Create a stable of conservative nut jobs who felt it was their duty to
cover up the half-naked women on *Raw*. Their name? Right to Censor,
or RTC (as a play on the PTC). Heck, the RTC was so powerful they
were able to transform WWE's resident hemp-smokin' pimp, the
Godfather, into the Goodfather, a wholesome man who disdained his
former lifestyle. We're willing to bet L. Brent was never able to accomplish that one in real life. As this was Vince's return volley, the group
members were naturally portrayed as villains in storylines. And in the
end, Vince did get the last laugh, as he not only mocked Bozell's group
on air, but also prevailed in real life, forcing the PTC to settle a law-

suit out of court for $3.5 million. A very rare instance of a spite story-line actually making money.

2. **An Extreme Example of Biting the Hand that Feeds:** Though it was a distant third during wrestling's heyday in the late 1990s, Paul Heyman's ECW provided the formula for a lot of what made WWE so successful. By the end of 1999, however, ECW was in dire financial straits and needed cash, fast. The only way anyone believed it could stay afloat was by getting a national television deal, which it did by way of TNN. A Friday-night time slot was opened up, giving ECW a chance to show the masses what it was all about. From the beginning, the show was a disaster. TNN, which at the time was still The Nashville Network, requested that several changes be made to the product. According to Heyman, the network felt the theme music, for instance, was too "demonic" and demanded it be changed. (Sadly, ECW never opened with a Waylon Jennings ballad.) All this drove Paul completely berserk, as he was unwilling to make this or any other change. TNN responded by forgoing any and all advertising. The volleys continued back and forth, with Heyman finally cutting a shoot promo on television wherein he stated how much he hated "The Network." Yes, the same network that was airing his product. The following week, Don Callis, under the guise of a network executive named Cyrus, began to make life hell for the babyfaces in the promotion. TNN was not amused, and in just over one year they cancelled the show. All of this was done because Paul Heyman didn't want to "compromise his vision," a vision, we should note, that died in 2001 with ECW's bankruptcy. A not-so-rare instance of a spite story-line not making money — in fact, costing a company dearly.

1. **Virgil . . . or Is that Vincent . . . or Is that Shane?** While many of the items on this list required a performer or two to be pawns in a promoter's vengeful mission, only Mike Jones can claim an entire *career* based on such antics. Jones originally appeared in the WWF as "Million Dollar Man" Ted DiBiase's manservant, Virgil. He was given this name as a way of mocking Dusty Rhodes, real name Virgil Runnels, who was one of the NWA's top stars at the time. Eventually Jones left the WWF and headed to WCW, where he became Vincent, as a shot at WWF owner Vince McMahon. He would later be redubbed Shane, so as to mock Vince's son Shane. And the reason he was always asked to play these parts? Because the guy almost always lost. Some guys just can't buy a break . . . even with a million-dollar man as his employer.

But sometimes promoters just aren't satisfied with the scripted cheapshots at those both inside and outside the business. Sometimes they feel it appropriate to broadcast the all-too-real and tragic misfortunes of their former superstars to the entire viewing audience. We call it . . .

WRESTLING'S 6 MOST DISTASTEFUL EXPLOITATIONS

6. **Tammy Sytch Bares Her Soul . . . in Prime Time:** In 1997, Tammy Sytch had the whole world in her hands — not only was she regarded as the reigning queen of wrestling, but she was the most downloaded celebrity on AOL. Flash forward two short years to 1999. Long gone were the accolades and magazine covers, replaced instead by wars against those infamous "personal demons." She was released from not only the WWF, but ECW as well. In time, ECW head honcho Paul Heyman decided to give her one more shot — which not so coinci-

dentally coincided with him needing to boost the ratings on his new ECW show on TNN. Thus Tammy was reintroduced with a heavily promoted "shoot-style" interview, in which she cried her eyes out whilst talking about all the troubles of her past. In addition to a lengthy discussion of her painkiller addiction, she also spoke of the death of her cousin, finally concluding that sometimes she "wished I wouldn't wake up in the morning." Sytch would be gone from the company mere weeks later.

5. Sadly, the First Lady of Wrestling Has Died (So Let's Exploit Her): On May 1, 2003, the wrestling world lost one of its true female pioneers, Miss Elizabeth. Since Liz had died of a combination of painkillers and alcohol, this meant but one thing — WWE's sorta-shoot, mostly-BS program *Confidential* had one heck of an exploitation story on its hands. The fact that her boyfriend was former superstar Lex Luger (who Vince had heat with from way back) only sweetened the deal. And sure enough, fans at home were treated to the desperate 911 calls from Luger, as he had attempted to save Liz's life. WWE dragged the investigative Liz story out over the course of two weeks, and it seemed less like *WWE Confidential* and more like *CSI: Stamford*. In closing, Vince concluded that the downfall of Elizabeth was that in her time in WCW, she didn't have a family-like atmosphere to guide her away from the path to self-destruction. This would be in stark contrast, of course, to WWE, a truly caring environment in which male wrestlers were known to defecate in female performers' luggage.

4. Just Say No to Drugs — Especially Drug-Related Storylines: It was common knowledge among those "in the know" that Mike Hegstrand

(Road Warrior Hawk) was plagued by his fair share of alcohol and drug problems. Those who didn't know, however, didn't remain uninformed or left out, as during the summer of 1998, the WWF decided to bring a reality-based spin to its programming as it showcased Hawk falling off the wagon. For a few fun-filled weeks, fans were exposed to Hawk collapsing drunk both inside and outside the ring. One time he even wobbled down to the announcer's booth. "Why are you here?" Jim Ross demanded to know. "I was come down to help you out with a little color dysentery," Hawk replied. This diarrhea-like angle reached its climax when a depressed Hawk tried to commit suicide live on *Raw*, tossing himself off the top of the giant TitanTron screen. Sadly, any amusement this angle may have brought to people was dampened by the fact that a clean and sober Hawk died in 2003 of heart failure caused by too many years of a hard-living lifestyle.

3. **"Your Husband Just Died . . . How Do You Feel?"** If the Diva Searches of recent years have taught us anything, it's that there are a lot of women out there who would love to be showcased on a big prime-time show like *WWE Monday Night Raw*. Imagine being thrust in front of the bright lights for your moment in the sun, as the camera panned in on you for your big moment. A great moment to be sure . . . well, if your husband hadn't passed away just twenty-four hours earlier. Such was the case the day after Brian Pillman was found dead in his hotel room, as his wife Melanie Pillman was interviewed by Vince McMahon live from her house on *Monday Night Raw*. In a moment of true sympathy, Vince asked a tearful Melanie the heartfelt question of how she, as a newly widowed mother of five, was going to be able to support her children. Maybe Vince could have offered her

a role as an on-screen performer, preferably as a heel. Hey, now there's an idea!

2. He May Be Gone, But He Won't Be Forgotten — Because We'll Just Keep Writing Him into Storylines: Not since the tragic death of Owen Hart in 1999 had WWE's active roster suffered such a gut-wrenching loss as when the legendary Eddie Guerrero passed away in November 2005. Perhaps it was too much of a blow to WWE's creative department, as they decided to keep Eddie involved in the storylines posthumously. For the better part of the next year, Eddie's name and memory were brought up frequently, whether in the form of JBL badmouthing him and Rey Mysterio standing up to defend his fallen friend's name, or the fun-filled sight of Randy Orton blowing up Eddie's famous lowrider, complete with the Undertaker inside. Guerrero's family wasn't left out of the mix either, as the ensuing months would see a downtrodden Chavo Guerrero "retire" because he wasn't the man his late uncle was. He would later "unretire" to face Mysterio in a match for Eddie's honor, inexplicably turning Eddie's widow heel in the process. ¡Viva la explotación!

1. My Kids Died, I Might as Well Too . . . If It Will Pop the Gate: Fritz Von Erich has been criticized for years for his poor treatment of his family. Let's face it: when a father — a father who has seen several of his children kill themselves — tells his final living son, "You don't have the guts to kill yourself," obviously something is awry. Still, when it comes to exploitation, nothing could compare to an infamous angle Fritz booked himself into as World Class (his wrestling promotion) was collapsing in the late 1980s. Following an attack by Terry Gordy,

Buddy Roberts and Iceman King Parsons, Fritz suffered a heart attack. Wait, scratch that. He suffered a "heart attack," in quotations to clarify that he was, in fact, not ill at all. Rather, he just used the heart attack to increase attendance at events. On television, Fritz's condition would get better or worse, depending on how many people were at each show . . . with the hope that fans would turn out to support him as his condition worsened. After all, his David and Mike memorial shows were always huge draws, so why not try an angle based on his own

PHOTO: MIKE LANO

The Von Erich family roster. Not pictured, Lance Von Erich and Fritz's cardiologist.

death as well? Despite the fact that several Dallas news stations bought into the story, it didn't help the promotion, which died itself, and Fritz sold it off in late 1988.

But hey, what would you expect of a Nazi? Okay, okay, we jest — Fritz wasn't a Nazi, he just played one on TV early in his career. The folks who ran WCW, though . . . we're not so sure they weren't descendents of Der Fuhrer himself. Don't believe us? Well, then let us present to you, dear reader . . .

THE 6 PIECES OF DEFINITIVE PROOF THAT WCW MAY HAVE BEEN RUN BY NAZIS

6. **Blitzkrieg:** Jay Ross was a highly impressive young prospect from California. In the late '90s, he would enter WCW and have many great matches with the top cruiserweights of the time, including Rey Mysterio Jr. and Psychosis. Heck, he was even named the *Wrestling Observer* 1999 Rookie of the Year. So, why on earth did he name himself after a Nazi Germany war formation? No idea, other than perhaps the name Swastika had already been taken.

5. **Berlyn:** After "Das Wunderkind" Alex Wright and his homoerotic "penile pump" dance had grown stale in the late '90s, WCW management decided to take him off television for a while and repackage him as a heel. Seeing as Wright looked about as menacing as a Care Bear hopped up on Prozac, this was gonna take some doing. When he returned under the name Berlyn in the fall of 1999, he looked liked he had enrolled in Neo-Nazism 101. Decked out in a black trench coat and mohawk, with an entourage of German baddies in tow, it

looked like Berlyn was gonna try to reenact 1942 in the WCW. What were his evil goals? We can only guess, as Berlyn refused to speak any English. While haters of horrible angles no doubt rejoiced at successfully avoiding Alex Wright interview segments, we should probably mention that he did have an interpreter . . .

4. Ute Ludendorf: As bad as it would have been to listen to Alex Wright drone on philosophically in Deutsch, we'd rather hear him read the phone book aloud than suffer the pain of listening to his prudish German translator, Ms. Ute Ludendorf. When Berlyn would spout off German phrases during interviews, Ute would grab the mic and translate in the most screech-filled, hate-filled, annoying-filled voice in the history of man. As loud as she would yell, sometimes it was hard to hear Ms. Abomination of Verbal Skills very clearly, as the live crowds tore the Berlyn gimmick apart with a loud chorus of boos. Thankfully, after a few weeks, Berlyn gave in and decided to start speaking in English, kicking Ludendorf to the curb, and in effect putting an "M" in front of Ute.

3. The Wall: The final member of Berlyn's entourage was his giant bodyguard, the Wall. And to complete his pseudo-Hitler gimmick, the Wall was a stereotypical blond-haired, blue-eyed soldier. While obviously named after the Berlin Wall, which separated East and West Germany for decades, this character was actually a metaphor, a huge man stuck right in the middle of WCW. On one side of him was the held-down undercard. On the other side, Hogan, Nash and the upper-card politics. Despite being a monster of a man, WCW totally botched his initial push and feud with Hulk Hogan. He never got another chance to break out of the midcard, going through a series of gimmick modifications that made his character's history about as confusing as Pink Floyd's movie, *The Wall*.

2. **Jack Boot:** Veteran WCW grappler Dwayne Bruce portrayed a ton of different characters in WCW over the years. Whether he was playing the role of grouchy policeman Sgt. Buddy Lee Parker, or Brawn the Leprechaun, you could always count on being amused by the pint-sized wrestler. One character, however, might've been best left on the idea table. That of the extreme militant man — Jack Boot. In case you dozed off during history class in school, *jack boot* is the term for the leather boots that Nazi soldiers wore into battle during World War II. To be fair, that's probably obscure enough to let slide. But after looking at the list thus far, you have to admit we're kind of right to have kept our eyes on these jokers. And if you don't think so, we present to you . . .

1. **The Final Solution:** By 1995, WCW high-ranking officials were trying to put on a more family-friendly, politically correct wrestling product. Gone were any scenes of blood, and televised chair shots were all but part of the past. Even the long-standing phrase for a weapon, *foreign object*, was replaced with *international object*. With such strict policies in place, surely there would never be a wrestler named after the Nazi's genocidal plan to wipe out the entire Jewish population? *Nein!* On the eve of *Uncensored '96*, the final character for the heel side of the main event was revealed: the Final Solution. The Solution (played by Jeep Swensen) was introduced by Kevin Sullivan in a giant in-ring rally of heels promising the demise of Hulkamania. It wasn't the only

rally that week. A group of Jewish people protested the offensively named Solution, and by the next week, WCW had smartened up and renamed him the Ultimate Solution. If you can't be named after a bunch of German gas chambers, we suppose the next best thing is to sound like you're a 400-pound calculator.

It doesn't happen often, but sometimes real life actually grants wrestling promoters favors, ones they wouldn't need to callously exploit. Maybe that's why they so rarely take advantage of them. We call 'em the . . .

"WE DIDN'T COME UP WITH IT SO WE CAN'T USE IT" LIST OF MISSED OPPORTUNITIES

6. So You Broke Your Neck? Let's Turn You Heel: In 1998, Marcus "Buff" Bagwell had a very real scare in the ring, suffering a broken neck at the hands of a Rick Steiner botched bulldog. Several months later, when Bagwell returned in a wheelchair, fans applauded his courage and perseverance. In short, WCW had just been handed a true baby-face, one the crowd wanted to see fight the dastardly New World Order. When he was finally green-lighted to return, he came out to face the nWo with Rick Steiner . . . who he promptly hit with a chair, turning heel — and therefore becoming completely and utterly irrelevant — in the process.

5. Swing and a Miss: In 1998, there was no hotter story in the sports world than Sammy Sosa and Mark McGwire's chase of Roger Maris's single-season home-run record. You could not turn on a newscast without seeing the constant updates of how the race was progressing.

During this summer when America seemingly rediscovered its supposed pastime, McGwire became buddies with one of WCW's biggest stars: Bill Goldberg. In fact, Goldberg even took batting practice with McGwire on at least one occasion. Since it was not their idea, though, WCW chose to completely ignore this.

4. **WWE Goes to the Dogs:** One of the reasons WWE decided to leave its longtime cable home of the USA Network in the late '90s was because *Raw* was preempted several times per year. Although its new network, Spike TV, did not have such preemptions, the relationship between the two parties didn't last long and soon enough WWE was back on USA. Suffice it to say, Spike TV, which had invested much time and money into making *Raw* the cornerstone of its "network for men," was livid to see Vince take his show elsewhere. In fact, it brought on a new wrestling promotion known as TNA in an attempt to appeal to wrestling fans. Soon enough, *Raw* was once again preempted for a dog show, opening the door for Spike to present its new product to wrestling fans on a night when they'd be looking for wrestling: the longtime *Raw* Monday night block. Despite this opening, Spike decided not to give TNA the opportunity and instead aired an old *CSI* rerun.

3. **Dancing with Myself:** Stacy Keibler was a top act for WWE for several years, and with good reason: not only did she possess movie-star good looks, but also an insane sex appeal that made her one of the most popular women in wrestling history. The key to that appeal would be her shapely forty-two-inch legs that left male jaws on the floor (and more than likely their hands in their naughty regions). She put those legs to good use on the popular reality show *Dancing with*

the Stars, finishing in the top three and becoming a mainstay on entertainment magazine shows. Despite this unending publicity, following her first couple of appearances on the show, WWE simply ignored her and never brought her back.

2. ***Tough Enough* Winner Actually Too Tough:** During the third season of *Tough Enough* (which, due to diminishing ratings, actually took place within *Smackdown* episodes), WWE had the brilliant idea to have its wannabe wrestlers actually try to take down one of their top stars, Kurt Angle. The idea behind this was stupid, but sound: while it made zero sense to actually have wrestlers shoot on each other, at least they had the guy to handle things in Angle. After all, who could take down a legit Olympic gold medalist? The answer to that would be a shootfighter by the name of Daniel Puder, who had trapped Angle in a keylock and nearly forced him to tap out. Instead of building up the natural rivalry — especially after Puder did, in fact, win the contest — WWE instead buried Puder in its developmental territory and fired him after his first twelve months were up.

1. **Two World Champions, Delivered:** It's a rare occasion when a wrestling promotion is fortunate enough to have a top star leave his former promotion while still wearing its top belt. For decades, as soon as a performer gave notice, he was given something in return: a list of men he was going to lose to on the way out the door. By doing this, the promotion accomplished two things. Not only were the men who remained in the company getting a "rub" by beating a top star, but the guy who was leaving saw his star power being diminished in the process. In the days of big-money contracts, promoters knew exactly

when a guy was leaving, so there was rarely a chance for a performer to walk at the height of his popularity. But in the Monday Night War era, it happened twice: once when Bret Hart left the WWF for WCW following the infamous Montreal screwjob, and once when Chris Benoit left WCW for the WWF following a dispute with management. Hart was the WWF world champion until his last match with the WWF; Benoit was WCW champion when he left the company. In fact, Hart had even more momentum, as the documentary *Wrestling with Shadows* also hit the airwaves during his time in the company. And how did their new employers maximize the opportunities that fell in their laps that detailed the entire Montreal fiasco? Hart's first WCW PPV appearance with WCW was as a special referee for a Larry Zbyszko-Eric Bischoff match. Benoit's first WWF match was a clean pinfall loss to Triple H. When opportunity knocks, wrestling promoters rarely listen.

Sometimes that's by design. If you've been paying attention for the past, say, twenty years, you'll note that the guys Vince McMahon likes to push are big muscleheads. Talent inside the ring is secondary to looking larger than life. In fact, at some point during 2006, the mandate was set forth that no talent under six-foot-two should even be considered. Odd, then, to take a look at . . .

THE 7 MEN WHO'D NEVER MAKE IT PAST PRE-HIRE REQUIREMENTS TODAY, YET WHO SOMEHOW WERE WWF CHAMPIONS (AND, OH YEAH, THEY DREW LOADS OF MONEY)

  7. **Shawn Michaels:** Sure, Shawn is still a big name in WWE these days, but when he first came in, he was viewed as nothing more than one

half of a teenybopper tag team known as the Rockers. And, according to some who were in WWE at the time, he was considered the weak half of that duo. Time certainly showed that to be incorrect, as was the original assumption that he really couldn't work and had little personality. Of course, you can't blame Vince for having such preconceived notions: after all, Shawn's under six feet tall and weighs less than 230 pounds. Who ever drew money at that size? Heck, the only thing worse would be if he were a minority.

6. **Rey Mysterio Jr.:** At five-foot-three and weighing a legit 140 or so, Hispanic Rey Mysterio has to be considered the man least likely to have worn major WWE gold. So can you imagine how he'd be viewed under the current prerequisites? You might even question how he made it as far as he did. Of course, the answer to that would be two words, and the next on our list of folks who'd never make it into the big leagues under the current rules.

5. **Eddie Guerrero:** Eddie Guerrero was a guy who was viewed as too small to make it back in the day . . . so you can only imagine what the take would be today. The difference, of course, as is the difference with virtually all the men on this list, is one of talent. Though he had fantastic in-ring ability, we'd argue that Eddie's greatest attribute was his personality. Fans just loved him, and at that point, WWE had no choice but to push him to the top in spite of his size.

4. **Bret Hart:** Stop me if you've heard this one before. When Bret Hart first entered the WWF, he was viewed as the weaker half of a tag team (yes, Jim Neidhart was initially considered the star of the Hart

Foundation). When the WWF and Vince McMahon were being investigated for steroid abuse, the company immediately needed a top star who was obviously not on the juice. It was, ironically, the fact that Bret did *not* look like a giant that got him the gig atop the federation. And it was his skill that kept him there for years afterward.

3. Pedro Morales: And now we enter the big three stars of yesteryear who *really* would never have made it in the company. Pedro Morales was a big name in New York City, a beacon of light for the Hispanic community. Despite being short and slightly pudgy, Morales was a huge draw for the company and held the WWWF (the precursor to both the WWF and the WWE) title for almost three years in the early 1970s. If he walked into the company today, he'd be laughed right out the door.

2. Bob Backlund: As would Bob Backlund. Though Backlund was fit and had an extensive amateur background, his personality was such that staring at paint drying on the wall would be far superior to watching him be interviewed. And yet, somehow, some way, he drew tons of money and was the champion for six years. *Six years.* But even that pales in comparison to . . .

PHOTO: MATT BALK

Bob Backlund takes down a Yankee.
Perhaps Catfish Hunter.

1. **Bruno Sammartino:** Younger WWE fans either know Bruno as a commentator (and a pretty bad one at that) during the late '80s or, worse yet, not at all. These fans would be shocked indeed to know he held the WWWF title for a whopping eight years straight, then came back years later for another three-year run. Yes, he held the title for eleven years! Steve Austin's entire WWE career as Stone Cold didn't last that long. Nor did Dwayne Johnson's run as the Rock. In fact, the number of guys who have remained with the company for that length of time could be counted on one hand. And yet here was this pudgy little Italian guy who held the belt for *eleven years*.

Hey, and speaking of champions, we'd be remiss if we didn't point out that sometimes promoters come up with the grand idea to put their straps on those who likely shouldn't hold them. At that point, the belts, which once actually meant something and could be used in angles that drew money, become worthless pieces of tin. There are bookers who over the years have treated belts as mere props, especially when they gave titles to . . .

THE 5 WORST CHAMPIONS IN WRESTLING HISTORY

5. **Chyna:** Now, we know what you folks are thinking: Chyna was a great woman wrestler, and including her on this list is borderline blasphemy. To which we reply, "Well, actually she was a not-so-good woman wrestler, and calling it blasphemy indicates that you are a borderline — nah, an all-out, 100 percent — moron." But we're not taking Joanie to task for being WWF Women's Champion. That's something we have no beef with whatsoever. What is an issue, though, is her run as an Intercontinental title holder. What the belt had once symbolized

— honor, prestige and, let's face it, the most important thing, money (meaning that fans were willing to pay to see bouts in which a championship match was contested) — all went out the door once a woman held the strap. Although, we suppose, you could make the argument that Chyna was more masculine than the man she defeated, Jeff Jarrett. So she does make it on the list, but just barely.

4. **Terri Runnels:** Whereas the Intercontinental title was traditionally a big deal, we have to admit that the WWF Hardcore title was largely a joke throughout its brief history. Still, putting the strap on Terri Runnels, who was barely five feet and couldn't have weighed more than 100 pounds, seems to us like a very, very bad idea. To be fair, at the time she won the title, the Hardcore championship was so prestigious that it was being defended not only in the ring, but at other locations, such as airports, hotel rooms and the local Chuck E. Cheese. Sadly, her reign lasted only five minutes, and therefore any potential Terri vs. Crash Holly best 2-of-3 Skeeball battles were nixed.

3. **Madusa:** Now, we must state we're not psychics, but we know what you folks are thinking again: Madusa was one of the greatest female wrestlers of her era, and including her on this list is a case of outright blasphemy. To which we reply, "Well, actually you're right — she was a great woman wrestler, but still, calling it blasphemy indicates to us that you have no inkling as to what the word *blasphemy* actually means." Anyway, as with Chyna, we're not dissing Ms. Miceli for her runs as Women's Champion, but rather her Cruiserweight championship run. A run, we should add, in which victory was obtained by seducing her opponent, Evan Karagias. We'd point out that this

title was also won by another woman, Daffney, but looking at this list you might think we were sexist, and we really can't afford a class-action suit by the local Lesbian Avengers chapter.

2. Judy Bagwell: But even the threat of flannel-wearing butches can't stop us from bringing up the next champion on the list. While Chyna and Madusa (and even Daffney, to some extent) had been trained in the business and were physically fit, the same could not be claimed of Judy Bagwell, whose climb to the top of the WCW tag ranks was solely thanks to her son, Marcus "Buff" Bagwell. Why someone felt that having a sixty-year-old woman as a tag team champion of the world was a good idea has never been fully explained. Why the same woman would later be an object for retrieval in a "Judy Bagwell on a Pole Match" is probably equally best left unexplored.

1. David Arquette: By far the worst champion in the history of the business, David Arquette, WCW World Champion, wasn't just a bad idea that everyone laughs at now, but a monumentally damaging blow to a company that was already at death's door. The logic behind the move, as explained by WCW's booker at the time, Vince Russo, was that it was something different that no one was expecting and it would get people talking. It's a move Russo still defends to this day — as he said in a 2006 interview with us, "Seven years later, and you guys are still talking about it." Using this logic, one could argue that we're still talking about the Hindenburg incident from seventy years ago. And look what that did for the budding zeppelin industry. We don't begrudge Russo for doing something so unexpected, and it did get the company mainstream publicity on several entertainment shows and in *USA Today*. But to whoever said there's no such thing as bad publicity, we offer up the following indisputable proof: once Arquette was wearing the world-title belt, fans stopped buying tickets. Pay-per-views featuring him in main events drew the absolute lowest buyrates in company history, and within months the company itself was purchased by Vince McMahon for virtually nothing. As for Mr. Arquette himself, we'd like to thank him. Yes, thank him. Not for helping to kill the company, but for being a truly great human being. You see, not only did Arquette argue vehemently that he should not be made champion (he was a lifelong fan himself and knew the ramifications), but he very quietly donated all his earnings from wrestling to the families of deceased wrestlers Owen Hart and Brian Pillman, and to recently paralyzed Darren Drozdov. Bravo, Dewey — bravo.

Not all celebrities have been so noble. Or notable, for that matter. One of the keys to the first *WrestleMania* was that Vince McMahon was able to get major stars, such as Muhammad Ali and Cyndi Lauper to appear, thus giving his wrestlers a celebrity rub. Over the years, though, it seems that just about anyone who ever appeared on a television screen, no matter what the reason or for how long, had an open invitation to WWE's biggest show of the year. Heck, we could scarcely remember . . .

THE 10 MOST OBSCURE *WRESTLEMANIA* CELEBRITIES

10. **Gennifer Flowers:** We seriously had zero clue who this even was when researching this list, which is odd — you'd think a Gennifer with a G would be something we'd remember. Maybe we should bone up on our presidential trivia. Like Bill Clinton, who apparently did the same

with Miss Flowers back in the day and thus generated her fifteen minutes of fame — which included a *WrestleMania XIV* stint as a backstage interviewer. But really, can you blame us for not remembering a woman who claimed to have ridden Bill's baloney pony? After all, aren't there like three dozen other skanks out there who claim the same thing?

9. **Jennie Garth:** Remember that pasty-faced skeleton by the name of Kelly from *Beverly Hills 90210*? That was Jennie Garth. Sure, these days she resides in the "Where Are They Now" file, but back in the day, *90210* was all the rage. In fact, we believe that the WWE creative staff were huge fans of the show, and of Garth's character in particular. In addition to giving her a job at *WrestleMania X*, they stripmined her character's storylines for the wrestling world. Check this out: Kelly was once trapped in a fire (like Kane), was in a cult (see Darkness, Ministry of) and even had a miscarriage (paging Amy "Lita" Dumas). Sheesh, they need to be sending Miss Garth and the *90210* writing crew royalty checks.

8. **Cy Sperling:** Baldness. After erectile dysfunction, there is no problem more humiliating for a man getting up there in the years. Back before the days of hair-follicle transplants and fancy drugs to make your dome sprout like a Chia Pet, bald men everywhere who wanted to be deemed ineligible for a Telly Savalas look-alike contest depended on one man: Cy Sperling. You see, not only was he the president of the Hair Club for Men, the once-bald Cy was also a client, as his famous tagline went. What Mr. Sperling did to put hair back on a man's head in the days before Rogaine is still unknown to us; after seeing some of the other "clients," though, we'd urge PETA to do some investigation into beaver

populations in the early 1990s. All of this "stardom" was enough for WWE to give Cy a spot at *WrestleMania X*. Guest referee? Guest ring announcer? No, he was there in the one role for which he was best suited: guest hair-makeover artist. With the help of a little superglue and the pelt from the most famous star from *Caddyshack*, Howard Finkel got to have a full head of hair again and feel younger for an evening. Thankfully, he removed said hairpiece before Bill Murray showed up ready to take his head off with a shotgun.

7. **Jonathan Taylor-Thomas:** While we cover mullets elsewhere in the book, had he been a wrestler, young Jonathan Taylor-Thomas might've had just a crappy enough 'do to hit the top of the mullet chart. The annoying son from the annoying Tim Allen show *Home Improvement*, Jonathan showed up to be the token timekeeper at *WrestleMania XI*. But that was just the start of the evening; Thomas would later engage in a battle for the ages, a bout more epic in nature than anything else on the card: a chess game against Mr. Bob Backlund. Sadly, we never got to see the conclusion of this battle, as it was cut short due to time constraints. Which sucks, because it was a five-star affair compared to Undertaker vs. King Kong Bundy.

6. **Marla Maples:** If you wanted to be a *WrestleMania* celeb in the late '80s/early '90s, you could do worse than be involved with Donald Trump. The Don's casino housed a couple of the early *Manias*, and he was often seen lurking at ringside. So it should come as no shock that his trophy wives/girlfriends would also appear, including Marla Maples, whom you have no doubt either a) never heard of, or b) never heard from since she and Trump split a decade ago. And if you

claim you know her from *Maximum Overdrive*, that Stephen King movie in which the Green Goblin truck began attacking people, you're a liar. Because that movie sucked.

5. Robin Leach: Another celeb from the '80s cashing in his fifteen-minutes-of-fame card, Robin Leach was the host of *Lifestyles of the Rich and Famous*, a reality-show pioneer who showcased filthy rich people's houses and obnoxiously luxurious lives. Leach, the appropriately named host of the show, would be brought onboard at *WrestleMania IV* to present a shiny new WWF Championship belt to the winner of the elimination tournament. While you might not remember Leach himself, odds are you remember his catchphrase: "Champagne wishes and caviar dreams." Judging by the way he wobbled down the steps toward the ring that night with the belt in hand, there was a wishing well filled with Dom Pérignon somewhere backstage.

4. Billy Martin: Coming in at No. 4 on our countdown is a man known for being such a hardcore drinker he makes Leach look like the poster child for O'doul's. The notorious, on-again, off-again manager for the New York Yankees was chosen to be the special-guest ring announcer for the main event at the first *WrestleMania*. He responded with a monotone, slurred, run-on sentence that sounded like Dustin Hoffman in *Rain Man* suffering from post-concussion syndrome.

3. Larry Young: "Wow!" you no doubt just exclaimed. "Larry Young once appeared at *WrestleMania*?! The Larry Young?!" Okay, that's a total fib. More likely you muttered, "Who the hell is Larry Young?" Good question. We honestly had no idea, and it took us like a week to figure it out. Apparently he was a baseball umpire, and baseball, as you might recall, was on strike in 1995. This, it turns out, was fame enough to garner a guest referee gig at *WrestleMania XI*. Our guess is that if you appeared in your high school's production of *Arsenic and Old Lace* you might have stood a pretty decent chance of appearing on the WWF's biggest stage that year.

2. **Clara Peller:** *WrestleMania 2*, with the distinction of being held in three different cities, also featured three times more celebrities than its predecessor. And the list of celeb activities that day was not limited to the usual special guest referees or managers. We saw guest ring announcers, guest TV commentators and the stupidest guest spot of all — guest timekeeper. To us, that sounds barely one step up from having someone as the guest coat-checker. Regardless, if you've got to know how many milliseconds the "Adorable" Adrian Adonis vs. Uncle Elmer match lasted, you might as well have someone famous keeping track. Manning the stopwatch was a woman whose own stopwatch read that her fifteen minutes of fame had already expired — the Wendy's "Where's the beef?" advertising star, Clara Peller. Clara herself was about to expire by this point, so we're surprised the WWF entrusted her with such an important task, especially one that occurred way after her normal post-bingo-playing bedtime. Thank goodness Howard Finkel made all the announcements about the victor and the official time of the match, as it would've been embarrassing for Clara, not to mention all us wrestling fans, if she got her hands on the mic and stated, "Time of the fall . . . Hey, my Depends are wet. And where the hell am I?"

1. Herb: If you ever wanted to know just how big *WrestleMania 2* was, consider this fact: not only was Wendy's represented, so was Burger King, in the form of Herb. While you likely remember "Where's the beef?" (well, at least if you were alive in the 1980s), you probably don't remember Herb. Herb, you see, was the only man on the planet who had never gulped down a Whopper, a nerd who, if you spotted him at your local BK, netted you $5,000. Amazingly, the idea of hanging out at the local Whopper emporium waiting for some geek to show up wasn't a commercial success; in fact, *Advertising Age* magazine dubbed the campaign the "most elaborate advertising flop of the decade." But Herb shouldn't feel too bad — after all, not every flop winds up at *WrestleMania*. Though this list may indicate otherwise.

But sometimes celebrities who were, you know, legit didn't add much to the big event either. While everyone knows the following folks, one has to question the idea behind promoting . . .

THE 5 MOST POINTLESS *WRESTLEMANIA* CELEBRITIES

5. Burt Reynolds: Oh, how we love Uncle Burt. Love him in a way that shouldn't be legal (and in some states, probably isn't). But as much as we hold him near and dear to our hearts, his stint at *WrestleMania X* was without question one of the biggest wastes of money Vince & Co. ever funded. Uncle Burt looked like he wanted to be anywhere else on the planet during his announcing gig: filming *Cannonball Run 3*, going through divorce proceedings with Loni, you name it. Now, had he driven a black Trans Am to the ring, the WWF just might have been onto something.

4. Alex Trebek: The answer is: The know-it-all game-show host who unnecessarily shared the backstage-announcing duties at *Wrestle-Mania VII*. The question: Who is Alex Trebek? While the *Jeopardy* host did a decent enough job in his gig as a wrestling personality, we're guessing his show is a little too intellectual for us knuckle-headed wrestling fans to fully enjoy. We'd much rather check out the "Daily Double" offered up by a less brainy, but much hotter, game-show celeb of the time . . .

3. Vanna White: As the vivacious letter-turning hostess of *Wheel of Fortune*, Vanna was undisputedly one of the hottest babes of the 1980s. With a resumé that basically consisted of her turning illumi-nated letters on a game-show board, Vanna would be put to the ulti-mate test at *WrestleMania IV*, where she would man the tournament bracket. Holy cow, she was going to have to read actual wrestlers' names on a live PPV broadcast, not just the single letters that were her norm. How well did she do? Does it matter? She was freakin' Vanna White. She was there for one thing and one thing only. Her b_ _bs. Hey, Pat, we'd like to buy an "O."

2. George Steinbrenner: The most infamous owner in professional sports history, George Steinbrenner was part of a special *WrestleMania VII* debate with NFL announcer Paul Maguire over whether or not instant replays should be used in professional wrestling. This has to be one of the most asinine concepts ever. Reminiscent of the NFL replay system of the time, which had no time limit and often caused delays of up to ten minutes, this boring segment just dragged on and on, culminating with the instant-replay reviewers, the Bushwhackers, eating the videotape of the match they were reviewing. Steinbrenner, who is notorious for firing his employees, should've terminated his agent for getting him into this disaster of a segment. In fact, he should've put him in front of a literal firing — a firing squad, that is.

1. **Ozzy Osbourne:** Before he was known as the silly, drugged-out and burned-out dad from the VH1 hit *The Osbournes*, Papa Ozzy had a gig at *WrestleMania 2* as, well, the silly, drugged-out and burned-out guest manager for the British Bulldogs. They were perhaps the greatest tag team of the moment, and one that really didn't need any outside assistance, so we're not quite sure what kind of help Ozzy could bring to the table. Rumor has it he possessed a "white powder" substance that was even deadlier than Mr. Fuji's ceremonial salt. Not only did WWF officials not allow this mysterious substance at ringside, the DEA also showed up to be sure it wasn't used. Thankfully the Bulldogs didn't require the use of Ozzy's ceremonial white powder to win the WWF tag team belts that night.

Looking over those last couple lists, you might wonder why the WWF didn't take a few of these guys under its wing for a week or so, or why the celebs didn't watch a tape or two to get a feel for how to be a good guest announcer. Well, maybe they did and decided they could do better, which we wouldn't argue, given . . .

THE 6 WORST WRESTLING ANNOUNCER CLICHÉS

6. **"How much does this guy weigh?":** The only reason former Baltimore Colt turned wannabe wrestling announcer Art Donovan didn't make

the list above is the fact that his stellar WWF appearance occurred at a *King of the Ring* PPV instead of *WrestleMania*. No doubt had Art graced the biggest stage in the business, he would have topped the list, as his announcing duties consisted primarily of asking how much each competitor weighed. Dude, if you're that interested, buy a fucking scale.

5. **"Uh Oh!":** Yet another entry from the celebrity realm, this one comes from Susan St. James, a guest commentator at *WrestleMania 2*. While Art Donovan at least aspired to further conversation by asking a question, Susie Q added her two syllables with all the emotion of a statue on ludes.

4. **"A miscarriage of justice":** Former *Prime Time Wrestling* host Gorilla Monsoon had an arsenal of horrible clichés; we could probably fill a list with just his announcing gems, such as "Give me a break" and "Will you stop?" But without question, this is the top Monsoon classic, often used right after the three count, when his beloved babyface went down in defeat to a cheating, dastardly heel. After hearing about these "miscarriages" for so many years, we began to seriously wonder about Justice's uterus problems. Would she ever give birth? Imagine how happy *WrestleMania VII* would've been if Gorilla Monsoon had stood up and proclaimed at the top of his lungs, "Justice just gave birth to twins!!!" Unfortunately, after decades of having to deal with heel screwjobs ruining her life, Justice finally turned to adoption.

3. **"Brother":** At first you may think we're about to take Hulk Hogan to task, but, you've got it all wrong. Before the Hulkster became a

"brother, dude and jack" spitting caricature of himself, one man truly owned the word brother: Superstar Billy Graham. Back when he was a wrestler — and one hell of a showman, we should add — that was fine. But when he became an announcer? Man, did that shtick get old fast. Example: *SummerSlam '88.* The recently retired grappler-turned-announcer Graham teamed with Gorilla Monsoon for one hell of an infamous evening, with Graham nearly having an aneurysm after his protégé Don Muraco lost to Dino Bravo, both men having multiple on-air orgasms at the sight of Miss Elizabeth removing her dress to distract the Megapowers, and Graham using the word brother approximately 1,345 times in a three-hour span. A few weeks later, Bobby "the Brain" Heenan, always on the cutting edge, told *Prime Time* viewers to count the number of times Graham uses the word in an upcoming televised match, turning the show into a truly interactive experience. Sadly, feeling no "brotherly love," Vince pulled the plug on the Superstar's announcing career after only a few short months.

2. **"Look at him!"** Some people work their tails off their whole lives and earn a job as the result of their efforts. Then there are those who are born into it. More often than not, they suck. To illustrate this point, we give you the NWA's David Crockett. Since his family owned the Mid-Atlantic territory, a lifetime job was in the cards. Cards that, unfortunately for the eardrums of fans worldwide, included David taking the mic every week to showcase his bizarre commentating style, a style that would lead one to believe he had picked up rabies from a diseased, chattering jungle monkey. David would yell uncontrollably, imploring co-host Tony Schiavone to, quote, "Look at him!" Blind fans, tuning in to at least listen to the sport they used to enjoy

watching, no doubt sobbed in disappointment as David mocked them week after week.

1. **"One, two, three . . . he got him!!! Oh, no he didn't."** One would think the owner of the WWF would try his best to look like a competent announcer, or at least appear to be remotely paying attention to the match he was calling. In the case of Vince McMahon, though, you would be wrong. As the lead announcer on WWF broadcasts throughout the late '80s and early '90s, he was perhaps best known for his "premature pinfall" cliché. For example, Hulk Hogan would have Randy Savage pinned to the mat, and Macho Man would kick out after the two-count, while Vince is yapping, "One, two, three . . . he got him!!!!" Then a second later Vince realizes, "Oh, no he didn't." Imagine, for a moment, Al Michaels calling the 1980 Winter Olympics hockey final: "Do you believe in miracles?!? No!! The Russians have won the gold. Oh wait, no they didn't." Just imagine the fun if Montreal hadn't turned Vince into the company's No. 1 heel and he remained an announcer:

"Bret screwed Bret. Oh, no he didn't."

"The XFL is the greatest football league in the world!!!! Oh, no it's not!!"

Yeah, that would have been fun.

No doubt you're chastising us for excluding a certain chubby, obnoxious WCW announcer from our list. Fear not — we just felt he deserved a list all to his lonesome. And thus we present . . .

THE 3 WORST TONY SCHIAVONE COMMENTS EVER

3. **"David Arquette just won the World Title":** To be fair, not everything Tony said was his own doing. After all, how would *you* announce the fact that David Arquette had just captured your company's most prized possession? Probably not like Tony did, which was to scream like a hopped-up fan boy: "David Arquette just won the world title!! David Arquette just won the world title!! David Arquette just won the world title!! Did David Arquette just win the world title? Did I see that? David Arquette's got the belt!! DAVID ARQUETTE IS THE WORLD CHAMPION!!!" Despite his best attempt, Tony's screaming was not quite as goosebump-inspiring as the call from the famous 1951 Giants-Dodgers playoff game, where announcer Russ Hodges yelled, "The Giants win the pennant! The Giants win the pennant!! The Giants win the pennant!!!" On a baseball-related note, couldn't someone in attendance the night Arquette won the belt have launched a ball at Schiavone's bean and shut him up for a second? Just an idea.

2. **"That's gonna put some butts in the seats."** January 4, 1999, was a day that will live on in infamy for everyone involved in WCW at the time, and for Tony Schiavone in particular. With *Nitro* running against a taped *Raw* that evening, Eric Bischoff instructed Tony to reveal what would happen in *Raw*'s main event. Not a bad idea, except they were revealing that one of the most beloved wrestlers in the world, Mick Foley, was going to win the WWE championship. Tony proceeded to mock the move, stating, "Huh, that's gonna put some butts in the seats, heh." As the years have gone by, Foley has gone on to even greater acclaim, while Tony has virtually disappeared, save for the times he must venture out to the store to buy a new seat, replacing the old one

his out-of-work and expanding rear can no longer fit into. Ah, the irony.

1. **"This is the greatest night in the history of our sport":** This is the wrestling equivalent of the riddle of the sphinx: how could one man think that every single *Nitro, Thunder* or pay-per-view was the greatest one he had ever seen? We can only assume Tony must've been suffering from an undiagnosed case of Anterograde amnesia, a disorder that renders a person unable to remember anything that occurs after his attention is shifted for more than a few seconds. Well, if you're going to be diseased, we suppose it could be worse. After all, every girl you make out with would feel like the first time. And that Stevie Ray vs. Bunkhouse Buck match on *WCW Saturday Night?* Greatest thing since sliced bread — or at least since WWF Ice Cream Bars. On second thought, diseases are never funny, nor was hearing about how great every single *Nitro* was . . . especially when they weren't.

Of course, every wrestler's dream is to compete in WWE. It's where you make the big money, but more than that, for most wrestlers it was the promotion they watched growing up and the one that inspired them to get into the ring in the first place. But as in any professional sport, very few hopefuls ever made it to the big time. And that's a shame, because there are at least . . .

4 INDEPENDENT GIMMICKS WE'D LOVE TO SEE GET A CHANCE IN WWE

4. **Curry Man:** Fans of Christopher Daniels will no doubt cry that he has, in fact, made it to the big time, that being TNA (and a blink-and-you-missed-it stint in WCW). While that's all well and good, the fact remains

PHOTO: MATT BALK

Any guy that bites someone in the ass, with a mask on, no less, is alright with us. Especially if he's a Shark Boy!

that we'd love to see this talented performer ply his trade on our TV every Monday night. But let us be more specific: we don't want to see him as The Fallen Angel, no no no. Nay, we want to see him as his Japanese alter ego, Curry Man, a masked avenger who loves curry, loves it to the point that he has named himself after it. Oh yeah, and he wears a mask with a plate of curry (complete with a side of rice) on the top of it. One can only imagine the marketing possibilities WWE would be able to take advantage of with this guy on the roster. With that crack staff, we see all sorts of great items, like Curry Man Masks. And Curry Man Curry. Eh, he's better off in TNA.

3. **Shark Boy:** Tremendously talented and possessing an obvious sense of humor, Shark Boy has been plying his trade on the independent scene for years and years. Wearing a blue singlet, matching fins and a mask so fabulous that Mil Mascaras might attempt to swipe it when he isn't looking, it's obvious that Shark Boy doesn't take himself too seriously. Which is why you are so caught off guard when you see him perform inside the squared circle; he's freakin' awesome. And this time, we're not joking when we say that WWE would have a field day with merchandise, much as they did with the Hurricane, who sold loads of masks and other Hurricrap to younger wrestling fans. This one is such a can't-miss that we truly cannot believe it hasn't happened already.

2. **Chicken Neck:** Weighing in tonight at $2.49 a pound is our next WWE hopeful, the ever unflappable Chicken Neck. For those of you who've never seen our hero (and that would be 99.999999999999999999 percent of the human race), Mr. Neck comes to the ring wearing a chicken suit and chicken mask, complete with chicken beak and chicken wattles (the red rubbery-looking thing that hangs down beneath his beak). And while his less-than-Herculean physique may be part of the reason Vince & Co. have never given the guy a look, we believe his lack of superstar status is more attributable to the fact that he just wore plain old wrestling boots to the ring. Dude, you're Chicken Neck.

You look like a chicken, you wrestle like a chicken. Wear some claws to the ring, and we bet you'll be on *Raw* next week.

1. **Pool Star:** While Chicken Neck is certainly obscure, he's Hulk Hogan in comparison to the next entrant on our list, the sadly unknown Pool Star. In fact, we're pretty sure the guy only ever wrestled one match, but he had the good fortune of wrestling that match in the presence of one of the authors of this book. So how did a man who performed only once leave such an indelible mark on us? By having quite possibly the greatest gimmick known to man. See, he was a pool cleaner. That's right, a guy who cleaned pools for a living. But he wasn't just any old pool cleaner, oh no. He was the world's *greatest* pool cleaner. And as he splish-splashed his way down to the ring, wearing a rubber-ducky floaty device and carrying his skimming net, it was apparent this was not hyperbole: he was, without question, the greatest cleaner of pools to ever walk God's green earth. If ever a man deserved to be called Pool Star, it was him. We cannot believe he has never been given an opportunity, if not to wrestle, then to at least clean Vince's pool.

Of course, there are times when even if shows are great, things just don't turn around. Even a tag team of Pool Star and Chicken Neck couldn't save the day. Contrary to what you might read elsewhere, this lack of interest never, ever has anything to do with the booking of the promotion, but rather with outside factors over which they have no control. It's true. Just listen in on a WWE financial report sometime if you don't believe us. In fact, just to save you time, here are . . .

THE TOP 8 ISSUES PROMOTERS HAVE NO CONTROL OVER THAT CAUSE FANS TO NOT CARE ABOUT THEIR (USUALLY HORRIBLE) PRODUCT

8. **"It's the economy":** Sure, you might have a storyline on top that absolutely no one on the planet could possibly give two ass squirts about, but the real reason numbers are down is that the economy is bad. You could back this up with hard numbers, such as unemployment rates or what have you, but really, who's going to look into it? Face it, you just paid two cents more for that gallon of milk at the store. When folks are looking at that type of cost-of-living increase, there's simply not enough left in the bank account for frivolities like pro wrestling. Remember: cow juice > entertainment. That's just a fact of life.

7. **"We're on a weak network":** You want to know why ratings aren't good these days? It probably has more to do with the network the promotion is on rather than anything the promotion is doing. After all, if no one can find your show — which, of course, is due to them not being able to find the network — then ratings are down. To subscribe to this argument, you'd probably also need to subscribe to the theory that your potential viewers are so stupid they are incapable of properly operating a television remote control. Which probably also makes them incapable of sustaining employment long enough to afford tickets to an event. Hey, that explains why house-show business is down too!

6. **"Kids are playing more video games":** It's true: video games are the very same evil that rock-and-roll music was back in the 1950s. Before that, life was grand and the world was perfect. Same thing

with life before video games. Folks came out to the matches and watched them on television because, apparently, there was nothing else to do in the whole entire world. Now kids play video games, and that's the cause of many wrestling woes. This somehow despite the fact that video games have been popular since the mid-1980s wrestling boom.

5. **"Wrestling is cyclical"**: Wrestling popularity goes up and down. It's a fact. And there's absolutely nothing promoters can do about it. It gets hot, then it cools down. Promoters can try all manner of stunt, but none of it matters, because that's just the way things are. Sure, you could try to push new talent, or try new things, but things that worked in the past will surely work now. After all, it did back when wrestling was hot.

4. **"It's spring"**: Spring is a busy time of year. The kids are gearing up to get out of school. Older kids are off at spring break. Adults are mowing the grass and gardening. Wrestling shows don't draw in the spring.

3. **"It's summer"**: Summer is a busy time of year. The kids are out of school. Families go on vacation. People spend most of their nights watching fireworks, not wrestling. Wrestling shows don't draw in the summer.

2. **"It's fall"**: Fall is a busy time of year. The kids are back in school. Oh, and don't forget about Halloween and Thanksgiving. Those keep folks very busy. Wrestling shows don't draw in the fall.

1. "It's winter": Winter is a busy time of year. Everyone is always busy with Christmas. Folks also have to spend time shoveling snow. Don't forget about that. Wrestling shows don't draw in the winter.

Really it's amazing that shows ever draw. In fact, you have to question why anyone would want to be a promoter.

Oh yeah, it's what we mentioned briefly at the beginning of this chapter — that business about Vince McMahon being a billionaire. We'd almost forgotten about that, probably because he doesn't talk about it much. No, there are actually other topics he'd rather espouse. To wit . . .

THE TOP 4 THINGS VINCE MCMAHON LOVES TO TALK ABOUT

4. Grapefruits: No, Vince hasn't secretly purchased a citrus fruit farm in Texas. You see, when he talks of grapefruits — or more specifically, his grapefruits — he is speaking of his testicles. This is said to explain how gutsy he is, you see, because apparently he has balls the size of grapefruits. Now, we're no doctors, but we'd strongly suspect that having gonads the size of softballs would, in fact, be bad. Because we love WWE's head honcho so much, we took it upon ourselves to research this medical condition. The technical term for such a malady is *macroorchidism*, and it is generally found in mentally retarded males. There's a joke to be made here, but since we're such upstanding members of society, we'll pass.

3. "This very ring": It seems that whenever Mr. McMahon is making a match, he always declares that said contest will be taking place, and we're quoting here, "in this very ring." Perhaps he fears that fans might assume that the bout will be taking place in the rafters, the parking lot or perhaps some unnamed wrestling ring down the street. You know, if Vince really wanted to change things up, he'd say, for example, "Triple H, you have crossed me for the last time! Quite frankly, I've had enough of your shenanigans, and therefore, later this evening you will be facing Randy Orton in some ring other than this very ring." Sheesh, even in our fantasy world, where we dream of Vince not saying "this very ring," he still somehow sneaks it in. Bastard.

2. **Firing people:** While we cannot begin to fathom what it is precisely that makes Vince tick, he seems to derive inordinate amounts of pleasure in sending people to the unemployment line. He will often quiver almost uncontrollably as he readies himself to make the announcement, much like Bruce Banner before his transformation into the Incredible Hulk. And then, when he has reached the zenith of his rage, Vince spits out the following two words in a manner most venomous: "You're fired!" The way he verbalizes this cannot be adequately described as him *saying* it. Even *yelling* doesn't begin to approach what is emanating from his vocal cords. Upon further reflection, he basically *phlegms* the words right out of his mouth, as though each syllable is riding its own wave of spittle. Some have made unkind accusations against Vince over the years, claiming he has perhaps chemically enhanced his body. We feel it is much more likely that if he has done anything to alter his being, it would have to be in the form of saliva-gland implants.

1. **The product of his semen:** One thing that is blatantly obvious about Vince is that he truly loves his family. In fact, some might claim nepo-

tism is the sole reason that folks like his daughter Stephanie appear on WWE TV so often despite the fact that she is not a wrestler (nor, come to think of it, a decent performer in any capacity). We disagree with this assessment. The *real* reason his children enjoy so much screen time is that it allows Vince to talk about his semen. When he discusses his son Shane, he refers to him as "the product of my semen." Why a man would feel the need to discuss his ejaculate with a worldwide audience is anyone's guess. Maybe it's because that semen comes from his oversized testicles. Which, of course, means he's a retard.

Ah well, so much for taking the high road.

THE 17 PHOTOS THAT DON'T FIT IN ANYWHERE IN THE REST OF THE BOOK

(THAT WE SOMEHOW HAD TO SQUEEZE IN):

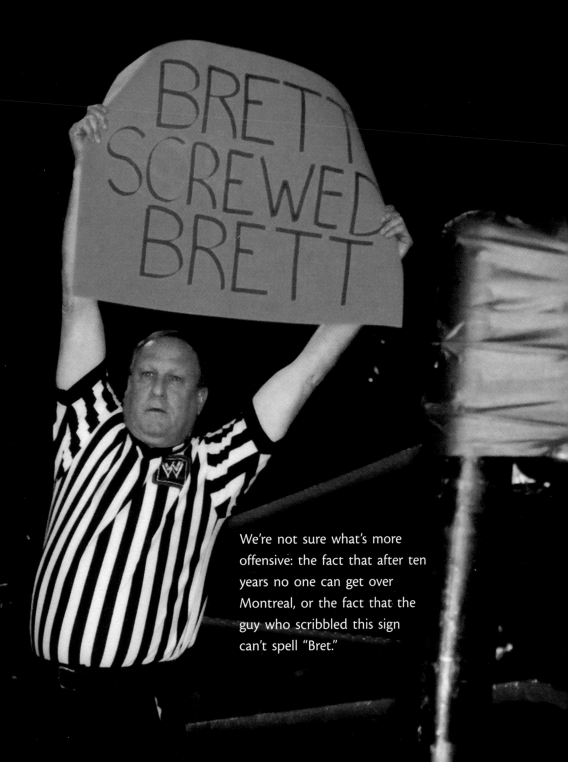

We're not sure what's more offensive: the fact that after ten years no one can get over Montreal, or the fact that the guy who scribbled this sign can't spell "Bret."

As you can see, the Big Show thinks *The WrestleCrap Book of Lists!*

It took an army of 10 year-old overseas sweatshop workers almost half a year to manufacture this extravagant extra-extra-extra-extra large sized bathrobe for Viscera.

You'd walk around with a constipated look on your face too if you saw your extreme creation turn into a stomping ground for zombies, vampires, and guys imitating Jim Morrison.

We're not sure if John Cena* is in pain, or if he's doing an impression of Ebert and Roeper after watching *The Marine.*

Look, it's the immortal Hulk Hogan hanging out in the Wal-Mart clearance aisle — oddly enough the final resting place for products like the *Mr. Nanny* DVD and the Thunder Mixer.

When the Boogeyman was done biting this hideous mole off of Jillian Hall's face, he should've shoved it down her throat. It might've actually improved her singing voice.

WCW's rabid mascot Wildcat Willie (yes, they actually paid money to design this atrocity) was euthanized shortly after this picture was taken. PETA (and everyone else for that matter) could've cared less.

While she may have taken the WWE Women's title from her at *WrestleMania 22,* Mickie James was polite enough to extend an invitation for Trish Stratus to eat out at her spot.

Hey look — it's everyone's favorite blind hillbilly redneck stripper, Nidia. Love the shoes, kid!

After the success of his finishing move the 6-1-9, Rey Mysterio decided to take it up a notch by introducing the 3-1-4. That's the California police code for indecent exposure. Booyaka!

Do we really need a witty caption for beauty personified? We loves ya, Patty.

Good Gawd! It's the lovely Kimberly Page wearing stockings and a mini-skirt. As soon as we're done drooling, we'll insert a dirty limerick here.

That mouth is wide open, which means either
a) Vince is about to talk about his grapefruits or
b) he's about to put his foot in it. Yes, again (in both cases).

Your Olympic hero, Kurt Angle. Preacher of the three I's:
Intensity, Integrity and "I Can't Drive 55."

Oooooh Yeahhh!!! Say hello to the awesomeness that is "Black Machismo," Jay Lethal. Rumors that TNA has signed his brother, Lanny Lethal, to a two-year, you-do-nothing-and-get-paid-for-it contract are unconfirmed at this time.

He's back from the grave and ready to kick ass, take names and eat some brains (not necessarily in that order) — the Zombie.

6

The Porntastic World of Pro Wrestling

If there's one thing we've learned from wrestling promoters over the past decade, it's that sex sells. Don't believe us? Then just flip on a wrestling show, any wrestling show, and try to name all the tanorexic, balloony boob skanks whoring around. Unless you're some weird cross between an octopus and a man, you will run out of finger, toes, tentacles and other assorted extremities to keep count.

Now don't misunderstand us, dear reader — we love beautiful women as much as the next guy. And there are many fine ladies that prance about for our enjoyment. Still, after a while, you just kind of get sick of seeing the silicone-enhanced skanks week after week.

But it wasn't always that way, no sir. Ever since Sable broke the "women shouldn't appear nude" barrier back in 1999 with her layout in *Playboy*, life has been good for male wrestling fans. From Sable to Torrie Wilson to Christy Hemme to Candice Michelle to Ashley Massaro, it seems every year wrestling fans get new whacking material courtesy of Mr. Hefner. It's just too bad there was a time when such a thing wouldn't have been acceptable. To be sure, a lot of beautiful women have dropped their skivvies for our pleasure, but we can't help but think . . .

THE WORLD WOULD HAVE BEEN A BETTER PLACE HAD THESE 4 WOMEN POSED FOR *PLAYBOY*

4. **Madusa Miceli:** It may seem odd to have Debra "Madusa" Miceli on this list. The kickboxer turned pro wrestler turned monster-truck driver (yes, seriously) has morphed over the years, from a fit and trim, almost svelte femme fatale to the most stereotypical blond bimbo around. No doubt she is a prime example that bigger is not always better, especially when you get bigger to the point that it appears you're shoplifting watermelons in your shirt. But back in the day, say 1992 or so, when Ducey first showed up in WCW . . . wow. It would have been at this stage that we wanted Ms. Miceli to bare all for the cameras, a) because she was so smokin' hot and b) because it would have opened the doors for other women to follow. Women such as . . .

3. **Tammy Sytch:** In our book — and since this is, in fact, our book, we can say whatever the hell we want — Tammy "Sunny" Sytch was the original WWF Diva. There may have been the odd woman who garnered some semblance of fame prior to her arrival on the scene, but she was the first to take her sexuality and shove it right in the fans' faces. Unfortunately, she never did this for *Playboy* during her prime. While the Sable issue was one of *Playboy*'s top sellers ever, we guarantee that had Sunny been spread-eagle, they would have sold ten gadzillion more copies. Well, maybe not ten gadzillion, but at least a dozen to the authors of this book alone. You know how pages get stuck together and stuff.

2. **Stacy Keibler:** We can only theorize that the luscious Stacy Keibler wasn't what *Playboy* is looking for. We can only further theorize that *Playboy* is run by a bunch of monkeys (and a senile geezer who must be pushing

127). Let's face it: Stacy was lacking something all the other WWE Divas and nearly all *Playboy* centerfolds have: a giant rack. If Ms. Keibler heads to Frederick's and picks up anything for her top over a AA cup, color us shocked. We don't care. When it comes to wholesome good looks and sex appeal, Stacy clobbers all the Divas who have posed like baby seals. On the one hand, it sucks that we never got to see everything she had to offer. On the other, her most glorious assets, namely her forty-two-inch legs, were always on display. So we guess not all was lost.

1. **Miss Elizabeth:** She was the one girl that every wrestling fan, male or female, loved in the late 1980s. Brunette and stunning, Liz Hulette was an anomaly in the world of professional wrestling. She looked like a movie star among a bunch of overgrown apemen and, to be frank, apewomen who roamed the sports-entertainment landscape at the time. It made sense that both men and women were fans, and the lovely Miss Elizabeth had tons from both camps. It would have been unheard of for her to pose naked. In fact, when she merely dropped her skirt at *SummerSlam '88*, revealing a very modest bikini bottom, all kinds of folks were in all kinds of uproars. Keep in mind that wrestling was very different back then, and the WWF's core audience was mainly kids. Had she dropped those bottoms (not to mention her top), the world might have stopped spinning on its axis entirely. Still, that can't keep us from dreaming about what might have been . . .

You know, while we yearn for the lovely ladies above to splay about in their birthday suits, we should probably give thanks for those who didn't. Because, after all . . .

THE WORLD IS A BETTER PLACE BECAUSE THESE 4 WOMEN DID NOT POSE FOR *PLAYBOY*

4. **The Fabulous Moolah:** She's the greatest woman wrestler of all time. If you don't believe us, just ask her. She's been spinning the same yarn since Lincoln was in the White House. The story goes something like this: she won the WWWF women's title back in the Stone Age and held it until being dethroned by Wendi Richter in 1984. The only reason she lost the belt was because of that no account Cyndi Lauper, darlin'. She then won the belt back and lost it once more, this time to Sherri Martel. This would have been Sherri Martel pre-catface, so Moolah had no excuses, and thus hung her head in shame and retired. Of course, we'd be remiss if we didn't mention that the primary reason she held the belt forever and a day was because she trained all the girls and kept them under her thumb, thus always securing her spot at the top of the cards. She wasn't a particularly attractive woman, and to be frank, looked a lot like Tammy Faye Bakker — if Bakker were a shaved bear. That's not what Hugh would look for in a Playmate, and so we are forever in Mr. Hefner's debt.

3. **Mae Young:** Moolah would have been bad, but to be fair, her running buddy in the late 1990s would have been far, far worse. And sadly, probably far more willing to do a nude shoot than any of the other Divas who did. Young was a tough old bird, willing to take any bump, no matter how extreme, to get a rise out of the fans. For this, she is to be commended. Any eighty-year-old who would put her life on the line for the sake of a powerbomb off the top rope — through tables, we should add — that's one old bitch who

deserves your respect. Unfortunately, Mae brought more to the table than just the ability to absorb tremendous amounts of pain. She brought an exhibitionist mentality that meant she always wanted to show the world her breasts. That's not a joke; she was hell-bent on putting her withered old funny bags on display for all. And in at least one instance, during a *SummerSlam* bikini contest, she did just that. Thankfully it was just a prosthetic prop like the one used in *There's Something About Mary*. Though, come to think of it, seeing withered old fun bags, whether they are real or synthetic, is something we really shouldn't be subjected to.

2. **Stephanie McMahon:** This is the one that keeps us up at night. And not in a good, "I've got a tent in my pants" kind of way. No, this would be in an "I'm scared of seeing that like I'm scared of the *It* clown" kind of way. Adding to this fear would be the fact that we know it could happen. In fact, we're shocked it hasn't already. The ego of the McMahon family knows no limits, and it would appear that the lion's share of Daddy's massive self-indulgence has been passed along to his daughter. Should she ever pose (and again, it's something we feel is inevitable), it would mean weeks — no, scratch that . . . months — of buildup to the mag hitting newsstands. Hell, they might even make the *WrestleMania* main event the unveiling of the cover, all in an attempt to make it a bigger seller than any of the prior WWE Diva spreads. Laugh if you will, but trust us, one day this will happen and no one will be laughing. Except, of course, for Stephers herself, who will be cackling with glee as the world revolves around her balloony boobs and even more balloony ego.

1. **Trish Stratus:** "What's this?" we hear you gasp. "You didn't want to see Trish nekked as the day she was born? What are ya, a queenie?" Calm down, Buford, let us plead our case. Trust us, we're not "quee-nies" (didn't that term go out in, like, 1989 anyway?). We're just like you — we love Trish Stratus. In fact, we have been accused of being such slobbering dogs when it comes to Patty (as she likes us to call her — we're tight, you know) that some have claimed we were the inspiration behind the Mickie James stalker angle. That's not true either, by the way. As Diva after Diva showed her goodies to *Playboy*'s cameras in the early 2000s, we waited ever more impatiently for Trish's turn to display her wares like a stripper at the local gold club. But it never happened. It wasn't due to lack of interest from either WWE or *Playboy*, as she was asked at least twice a year during her entire tenure to do the shoot. And every six months, like clockwork, she turned them down. After a while, it almost became a game. At some point, we believe pretty much every fan concluded she would do it, but she held steadfast and refused. In a 2004 interview with the *Ottawa Sun*, Trish said, "I don't think [*Playboy*'s] an option for me. I've never really been interested in that . . . I want to leave my mark in wrestling." Somehow, that's even cooler than if we'd seen her nipples and fur patch. Good for her for making us better people.

Of course, there was another very famous woman who went spread-eagle for Hef's cameras, a woman we'd truly want to forget. Alas, you cannot forget her, no matter what form she takes. And each of those forms brings on night terrors the likes of which will make the most macho of men wet the bed. Terrors we've dubbed . . .

THE 3 FACES OF JOANIE

3. Chyna — Silent Shemale: When Joanie Laurer made her debut in WWE, she was a bodyguard for D-Generation X. Nothing more, nothing less. And she fit the bill well — a muscular female who looked for all the world like she could, and most likely would, kick your ass. In fact, she bore a striking resemblance to a vicious pit bull, with her gigantic square jaw, a muscular (though flat) chest and biceps that put to shame half the males on the roster. She rarely spoke a word, preferring to let her actions in the ring (which primarily revolved around punching dudes in the nutsack) speak for her. And due to both her unique appearance (clearly, she looked nothing like the other women on the show) and her "actions speak louder than words" mentality, she began to get over with both the guys and the gals in the crowd.

PHOTO: MIKE LANO

2. *Playboy* Model Bigmouth: The next stage of the evolution of Chyna saw Joanie take a few weeks off from *Raw* to undergo some rather drastic enhancements. Gone was the square jaw, and the muscular chest had transformed into a landing strip for a pair of Goodyear blimps. But more apparent than any of the physical changes was her new attitude. Rather than let her actions (which still primarily revolved around punching dudes in the nutsack) do the talking, now she let her increasingly nasal and ever-grating voice carry the load. And it was awful — all she ever talked about was her favorite subject: herself. Since she was one of the most popular performers in WWE prior to her absence, she was brought back and pushed to the moon, given titles and the coup de grace, an appearance in *Playboy*. At the unveiling of the cover, she thanked the countless people who had made it happen. Okay, that's a total lie. She thanked *herself* for working so hard. Now, unless she somehow gave herself a boob job, we think that might have been selling her plastic surgeon (not to mention the WWE promotional machine) a bit short. About this time, she also had a new theme song that requested, "Don't treat me like a woman/Don't treat me like a man." Which, given the fact that during her first and second phases she resembled both, made it rather easy to do.

1. **Howard Stern Show Punching-Bag Chynna Doll:** Of course, the one thing we've failed to mention thus far is why this strange, strange woman was ever pushed in the first place. Glad you asked. It was because she was the girlfriend of Triple H, who at the time didn't wield the power he has today, but still had quite a bit of pull. So his bedmate was given all kinds of on-air attention . . . until he decided that it was better for his career to dump the weirdo and start making googly eyes at the boss's daughter. Once that happened, the writing was on the wall and it wasn't long before Chyna was no more and back to being plain ol' Joanie Laurer (because WWE owned the rights to her ring name). She also began to appear in public in stranger and stranger outfits, looking like a runway-model hobo.

Much like Rena Mero, Joanie felt she could make it on her own, pursuing an "acting" career and releasing a rap CD (!!) under the name Chynna Doll. She also appeared on MTV's *Surreal Life*, and boy, was that ever an appropriate title for a show starring the increasingly unstable former Ninth Wonder of the World. She eventually unraveled to the point that even Howard Stern got bored of making fun of her. Finally, in a last-ditch effort to regain the public's attention, she and her boyfriend at the time, Sean Waltman (formerly X-Pac), released a sex tape called *One Night in China* (as a play on the Paris Hilton skin flick *One Night in Paris*). All we'll say about it is that between her legs there appeared to be a penis. And that's not a joke. We wish it was.

Of course, the women listed above aren't the only folks in wrestling we have no desire to see nekked. To prove we're not sexist, we'd like to point out . . .

THE 3 THINGS WRESTLING FANS, MALE OR FEMALE, SHOULD NEVER SEE AGAIN

3. Big Dick Johnson's Barely Covered (Supposedly) Big Dick: Not sure if you know this, but big fat strippers are funny. It's true. Don't believe us? Then ask WWE, who likes to bring out an overly paunchy ladies' man named Big Dick Johnson now and again. Maybe we're just prudes, but we needn't witness Johnson, who makes one long for the heyday of "Playboy" Buddy Rose. At least that dude wore more than a thong to the ring. Given that this company prides itself on doing huge numbers in the coveted eighteen-to-thirty-four demographic, we have to question the means by which it attempts to lure them in.

2. Ric Flair's 58-Year-Old Anal Cavity: This just in: Ric Flair loves to show the world his ass. Wait . . . what's this? This piece of paper has actually been lying around since 1987? Who knew? Oh yes, happens all the time. The spot generally works like this: an opponent goes for a sunset flip. In that move, you jump over your opponent's back and hook his hips to bring him down, then put your legs over his shoulders, leaving your face approximately four inches from your foe's crotch. What a gay move. Anyway, Flair takes the fudge factor even further and has his opponent grab his tights and yank them down, leaving you with this visual:

PHOTO: MATT BALK

But see, in the old days, he'd appear embarrassed and almost immediately yank his panties back up. Flash forward to today, when following a depantsing, he tends to compete the remainder of the match showing us his cornhole. Sometimes he'll just walk around doing chops or climbing the ropes with his Nature Buns out in the open:

PHOTO: MATT BALK

It's almost a time-honored tradition, like putting your hand over your chest and looking at the flag during the national anthem prior to a wrestling show. Honestly, though, we'd be content to never witness Flair's Old Glory ever again.

1. **Vince McMahon's 60-Year-Old Anal Cavity:** On some of these lists, it's tough to determine a "winner." Of course, we all know who the losers are: the poor saps who sit in the stands. In the case of this particular list, it was very difficult: is it the fat-ass stripper? The legend with a penchant for showing us his brown eye? Or the promoter who takes joy in doing the same? After months of soul-searching, we decided to give Vincent Kennedy McMahon yet another accolade. The deciding factor was that, unlike the other two, Vince's gluteus has been an ongoing storyline prop for years. In fact, he has a club in which he forces his employees to literally kiss his ass. Imagine trying to explain this to non-wrestling friends of yours. Better yet, go do that and let us know how it goes. Regardless, it's time to cancel membership to that club — our eyeballs needn't be sullied in such a manner again.

In addition to men in wrestling who can't resist showing off their bung-holes, there are also guys who seemingly long to be women. We'd explain, but honestly, it makes us a wee bit uncomfortable. Still, we will persevere and give you the official list of . . .

WRESTLING'S 9 WORST DRAG QUEENS

9. **WWE's Mystery "Woman":** In 2004, Victoria was embroiled in a feud with WWE women's champion Trish Stratus and various other evil Divas. She found herself outnumbered in battle, but thankfully help would come in the form of a mysterious woman who would regularly run into the ring and interfere on her behalf, helping her to achieve some victories. Who was this great female humanitarian? Why,

none other than the love of Victoria's life, the always amusing Stevie Richards in a drag queen disguise. I don't know about you, but if we were Victoria's main squeeze, we'd spend less time putting on her clothes, and put a little more effort in trying to get hers off.

PHOTO: KELLY PARMELEE

Hey Stevie — you're supposed to be a drag queen, not a blow up doll!

8. **Hildegard:** Back when Eric Bischoff introduced the world to HLA — Hot Lesbian Action — his ultimate goal was to make his rival, Stephanie McMahon, engage in rug-munching for the whole world to see. Bischoff had seemingly achieved this bizarre objective at *Unforgiven 2002*, when his team of Three Minute Warning defeated the quasi-gay duo of Billy and Chuck. In an effort to really humiliate Stephers, Bischoff hit the buffets and found the most obese woman imaginable, a beast named Hildegard. Of course, the joke eventually backfired on Bischoff when Hildegard did the ol' swerve by knocking Eric out, then taking off a rubber latex mask, revealing himself to be the Samoan hit 'n'

runner, Rikishi. He then proceeded to do the stinkface on the befuddled Uncle Eric. Those wrestling fans disappointed by the lack of a sexy make-out love session between Rikishi and Stephanie immediately turned channels to a reasonable substitute — a Discovery Channel documentary on the copulating tactics of farm swine.

7. Sammi: "Sweet Jesus, you've got a penis!" was the phrase Mark Henry uttered when his large, groping hands moved into the genital area of our No. 7 entry. When his advances toward Chyna were shunned, she was kind enough to hook Mark up on a blind date with her transvestite chum Sammi. Mark's weighing of the salami that night was just one of many kinky misadventures the man known as Sexual Chocolate would get into during the late '90s, though none were quite as disturbing as this encounter. A quick word of advice to you, dear reader: never, never, ever go on a blind date with any of Joanie Laurer's friends. For that matter, and for your own personal health, do not even come in close physical contact with Ms. Laurer or any of her clique. At least not unless you're wearing one of those bird-flu respirators. Gotta play it safe when it comes to dealing with those nasty viruses originating from China. Oops — Chyna.

6. Harvina: One of the least-remembered Divas of the Attitude era was also arguably one of the most successful. Harvina was the dress-wearing alter ego of longtime manager Harvey Whippleman, who in a clash-of-the-titans showdown topped only by Savage vs. Steamboat at *WrestleMania III*, defeated the Kat in a thrilling snowbunny/lumberjill match to capture the WWF women's championship. The scary thing is, the scrawny Whippleman exuded more raw sex appeal as a woman than he ever did in his normal guise as a nerdy-looking heel manager. Scarier still, we just analyzed how sexy a grown man, named Harvey, with a beard looked wearing women's panties. Next entry, please. Quickly!!!

5. **Kloudi:** If you ever get down about life, don't go to a psychiatrist, just look at the sad saga of Skip and Zip, the Bodydonnas. You'll feel better immediately. At the beginning of 1995, Chris "Skip" Candido and "Zip," Dr. Tom Pritchard, had it all. Candido had his arms around Sunny, arguably the hottest woman in the world at the time, and the good doctor was cruising around town with a perm that mere words cannot describe. Then disaster struck. First, Pritchard chopped off his locks to join Skip and Sunny in the Bodydonnas. Although they won the tag team championship at *WrestleMania XII*, the good times would not last, and Sunny soon bolted the team to join up with the Smoking Gunns. Skip and Zip's response to losing the best piece of ass wandering Stamford? They hired Kloudi, a tattooed man dressed up in Sunny's Bodydonnas fitness gear. We really wish we could make a joke about a cross-dressing man called Kloudi, but suddenly our sense of humor has been darkened, just as Kloudi did to the glorious sunshine that was the Bodydonnas. Even to this day, Dr. Tom Pritchard cannot go outside on overcast mornings, due to the emotional scars from his time experiencing such "Kloudi days."

4. **The Nature Woman, Ric Flair:** To be the man, you have to be . . . the woman? That's not quite how Ric Flair's catchphrase goes, but at *Uncensored '95*, a then-retired Nature Boy dressed up in Beth Flair's Sunday best, disguised as such to come out of the crowd and attack

Randy "Macho Man" Savage. With runny black mascara adorning his face, Naitch looked like he had been ridden hard and put up wet at Space Mountain himself for a change. Flair's wearing a dress was just one of many lowlights at one of the worst WCW pay-per-views of all time. The event was literally a drag.

3. **Miss Atlanta Lively:** Some people may say that Ronnie Garvin wasn't the most handsome man in wrestling history. The bizarre "Barney Rubble with a Marine Corps hairdo" look he had going on in the '80s was certainly less than popular with the weaker sex. However, just because you're having problems scoring with the ladies doesn't give you an excuse to *become* one. In 1985, to complement his "fists of stone," Garvin decided to add "tits of tissue" to his impressive physical attributes. With a new feminine attitude, a brown wig and a gorgeous dress, he hooked up with Jimmy Valiant to take on the Midnight Express at *Starrcade '85*. Oddly enough, even though he was a man, he looked more woman-like than Valiant's 100 percent female valet, Big Mama. Despite his sexy new wardrobe and a damn fine purse, there was one thing Ron possessed that would ultimately never fool anyone into thinking he was a woman — "the Garvin stump."

2. **Fabian Kaelin:** Some wrestlers on this list had it easy. They could slap on a dress and a little makeup, just go out to the arena for a five-minute bit and call it a day. Our No. 2 entry, though, didn't have it so easy. Before he was WSX's resident host and hype man, Kaelin's (Ryan Katz) first exposure on cable was on the TBS reality show, *He's a Lady*. He signed up to do a manly, *Fear Factor*–type show, but it was all a ruse. Katz recalls, "I went on this show thinking I was going

to get to do these crazy, death-defying stunts, but the stunt was living as a woman. We were told the show was called *All American Man*, and it was a contest to find out who was just that. Little did we know that we would be duped." When he arrived on the set, in a classic reality-show twist, it was revealed that all the guys had to live in a house together — and they had to dress in drag. Over the course of the following weeks, whoever was deemed most ladylike by a panel of judges would be declared the grand-prize winner.

Out the window went physical challenges the sometimes-wrestler Katz might've had a distinct advantage at winning, and in came competitive beauty pageants, gigs as bridesmaids at weddings and the grueling task of acting like a true lady while in public places. Katz performed well, until he slipped up on one episode, when he got a little too drunk. While most of the single men in America would love the company of a sauced party girl, guest judge Morgan Fairchild said Katz's drunken behavior was unladylike and he was eliminated. "The experience itself of doing the show was great," says Katz. "I had a blast, was treated well, and it was fun. But . . . it was uncomfortable as hell, and I knew it would be embarrassing." For Katz to walk around in real life wearing a dress took a true set of balls, and it was almost enough for him to win the top spot. However, there was one wrestler dressed in drag who made it seem like an all too familiar routine . . .

1. Pat Patterson: They say the best performers in the sport are those who live the gimmick. For the record, we're not going to say Pat Patterson had any experience dressing in drag prior to his "hardcore evening gown" match against Jerry Brisco at *King of the Ring 2000*, but . . .

Enough pseudo-women; back to the real deal. Somewhere along the line, it seemed that bookers and promoters weren't satisfied with just a moderately attractive or even a cute, girl-next-door female wrestler. In the '90s, the time-tested formula of a woman wrestler earning her keep by working a solid match was simply no longer enough. The combination of the Monday Night War and the dawn of the WWF Attitude era had organizations looking everywhere for the next breakout star, or at least someone who could help them win the next ratings quarter-hour. As storylines got sleazier, promoters would turn to the drop-dead gorgeous and impeccable girls who made a living as fitness models. However, for every model-turned-wrestler like Trish Stratus who made her mark in the wrestling world, there were dozens of surgically enhanced females whose wrestling career resembled that dud of a Roman candle you tried to light last 4th of July. In memory of their short, fizzled-out careers, we present to you . . .

THE TOP 7 FITNESS MODELS DEEMED EXPENDABLE BY PROFESSIONAL WRESTLING

7. **Marie Lograsso:** Before Vito Lograsso became known as the one who wore the dress in the family, he had to deal with another dress-wearing sibling, his feisty sister, Marie. She entered the WCW scene in the fall of 2000 and immediately caused her Italian brother grief, as she became romantically involved with Vito's friend and tag team partner, Reno. This caused a rift between the two, who were once like brothers. A few weeks later, however, it was revealed that they actually *were* brothers, and the Marie-Reno love affair took a Luke Skywalker–Princess Leia incestuous turn for the worse. Unfortunately, Marie and her gorgeous gazoongas were given the

pink slip before she was forced to don a metal bikini and be chained to a Jabba the Hutt-like Mark Madden at ringside.

6. **Scott Steiner's Freak, Shikira:** One of the hottest and most charismatic of the giant influx of fitness chicks hired by WCW in the late 90s was undoubtedly Shikira, played by model Kim Kanner. Of all the girls on this list, she had the best chance to succeed in the business. Not only did Kim and her co-Steiner hoochie-mama Midajah provide Big Poppa Pump no less than *four* melons bouncing in perfect unison, but Kanner also had a wrestling pedigree on her resumé. Turns out her father, Hal Kanner, was a former pro wrestler who once worked for Vince McMahon Sr. in the 1950s. However, Kim's fate was sealed when Vince Russo decided that all the females on the roster had to report to the Power Plant to learn how to wrestle. Wary of becoming an actual in-ring performer after witnessing the injuries her father suffered during his days as a pro, Kim declined to go to the training facility. Her refusal to train to be put in moves like the Torture Rack meant Kim and her incredibly wonderful rack were shown the door and never seen again.

5. **Jamie Koeppe:** Coming in at No. 5 is a true pioneer of the Diva phenomenon — Jamie Koeppe. Who in the hell is that, you say? Well, she was the winner of the first-ever, prototypical 2003 WWE Diva Search. Sadly for Ms. Koeppe, who possessed a J-Lo like rear end you could play a game of pool on, there was no $250,000 pot of gold at the end of her winning rainbow. All she got was a measly photo shoot for *Raw Magazine* and the satisfaction of knowing she caused judges like Edge and Maven to drop a combined ten pounds of water weight due to

massive loss of saliva from perv-induced drooling. Did we mention she had nice hooters? Too bad the WWE didn't give a hoot about her.

4. **Rochelle Loewen:** Almost halfway through the list, and we're running out of different ways to distinguish all these silicon-enhanced hotties. We won't have that problem with Rochelle, though. She will forever go down in infamy, but not due to her funbags. Instead it was a different kind of bag — her gym bag — that was responsible for her fifteen minutes of fame. To be more precise, it was allegedly the feces from Randy Orton's bunghole that somehow ended up in her bag that made the headlines. Seems Randy made the common mistake of mistaking a nylon bag with a Nike emblem on it for a toilet bowl. Either that or he was tired of putting up with all the crap from these models-turned-kayfabians, and he decided to stir up a little shit of his own. Deciding she didn't want to rely on a urinal cake in her gymbag to keep her belongings smelling fresh, Rochelle left the WWE before the shit hit the gym bag again. Her giant chesticles were not missed by the WWE. Longer waiting lines at the bathroom stalls were reported, however.

3. **Lauren Jones:** Another one of the . . . You know what, this list is getting rather repetitive. Here's all you need to know about this random, anonymous ho-bag. She had big fake tits. She didn't last long. Nor did her 2007 reality show, *Anchorwoman*, which lasted exactly one episode. Next.

2. **Joy Giovanni:** Joy had a nice ass. She had nicer boobs. Thanks for the mammories, Joy. Next.

1. **Amy Weber:** Sigh, let's put this to bed, shall we? Amy was a former fitness model. That meant she was in excellent physical shape, was hot and at one point probably had a breast augmentation. However, we can hold our breath longer than she was employed by the WWE. In conclusion, thanks to their knockers, these babes will never have a need for floatation devices should they ever be involved in a *Titanic*-style boating disaster. However, their cases proved that boobs alone cannot keep most fitness models' wrestling careers from rapidly sinking.

But hey, let's face facts — if you want to be hired by WWE, you pretty much have to be at least a D cup, preferably DD or DDD. In fact, we're pretty sure it's a job requirement. So when WWE decided to hop on the reality-show bandwagon in 2004 with an *American Idol*–style popularity contest known as the Diva Search, you knew what to expect. But we got more. *Much* more. Just as with *Idol*, the fun is not in seeing the best of the best crowned, but in seeing all the destined-to-lose contestants make a mockery of the process. We did some voting of our own, and here are . . .

THE TOP 8 WWE DIVA SEARCH REJECTS

Oh, and because remembering all these different girls' real names could be a chore, to keep things easier, we will refer to the wannabe Divas by what they are most infamously known for.

8. **Naked Girl:** Leyla Milani, aka Naked Girl, must have the worst luck of all. Despite actually having WWE script her to fall out of her top and parade around nude during an obstacle course competition, this incredibly hot chick eventually lost out in the finals to Ashley, who pranced

around looking like a punk rock tomboy. She wound up on NBC's *Deal or No Deal,* where she can be seen opening her box, or briefcase, rather, on a weekly basis.

PHOTO: MATT BALK

We had an awesome caption for this photo of Diva Search reject Leyla Milani, but sadly, we fulfilled our "blow up doll" joke quota eight or nine pages ago.

7. J.T. Titty: The 2006 Diva Search started off on the wrong foot, as the WWE decided to let MTV reality show star and WWE newcomer the Miz host all the weekly segments. Looking like a deer in headlights . . . No, that's not quite right . . . Looking like a fawn caught in an Earth-destroying meteor shower, the Miz was a total disaster in his debut segment. First off, he was lovingly booed by the crowd, and then he totally blew his first assignment by forgetting how you cast a vote for your favorite contestant. A host able to wing an impending live disaster would simply have directed the fans to the company Web site to obtain the details, but the Mizard of Uhhs forgot even that. After his massive brain fart, it was time for him to introduce all the ladies. With mature, sophisticated behavior reminiscent of a ten-year-old child whiffing nitrous oxide from a Reddi-wip can, Miz started introducing and mispronouncing most of the Divas' names. As he worked his way down, he got to an incredibly attractive brunette and screamed her name with glee: "J.T. Titty!!!" Breast lovers everywhere sat up and paid attention. After all, there was a woman on the screen with the last name Titty. And, to be sure, she was aptly named! Ms. Titty was back the next week, where Miz again loudly proclaimed "Titty" for the whole world to hear. It was the last time anyone would ever mutter the word *titty* on a WWE program. By the third week, probably to avoid FCC fines because of Miz's potty mouth, the WWE ceased having him say the girl's last names. J.T., whose real last name when pronounced by anybody other than a spaz with a modern-day Red Rooster hairdo, is actually Tinney, made it all the way to the finals of the Diva Search. She did not come out victorious, however, proving that sometimes the WWE does not save the breast for last.

6. The Blunder Twins: What is more annoying than one blond, generic Diva Search contestant? Why, a pair of twin Diva Search contestants, of course. Like a bad case of alcohol-induced double vision, Chandra and Julia Costello made their national television debuts during the 2004 Diva Search. If the first Costello didn't put you to sleep, being forced to sit through another one's shtick would make you comatose. Luckily, the viewers at home persevered (or were drinking enough YJ Stinger — WWE-endorsed caffeine in a can!) and kept themselves awake enough to vote for anybody other than the twins. Much as they looked the same, the Costellos' fates were identical too. Both were eliminated faster than a line of coke snorted by an Olsen Twin.

5. Blue Paint Girl: One entertaining part of the Diva competition is the ever-ultra-competitive talent contest. Oh, what fun this always is. But it takes a *special* talent to make it in this book. Diva hopeful Kristal Marshall has done just that, as her "talent" was her artistic ability specifically, her mastery of painting. Which she did using her boobs and ass. And thus she became "Blue Paint Girl" by pouring paint all over herself and then flopping around on a big white piece of paper on the mat, thus creating a "painting" in the process. Somewhere up in the heavens, resting on some fluffy white cloud, legendary Public Television painter Bob Ross no doubt wept enough tears at this bastardization of everything he stood for to flood an entire small village with his sorrow.

4. The Barbarian Girl: But painting isn't the only fine talent that wannabe WWE skanks have put on display. Inspired by one too many viewings of *Lord of the Rings*, Austrian-born Simona Fusco came to the ring wearing a loincloth and swinging a huge sword. Male fans, likely more interested in swinging their own flesh-colored wonder-sword across Simona's face rather than having a modern-day Lorena Bobbit in their midst, decided to make a cut of their own.

3. **Catgirl:** 2006 Diva Search contestant Jen England tried to work the Julie Newmar Catwoman gimmick into her behavior during the contest. She proclaimed herself an honest-to-God kitten. Not a sex kitten, mind you — just a cat! While she didn't drag out a giant-size box of Tidy Cat kitty litter and take a shit right in front of the TitanTron, she did ask the men in the audience if they wanted to feel her kitty-cat "bite." In theory, this offer for feline fellatio should've been enough to help Jen win the contest. However, it was her rival Leyla who walked away the winner, as it was too hard for Jen's fans to pick up the phone and vote for her when they had one hand on their penis and the other on a tube of Neosporin, disinfecting their gnawed-on Oscar Mayer weiner.

2. **Some people call her Maryse:** Steve Miller, who some people call Maurice, once spoke of the "pompatus of love" in his '70s hit song "The Joker." The 2006 Diva Search contestant known as Maryse, though, didn't sing anything. In fact, she could barely speak at all. This French-Canadian, imported hussy had an accent so thick that if Frenchy Martin tried to record the books-on-tape edition of *The Da Vinci Code* while simultaneously blowing author Dan Brown, he would've been easier to understand.

1. **Clumsy Girl:** Trish Stratus set the standard for attractive models-turned-wrestlers busting their asses to become successful. Summer DeLin, aka Clumsy Girl, simply set the standard for busting her ass

— literally. During one of the initial segments of the 2005 Diva Search, Summer was introduced, and to impress the crowd with her flexibility, she attempted to raise one of her legs over her head while remaining standing on the other leg. The horrible end result saw her crashing to the floor, right square on her ass. It's too bad she disappeared after she was eliminated. She was a blue *Star Wars* Stormtrooper helmet and a name change to the Shockmistress away from being crowned the All-Time Queen of *WrestleCrap*.

To be fair, while most of the women in the Diva Search were ho bags, none were full-blown porn stars. At least we don't think they were; maybe we should do a few more Google searches. After all, it's not like the world of porn has never invaded the squared circle — just ask . . .

THE TOP 4 PORN STARS WHO PAID PRO WRESTLING A VISIT

4. **Jenna Jameson:** Before she had achieved the mainstream popularity she enjoys today, in the '90s, Jenna Jameson was strictly known as one of the most popular stars in the adult entertainment business. Her biggest role in the sport of wrestling would cum — err, that is come — in the form of a cameo in one of Val Venis's 1998 debut vignettes in the WWF. That was her only shot in the WWF, but a year earlier in ECW, Jenna had stuck around a little longer, showing up on pay-per-views accompanying the Dudley Boyz and later handling some backstage interviews. But Jenna wasn't long for the wrestling world, as she quickly disappeared. As with most talent leaving ECW, her departure was probably money-related. Jenna loved to get screwed, but not when it came time for Paul E. to give her a paycheck.

3. Heather Hunter: A very beautiful African-American porno actress in the late 1980s, Heather Hunter was best known for her starring roles in such films as *Coming on America* and *Screw the Right Thing.* Say what you will about porn, but galldarnit, they come up with some great titles. Anyway, it was in the summer of 1989 when Heather received her first big break on WWF television, on the set of the far too short-lived *Bobby Heenan Show.* Heenan and his nerdy sidekick, Jameson, were surprised to find out Heather was not an actress from Eddie Murphy's *Coming to America,* but a full-fledged porno queen. As the Brain fired off one-liners, Heather started an erotic striptease, one which climaxed — quite literally — with the first-ever on-air ejaculation for a wrestling star. Seems Jameson just couldn't keep his twig and berries under control, so he shot his wad unto a pillow that was covering his lap. Try explaining that gooey mess to the Tooth Fairy.

2. Jasmin St. Claire: What do you do for an encore when you've just

PHOTO: MIKE LANO

Jasmin St. Claire assumes
the position.

been gangbanged by 300 men, in the legendary *World's Biggest Gangbang* (not, by the way, a theatrical release)? Why, you do what Jasmin St. Claire did. Go to a sport that includes *way* more men than 300 — professional wrestling. In ECW, XPW and TNA, Jasmin would show off her . . . her . . . well, basically her boobs, as she spent years doing her damnedest in any catfight/lingerie brawl/wet-t-shirt contest she entered. Along the way, she hooked up with the Blue Meanie and they started

3PW. They were good enough to get a respectable DVD distribution deal, but alas, things quickly took a downward turn, and Jasmin bolted on the federation, refusing to pay the workers, breaking up with Meanie and leaving him holding the bag. Although after a few years of dating Jasmin, he was probably all too familiar with holding a bag.

1. **Lizzy Borden:** Whereas the aforementioned girls merely dabbled in the wrestling business, the pornstar husband-and-wife duo of Rob Black and Lizzy Borden set out to make a big-time, mainstream, sleazier version of ECW, entitled XPW — Xtreme Pro Wrestling. Fueled by lots of blood, lots of Borden's flesh and a cast of goons that included pedophile clowns and bizarre religious icons, XPW was unquestionably the filthiest wrestling promotion around. One time, as a publicity stunt, Black went so far as to claim he was going to feed a live puppy to his pet snake on the XPW Web site (he thankfully didn't). With their connections, Borden and Black were able to build up enough of a following to see their product distributed across the United States. However, the house would come crumbling down on them in 2003, as both Borden and Black were arrested for sending bondage porn films from their home state to another state that deemed the films illegal. Lizzy Borden and Rob Black — making the world a more family-friendly place, one illegally simulated, forced gangbang at a time!

Oh yes . . . and we'd be remiss if we were to pen this little book and not mention . . .

THE 1 PORN STAR WHO NEVER MADE A WRESTLING DEBUT . . . BUT WOULD HAVE RULED THE WORLD IF HE HAD

1. Randy West: In 1988 and 1989, Pleasure Productions Studios released a series of films entitled *The Young and the Wrestling*. Starring in these

Have Mercy, Daddy! This Wildman would totally kick your ass!

PHOTO: RANDY WEST

porno-wrestling parodies was the porn legend Randy West. While West's impressive resumé includes performances in 1,200 films with over 2,500 girls, being the sex stunt double for Robert Redford in the movie *Indecent Proposal* and owning the adult entertainment studio that discovered Jenna Jameson, he's best known to us for one role. That of the wacky, eyepatch-wearing "King of Rock 'n' Roll Wrestling," the Wildman. West was an actor at heart, and other places as well, and his Wildman character displayed more charisma and better mic skills than about half of the current WWE and TNA roster combined — and he cut killer promos they could only dream of. Trust us, when the Wildman bellows, "I'm gonna rip your dick off and make you wear it for a bow tie, fool!" you damn well better run for Jack & the Curly Q's sake.

And then there have been those inside the squared circle whose names might make you think you were about to watch a peep show instead of a tag team encounter. Especially if the competitor had one of . . .

THE 6 MOST FILTHY, PORNTASTIC WRESTLING NAMES

6. **Wet 'n' Wild:** What fully grown adult on this planet doesn't like things to get wet and wild in the bedroom on a frequent basis? If you were a female who ever came face-to-face on the sheets with the GWF tag team of Sonny Beach and Stevie Ray, you probably wouldn't get wild, and you definitely wouldn't get wet. Stevie and Sonny, whose bright and flashy wardrobe was complemented by inflatable beach balls they brought ino the ring, looked like thirty-something, wannabe Dynamic Dudes in the midst of a midlife crisis. Their female fans were lovingly

christened the Beach Bunnies. Hey, Sonny, is that a carrot in your pants, or are you just excited to see your hare-brained fans?

5. **The Johnsons:** When one looks back at whatever legacy TNA ultimately leaves, one thought will always be there: how did it last even a month? Not an unreasonable question, considering one of the promotion's first grand designs to take over the wrestling world was the introduction of Richard and Rod, the tag team known as the Johnsons. Their gimmick? They wore flesh-colored masks and full-body tights designed to resemble condom-covered tally-whackers. Inside the ring, Richard and Rod had about as much success as a ripped condom has in preventing pregnancy. Thankfully, TNA quickly aborted the career of the condom-clad grapplers.

4. **Dark Journey:** Speaking of condoms, if you are into what our No. 4 entry's name sounds like, it might be a good idea to use one. And a good lawyer might also be useful, because in the United States of America, sodomy is illegal in fourteen states. One thing that will never be outlawed, though, are beautiful women in the wrestling business. And in the '80s, few were more attractive than Dick Slater's valet and real-life girlfriend, Dark Journey. So attractive, in fact, that while in the UWF, a young Sting took it upon himself to have a private "dark journey" behind closed doors with Slater's main squeeze. Sting got his rocks off, and then he got rocked — by a Dick Slater left hook to the noggin. With his little rebel heart broken, Dick moved on to more troubled love relationships, including one that would see him allegedly stab his ex-girlfriend in 2003. You know, Dick, when Bryan Adams sang the love song "Cuts Like a Knife," he didn't mean it literally.

3. Prince Albert: When you hear the name Prince Albert, you may think we're talking about a particular brand of pipe tobacco. Unfortunately, one of the higher-ups in the WWF must have been smoking some wacky tobaccy when they decided to give a wrestling newcomer the name Prince Albert under its second meaning — a piercing at the top of the penis. The site of the bald, hairy-backed and sweaty Albert was bad enough. Visualizing his pierced schlong every time Howard Finkel announced him in the ring was every bit as painful as getting said piercing done on your own weiner. In the end, Albert found himself living up to the other definition of his name — Prince Albert was canned.

2. Cheex: After a few genital- and sex-related performers, it's time to bring up the rear of this list. Literally. Another one of TNA's silly gimmicks from the early days, the 500-pound-plus Cheex, was one of the fattest, most immobile wrestlers ever seen on a mainstream wrestling show. With all that girth, you know he had to eat a lot, and with overeating comes a lot of time spent dropping some stinky bombs in the toilet. Being so big, how in the hell could Cheex clean his enormous . . . cheeks? Thankfully he had a loyal companion by his side, to not only keep his stinky behind smelling fresh, but to lend him some encouragement at ringside. Her name: Brown-Eye Girl. Why not just call her Sphincter Gal and be done with it?

1. Little Beaver: Every heterosexual man in the world daydreams about getting some beaver, from the time he hits puberty until the day he passes away from a Viagra-related heart attack. At *WrestleMania III*, we're sure the bulk of the male portion of the 93,000-plus in attendance at the Pontiac Silverdome got a little excited when they noticed the phrase

"Little Beaver" on the afternoon's card. Expecting a little slice of poon-tang pie to go with their entrée of Hulk Hogan vs. Andre the Giant, male testosterone levels shot up, only to come crashing down at the site of a harsh, unsexy reality. Little Beaver was a male Native American midget wrestler who looked like a three-year-old dressed up as Tatanka for Halloween. It's arguable what was more painful — tens of thousands of blue balls in the crowd or the black-and-blue body of Little Beaver, who got squashed by King Kong Bundy in their six-man mixed midget tag team match. The lesson learned here? The next time you see a beautiful woman walking down the street, be thankful for the existence of the female species. After all, if the only bush a guy could get was a fat midget named Little Beaver, a massive wave of celibacy would shroud the planet, and mankind as we know it would become extinct.

Of course, you can't write a sex chapter in a book like this without discussing a particular weird fetish that's popped up in this business over the years. Here are . . .

THE 2 WRESTLING PERSONALITIES WITH A FOOT FETISH

2. **Francine Sells Her Sole:** When some of the more popular and attractive women in wrestling decide to shed some clothing by doing a nude magazine pictorial, we're sure there are a few prerequisites before the photograph shoot. Before said naked layout, it's a must to get a nice fake tan, as well as doing a little trimming of the bush, so to speak. When longtime ECW manager Francine decided she was going to show some skin, she made an appointment with her podiatrist and got her bunions and corns removed. Huh?! Unfortunately for ECW

fans, Francine was one of the few Divas who kept 95 percent of her clothes on during the last decade, shedding only her socks as she offered up Polaroid pictures of her feet, available for purchase on her Web site. We can think of a lot of bizarre fetishes Francine could cater to, but how many people out there were going to purchase a photo just for the purpose of yanking it to shots of a pinky toe? Well, we can think of one person . . .

PHOTO: MATT BALK

Don't blame Gene Snitsky for his two bigget loves: feet and punting babies. It's not his fault!

1. Gene Snitsky — A man and his foot fetish: Even though he's been in the sport only for a few years now, Gene Snitsky has had a few memorable character tweaks. At first, he was a baby-killer, going so far as to punt a doll of an infant into the crowd. But that was patently normal compared to Gene Snitsky, foot perv. We somehow doubt he would have been happy just looking at Polaroid pictures of Francine's little piggies, as he seemed truly satisfied only when he had a gal's toes stuffed in his pie hole. When Edge was having problems with Kane and needed assistance in taking the Big Red Machine out, he came to Snitsky for help. However, it would take more than money or some bedroom action with Lita to persuade him. Snitsky's fee was a one-on-one encounter with Lita's stank-feet. In essence, Snitsky had become a foot-fetish bounty hunter for hire, one we lovingly dubbed "Boba Foot."

And hey, before we leave the land of porn, it seems only appropriate that we totally blow our wad. Figuratively, you pervs. Though we can understand your confusion, given . . .

THE SINGLE MOST BAFFLING BLOW JOB IN WRESTLING HISTORY

1. Triple H and Candice Michelle, Private Parts Picnic: In the summer of 2006, Shawn Michaels and Triple H put aside their years-long rivalry and reformed the team that was a driving force behind WWE's resurgence in the late '90s, D-Generation X. To celebrate their return, DX held a giant outdoor barbeque/picnic. As the party went on throughout the episode of *Raw*, they cut to Triple H chatting it up with Candice Michelle. After a few seconds, both started to quiver rather awkwardly. At first, we thought they were breaking out into convulsions because Shawn undercooked the hamburgers that evening, perhaps causing a rapid case of E. coli poisoning. After a series of moans and groans, it appeared both were on the verge of death. However, all worries about fatal intestinal tract failure ceased when two women came up from underneath the picnic table, wiping their mouths. These two anonymous skanks had apparently been servicing both Hunter and Candice from on their knees under the table for the entire segment. Two disturbing things to point out: 1) if Skank No. 1 had to wipe her mouth after munching on Candice's rug, Ms. Go-Daddy must have had enough yeast going on down there to start up the Rainblow Bread Company; 2) when the camera panned down on Hunter, it revealed that his pants were still on. So either he doesn't have much in his tank, or the gal blowing him had the last name Hoover. Either way, it's something we didn't need to see.

No doubt, reading the item above, you're thinking, "That Triple H . . . he's a real ladies' man." We laugh at such nonsense. Laugh, laugh, laugh, like the fools we are. For, you see, when we think of Triple H and his D-Generation X partner, Shawn Michaels, we think of other things. Stuff like ass shots, improper male touching and boatloads of overall homoerotic behavior, enough to fill a DVD and offer it up for rental in the gay section of your local adult entertainment establishment. They may have tried to fool us with that BJ skit, but we know the truth. And now you will too, with . . .

THE 8 THINGS THAT PROVE DX IS REALLY, REALLY GAY

8. Michael Cole, Wedgie Boy: Sometimes, you just have to feel sorry for

Michael Cole. A loyal WWE employee for over a decade, he has been forced to live in the shadows as the No. 2 play-by-play man behind Jim Ross, and even for a brief time, Joey Styles. By the time he's ready to take over the lead-announcing duties on WWE's flagship show, *Raw*

PHOTO: MATT BALK

Shawn Michaels prepares Vince McMahon for the dreaded rear admiral.

will probably be canceled by the USA Network that same week. You might say, metaphorically, his ass just never seems to catch a break. If you said that literally, you'd be correct too. Long before Heidenreich had his fun with Cole's Hershey highway, DX broke Cole's anal cherry with the mother of all wedgies. And, of course, there's only one thing more enjoyable than having Trips stick his hand in your ass crack, that being . . .

7. **Fun with Shawn in the Shower:** At the *In Your House: D-Generation X* pay-per-view, Michael Cole was once again attempting to be a respectable journalist and conduct an interview with DX. For their part as fun-loving heels, Triple H, Rick Rude and Chyna all took turns ripping off Cole's suit and undershirt, before throwing him into the shower where Shawn Michaels was waiting for him, clad only in a towel. Wrestling hijinx? Sounds more like a gay prison-rape scene to us. Cole's first boy-on-boy action concluded with him getting sprayed with a big, wet explosion erupting from Shawn's long shaft . . . the shaft of his shower head, that is. Geez, what is it with you guys and your dirty minds?

6. **HBK to Jim Ross, "Suck It!" . . . Literally:** Back in the early days of DX, Shawn & Co. really went out of their way to shock and offend viewers. Bret Hart often got agitated by their antics, such as during an interview with Michaels conducted by Jim Ross on an episode of *Monday Night Raw.* Shawn, coming to the ring clad only in his boxer shorts, with what appeared to be a sock or a very ripe banana stuffed in his pants, proceeded to spend the next five minutes doing every-thing in his power to shove his overly meaty crotch right in Ross's

face. Despite all the pointing to his package, and numerous Michael Jordan-style jumps in the air to put his schlong square in front of Ross's mouth, HBK was unsuccessful at receiving any Okie fellatio that evening. Not to sound insensitive, but we've kind of always wondered if Jim Ross really suffered from Bell's palsy or if his jaw just got stuck after clamping down too hard to make his mouth bulletproof against Shawn's love gun.

5. Merry X-M(ass): It was the winter of 1997. Christmastime. A time to show that it's better to give than to receive. A time of heartfelt joy. A time to see Shawn Michaels and Triple H strip off their boxers in the center of the ring, wearing nothing but thongs styled after red Christmas stockings, and having the words *Merry X-mas* painted on their buns?!? Had Jimmy Stewart been alive to witness these shenanigans, no doubt he would have loudly proclaimed, "It's a horrible life!"

4. DX Proudly Present . . . Midget Ass: What could be gayer than Shawn and Hunter showing a little holiday brown-eye? How about the exposure of ten additional ass cheeks? During their feud with the male cheerleading Spirit Squad, DX decided for a goof to bring out ten midgets to do a parody of their pep-squad rivals. And like far too many DX skits, it wasn't long before brownholes were exposed. With all this gaiety, we're surprised that Trips didn't rename himself Mr. Ass. Oh, wait . . .

3. Billy Gunn, Mr. Ass: Following his arrival in DX, Billy Gunn decided to start calling himself Mr. Ass. Read that out loud, and let that verbiage hang in the air for a second: he called himself *Mister Ass*. Not only that, Mr. Ass, likely known simply as "Ass" to his friends, entered the ring to the loud beat of a theme song entitled "I'm an Ass Man." While the singer belted such tasteful lyrics as "I love to stick 'em, I love to pick 'em, I'm an ass man," Billy would ever so gingerly pull his tights down, revealing his thong to an audience comprised of 85 percent men. Or maybe he was just showing his fanny to his partner, one Road Dogg Jesse James. After all . . .

2. **Road Dogg Likes It Doggy Style:** So when you are a man named Mr. Ass, what do you search for in a tag team partner? Similar looks? Similar ring style? Surely you wouldn't pick a guy who dry-humps another man in the center of the ring, would you? Sorry, kids, but we're too far down this list for the topics to go anywhere but waaaaaaay off the decency path. For one of his most famous moves, Road Dogg Jesse James's Doggy Style Pump Handle Slam, the Dogg would position himself behind his unlucky opponent and proceed to engage in an act of dry fudge-packin' prior to hoisting his opponent up and down to the mat. No word if it was the force of the slam or a raw asshole that rendered Road Dogg's opponents unable to kick out of the pin.

1. **Bondage and Spray-Paint Fun with the Coach:** Still not convinced? Still need more proof? Consider this: when DX made their comeback in 2006, it was thought that this version of the group might be slightly kinder and hopefully less homoerotic. Fat chance, as poor Jonathan Coachman could tell you. Coach, following an altercation with DX, would soon enough find himself tied to a couch, hands above his head, pants pulled down. For the grand finale, the poor guy would have his buttocks branded by HBK and Triple H, who used green

spray paint to write DX on their poor victim's ass. Sigh, with all this talk of stripping, ass shots, nude showers and doggy-style dry-humping, for a second we thought we were freelancing for *Penthouse*.

A very gay *Penthouse*.

Ick. Time to wash our hands, kids, and return you to your relatively filth-free *WrestleCrap: The Book of Lists*.

Wrestling . . .
You Know, Actual Wrestling

Well, we've had some fun here, but as you've purchased a book with the word *wrestle* in the title, odds are you probably want to read something about, you know, wrestling. And hey, we're all about the people, so here you go, kiddos — an entire chapter dedicated to it.

To be fair, however, we should also note that the book you hold in your grubby paws has another word in the title, a four-letter word at that: *crap*. Therefore, we are under the assumption you are likely not looking for a list of who does the best figure-four leglock. So let's just kick things off with a bang by naming . . .

THE 7 SILLIEST MANEUVERS IN THE HISTORY OF PRO WRESTLING

7. **The Garvin Stomp:** A lot of folks yearn for the "good old days" of wrestling, back when it was more — and I am just quoting these fans — "real." Many will point to the glory days of Jim Crockett Promotions and the NWA, bringing up the gritty action that was broadcast each Saturday night at 6:05 p.m. The company featured the likes of Ric Flair, Dusty Rhodes, Tully Blanchard and Ron Garvin. To many, Garvin was a workingman's champion, a blue-collar guy who just looked like

he could beat your ass. In fact, following a right from the man with the "Hands of Stone," opponents would be so dazed that Garvin could execute the dreaded Garvin Stomp. With his foe staring at the lights, Garvin would go to the man's shoulder and . . . *stomp!* Then he'd go to the waist and . . . *stomp!* The right foot, the left foot, then back up the side once again, *stomp stomp stomp*. One more *stomp* to the head later, and the move was complete. Which kind of begs the question: if the guy is so out of it he can't move when being *stomped*, why not just pin him?

6. **The Boomerang:** Remember that glorious time in the 1980s when *Crocodile Dundee* ruled the roost? When Men at Work had us all wishing that Burger King had vegemite sandwiches on the menu? No? Then you probably also don't recall the kangaroo-lovin', gap-toothed Aussie wrestler known as Outback Jack. In an effort to really drive home the fact that he was from the land down under, his finisher was dubbed the Boomerang and was performed thusly: first, he would clothesline his victim from the front. So far, so good, right? Well, from there, he would wait patiently for the guy to struggle to his feet. Then he would hit him with a clothesline from behind. Sadly, we only saw this maneuver once or twice, as Outback faded from the scene faster than you could say, "Yahoo Serious."

5. **The Check into the Boards:** This one is ridiculous for countless reasons, not the least of which is the fact that it was performed by a man called the Goon who wore boots that looked like hockey skates. See, because he was an evil, hockey-playing wrestler. Sometimes it's just best not to ask. Anyway, his finisher was a move in which he

simply ran into his opponent from behind outside the ring, thus pushing his foe into the barricade set up to protect the fans from the mayhem. The Goon would then presumably win by count out. We say "presumably" because in the 15,000 or so T-120s we have at WrestleCrap HQ, we couldn't find a single one in which the Goon actually, you know, won. Maybe if he had a different finisher . . .

4. The Noogie: Sergeant Slaughter, fresh off a heel turn during the middle of the first Gulf War, in which he became an Iraqi sympathizer, was looking for an edge, a leg up to help him wipe the mat with his flag-waving American foes. For whatever reason, it was determined that his Cobra Clutch finisher was no longer vile enough, and thus something more nefarious was called for, like, say, a knuckle in the temple. Yes, he began to use the dreaded *noogie*, the favored finisher of fourth-grade bullies the world over. It looked ridiculous, but it could have been worse. Can you say "titty twister"?

3. The Pit Stop: This brutal maneuver was a staple in the playbook of Brian Knobbs and his Nasty Boys partner Jerry Sags. Grabbing their opponent by the hair, Sags would drag him into the corner where Knobbs would wait with his arm held high in the air. Instead of looking for a tag, though, Sags would take his foe's face and cram it into Knobbs' armpit. The opponent, apparently rendered helpless by Knobbs' B.O., would be easy pickings for the pin. While you might find this disgusting, at least he wasn't shoving the guy up Knobbs' rectum or anything.

2. The Stink Face: So you have a fat guy named Rikishi, and despite being obese and wearing what is basically a thong, he is a babyface. Not sure why people would cheer upon seeing a guy's big cottage-cheese ass covered only in dental floss, but we wrestling fans are a strange bunch sometimes. Which might explain the euphoria exhibited when 'Kish would shove his ass right into the dude's face. You look at a move like this and you'd have to consider the physical damage laughable. But the psychological scarring would run deep indeed.

1. **The Stink Face, Version 2.0:** Torrie Wilson was one of WWE's top Divas for years, gracing countless magazine covers and appearing

PHOTO: MATT BALK

Torrie Wilson's ass gets ready to claim another victim.

buck-naked in the pages of *Playboy*. When she decided to resurrect Rikishi's deadly finisher, it was applauded by fans worldwide. After all, who wouldn't be up for seeing her barely covered keister going right into some other chick's face? Things went horribly awry, though, when she began bringing a poodle named Chloe to ringside and decided that it should be her *dog* who did the dirty work. Yes, she would stick her foe's face up the dog's ass. Thanks, but we prefer our poodles to crap on the floor.

But here's the thing. Sometimes moves don't just look dumb, they go beyond that and make no sense. Now, obviously watching wrestling demands some suspension of disbelief; otherwise, you'd scoff when two men repeatedly hit each other in the face and continue fighting for the next ten minutes. In real life, this would result in an entire legion of hideously scarred and disfigured men, and that's just not the case. Honestly, probably only about 63 percent of pro wrestlers fall into that category. So while we can accept that some moves require you to simply nod and smile, others are just a bit too silly to accept. Others like . . .

THE 5 MOVES THAT SIMPLY MAKE NO SENSE WHATSOEVER

5. The Back Suplex: It's one of wrestling's most basic moves, one that is seen on nearly every wrestling card. Yet, upon further reflection, it's also one that makes the least sense. Standing behind your opponent, you hook your arms around him, pop your hips and then throw him backward to the mat. This would presumably cause damage to your opponent's back. However, you might note that in doing so, you've also thrown your own back hard onto the canvas, at least as hard as you've thrown your opponent. Therefore, logic would dictate that you would be hurt just as badly as your opponent.

4. **The Stroke:** A lot of fans do not like Jeff Jarrett, and it's not in an "I will pay money to see you get beat up" kind of way. Actually, it's more in an "I would not pay money to see you get beat up, or really, for any other reason at all" kind of way. While many have complained that Jarrett is simply too bland to be a major player in the business, to be fair, he is a decent worker inside the squared circle. Unfortunately, that level of aptitude does not carry over to his finishing move, the Stroke, in which he hooks an opponent from the side, leans back with him and then falls face-first to the mat with him, smashing his adversary's schnoz right into the canvas. Of course, as his opponent is going face-first in a downward motion, so is Jarrett. And while we don't mind seeing Jarrett cause damage to himself, it really doesn't make a whole hell of a lot of sense.

3. **The Worm:** No doubt a lot of you read the name of the list above and immediately thought of the Rock's patented People's Elbow. After all, that move requires the stunned opponent to lie on the mat while Rock removes his elbow pad, throws it to the crowd, then runs back and forth across the ring before dropping, well, an elbow. That does seem a bit silly, but in the same vein would be Scotty 2 Hotty's infamous Worm, which is actually even more nonsensical in our book (and since this is, in fact, our book, we're allowed to get away with it). You see, with the Worm, Mr. Hotty requires his foe to: a) be driven face-first into the mat; b) roll over from that position to lie faceup; c) lie in this prone position while he does a dance; d) continue lying in this position while

he jumps on one foot four times, once for each letter of *w-o-r-m*; e) still lie there comatose while Scotty does a break dance move called The Worm; f) continue to lay there while Scotty does a chop motion in not one, but two different directions. In some states, not moving for that long is legal grounds for being declared deceased. This massive build culminates in a lethal . . . devastating . . . aggravating . . . mildly both-ersome — eh, hell, it winds up with a chop to the throat, one that never really seems to harm an opponent at all. In fact, we're not even sure he's ever won a match using it. Maybe it does make sense after all.

2. **The C4:** It's too bad the pirate known as Paul Burchill had such a short tenure in WWE rings; we'd have loved to see him attempt his finisher on anyone larger than, say, 150 pounds. In the move, Burchill locks his opponent from the front, much as the Rock would do with a Rock Bottom (or, for all you hardcore marks reading this, a urange). Instead of simply lifting the opponent in the air and driving him to the mat, though, Burchill propels himself skyward, doing a complete 180-degree move into the air, all the while somehow carrying his opponent with him. Logic would dictate that Burchill would not be able to accomplish such a feat without some assistance from his "foe." Stupid logic.

1. **The Canadian Destroyer:** While the other moves listed require folks to put aside logic, this move requires them to put aside the laws of physics entirely. We'll try to explain it, and please pay attention, as it is rather complex. The move, made popular in the mainstream by Petey Williams, starts off like a standard piledriver, with Williams' opponent's head between his legs. Williams then jumps over his opponent's back and does a full-front flip. This while somehow, inconceivably, carrying his

opponent with him. Yes, Petey Williams, all five-foot-seven, 180 pounds of him, is apparently strong enough to not only lift his opponent — who we would assume would be fighting him — into the air, but to flip both himself and the other guy a full 360 degrees. Once the rotation is complete, his opponent's head is where it was to begin with — in the piledriver position, and he is, in fact, piledriven. Still, while it defies pretty much all laws of physics, we have to admit it looks pretty damn cool (and we also concede that, in the overall wrestling fan base, there's probably not a great contingent of physicists to dispute its effectiveness).

There are also times when the move you see in the ring makes sense, but it's so poorly named that you can't help but laugh at it nevertheless. In fact, we'd go so far as to say that no matter how devastating any of the following moves might have been, their names meant you simply couldn't take them seriously. After all, who could keep a straight face around . . .

THE 15 MOST IDIOTICALLY NAMED WRESTLING MOVES

15. **The Ghost Buster:** This move was actually a brain buster, performed by a guy dubbed The Birdman, who sang a song called "Piledriver." In fact, the video for "Piledriver" showed him performing the Ghost Buster, which means the name of the move makes even less sense than it did before.

14. **The Bunny Hop:** Honestly, we don't even remember what type of maneuver Evad Sullivan was doing when WCW announcers screamed, "Look out, it's the Bunny Hop!" He could have punched the guy in the balls, ruptured his testicles, placed a gasoline-soaked rag on his gonads, set it on fire, then stomped said fire out as the announcers

screamed, "Look out, it's the Bunny Hop!" and it still would have made this list. Besides, we're pretty sure that crotch arson wouldn't have been something Evad (see, he was Dave, but then he became dyslexic) would have perpetrated.

13. **Uncle Slam:** Not to be confused with the time that Chavo Guerrero waylaid his uncle Eddie, this move was actually the finisher for the former flag-waving felon dubbed The Patriot. It was a full nelson slam. But it was a full nelson slam performed by a real Yankee Doodle Dandy, no doubt born on the Fourth of July. Sadly, he did not perform the move whilst wearing a top hat.

12. **The Five-Arm:** This would be a forearm thrown at you by Terry Taylor, one so devastating that it is actually more than a forearm — it's a five-arm. Geddit? This was to make it sound impressive. Sorry, but that name sucks our fiveskin. Personally, we would have named it the 7,873,784-arm. Much more deadly.

11. **The Moss-Covered, Three-Handled Family Credenza:** In his early days as a color commentator, Tazz had the bright idea of assigning the above nom de plume to a twisting suplexy-neckbreaky move used by Perry Saturn. No one is sure exactly why this was considered a good name, but we will give Tazz credit: we can think of no other finisher named after a Dr. Seuss short. But we are holding out hope for someone to bust out a "Hop on Pop."

10. **Cattle Mutilation:** No, Hillbilly Jim didn't turn heel when you left to take a leak. The Cattle Mutilation is a submission move in which one

wrestler traps another the way a cow is held and pummeled. Uh, yeah. We don't care how good a guy like Bryan Danielson is, the moment he named his finisher after a conspiracy theory involving aliens vivisecting bovines, he lost us.

9. The Mooregasm: As much as we love Shannon Moore, his neckbreaker will remain on the list until he begins going for the move, only to hit a different finisher altogether — which will then be dubbed the Fake Mooregasm.

8. Mizard of Oz: Mike Mizanin gained glory as a reality-show star. Not even sure if we can continue after writing a sentence wherein we claimed someone claimed "glory as a reality-show star." It just feels like we're somehow lying to you. But such was the case, as the guy appeared on *The Real World*, then on *Road Rules*, then on *Fear Factor*. The wrestling tie-in here is that he also appeared on WWE's version of reality known as *Tough Enough*. He didn't win, but he was mediocre enough for WWE to offer him a contract, and soon The Miz, as he became known, was a weekly mainstay on WWE TV. Although he began as an announcer, it didn't take long for him to become a wrestler, a wrestler with a finisher known as the Mizard of Oz. There's a fine line between being clever and being retarded, and naming a finisher after a seventy-seven-year-old Judy Garland film, no matter how famous, is approximately forty-eight miles over that line.

7. Molly Go Round: Let it be known that we believe Molly Holly (Nora Greenwald) is one of the most talented women to grace wrestling in years. In fact, one need look no further than one of her signature moves, in which she does a complete flip from the top rope. Sadly, for whatever reason, the decision was made to name this awesome maneuver after a lame carnival ride. Note to bookers, promoters, wrestlers, announcers and anyone else with the ability to name finishers: impressive moves named after carnival rides immediately cease to be impressive.

Molly Holly is so cute and wonderful we almost feel wrong including her in a WrestleCrap book.

6. The Feliner: It seemed that anyone could get a job during the glory days of WCW, especially if that person was the karate instructor of the son of WCW head honcho Eric Bischoff. Which Ernest Miller just so happened to be. Dubbed the Cat for, uh, his catlike reflexes, we guess, Miller primarily used karate moves inside the ring. One such move was a kick named the Feliner. Unless your opponent happens to be a mouse, we cannot imagine anyone being scared of something named after a kitty cat.

5. The French Tickler: In the wrestling world, it is a foregone conclusion that any French wrestler, especially after the year 2000, is a wimp. This is the case even if the wrestler is only half-French, such as a French Canadian like Rene Dupree. Of course, it doesn't really help your cause when one of your primary weapons is the French Tickler. No, Rene wasn't slapping people with a condom, nor giving them genital warts, he was dancing. Which, come to think of it, isn't much of a move either.

PHOTO: MATT BALK

Oui oui! Look at moi! Rene Dupree dancing for your enjoyment.

4. The Fame-Asser: You'd think being known as the Ass Man would be like the kiss of death. It may have worked for Cosmo Kramer, but realistically, is that something you'd want as your wrestling moniker? Having that working against him already, the last thing Billy Gunn needed was a stupid finisher named, of all things, the Fame-Asser. See, it's like the Famouser, but it has the word ass in it. Just for the record, the Famouser would have been a stupid name too.

3. The Five-Knuckle Shuffle: Want to know why John Cena is hated by some and loved by others? Why he gets mixed reactions from arenas the world over? Maybe it has to do with the fact that one of his primary moves is named after spanking the monkey. Next!

2. The Schoolboy: This move, which has been around for ages, has long puzzled us. Why would you call a move in which one man slides his hand over another man's crotch, and then takes his other hand and cops a feel on his ass while holding him down for a pin, the Schoolboy? That just seems wrong.

1. The Hollycaust: Old Bob Holly sure can be a horse's ass, whether he's taking liberties with poor newcomers to the business or just deciding to stop cooperating with whomever he might be in the ring with. Still, we consider his greatest crime to be naming his 1999 suplex-slam finisher after the worst tragedy in the history of the human race. Or maybe he just didn't know about the period in which the Nazis attempted genocide on the entire Jewish population. Nah, we think he's just a dick.

One of the most common complaints we've heard over the years while documenting the worst in wrestling is that we never seem to target Extreme Championship Wrestling. (This would be the original version, not the Frankenstein monster that Vince has created.) Just to show that the folks in Philly weren't immune to being craptastic, we give to you today . . .

THE 6 DUMBEST NAMED MOVES IN ECW HISTORY . . .
AND YES, THEY ARE MORE IDIOTIC THAN THOSE
IN THE LIST ABOVE, THANKS FOR ASKING

6. **The Simonizer:** ECW's Simon Diamond had a simple, yet somehow not too insulting, gimmick: he would play Simon Says with his foes. While this sounds like it would be moronic, let's face it — this book proves there have been much, much worse gimmicks. Part of the reason it wasn't awful was due to Pat Kenney, who was great as a smug, unlikable prick, and had a cool match-ender to boot: a fireman's carry into an inverted DDT. Sounds awesome, right? Well, what if we told you it was named after a car wax? Would that make you rush out and buy a ticket?

5. **The Whippersnapper:** Want to get a young guy who doesn't have much of a personality over? Why not name his finisher after an antiquated term for a young guy? Such brilliance was on display when ECW's Mikey Whipwreck was given a shot in 1995, becoming the company's champion and defeating the likes of Steve Austin. His finisher, though, was indeed the Whippersnapper. You can put the guy over Steve Austin, the Rock, Triple H and the Ghost of Andre the Giant and he's still not going anywhere with that finisher.

4. That's Incredible: Another guy ECW main man Paul Heyman pegged as the top guy, veteran Pete Polaco did a switcheroo from a lame-ass WWF gimmick, Aldo Montoya, Portuguese Man o' War, to a slightly less lame-ass ECW gimmick, Justin Credible. Yes, like "just incredible." The name was silly, but not as silly as the fact that his finisher was named after *That's Incredible!*, an obscure, early-1980s TV show that featured such amazing feats as a guy stuffing himself into a shoebox and another dude solving a Rubik's Cube in nine seconds. Come to think of it, Polaco should be thankful that Paul didn't decide to name him Rubik Scube.

3. Greetings from Asbury Park: Bam Bam Bigelow was a huge, agile man from New Jersey. In fact, when he debuted in the late 1980s, many had him pegged as the next big thing in wrestling. Sadly, that didn't quite work out, and less than ten years later, Bigelow was plying his trade in ECW. He still had all the gifts of years earlier and had added a new weapon to his repertoire: a reverse, over-the-shoulder piledriver, unquestionably a killer finisher. However, that finisher also had a killer name — Greetings from Asbury Park. You know, we're not fans of naming moves after Bruce Springsteen albums, but if you're set on doing it, maybe calling it Darkness on the Edge of Town would be better. Nah, that would have sucked too. Never mind.

2. The Nutcracker Suite: Your wrestler's name is Balls Mahoney, a rough-and-tumble guy who looks like he'd be equally at home at a rock concert or in a cardboard box taking a snooze. A mean, tough mutha. So why not name his finisher after Tchaikovsky's famous ballet? We can think of a million reasons, actually.

1. **The Jazz Stinger:** Poor Carlene Begnaud, aka Jazz, had what is, without question, the worst-named move in the history of the game: the Jazz Stinger. Maybe there really was something in the much-ballyhooed Kool-Aid in Philly, because we cannot think of a worse idea than naming a move after a best-forgotten Neil Diamond movie. Somehow we doubt that many in the audience — many of whom sported Metallica or Marilyn Manson T-shirts — had a whole hell of a lot of Neil Diamond albums in their collection.

Enough stupid moves, let's get back to talking about wrestling matches themselves. This is what everything is built up to, after all: two men, or two teams, squaring off in the middle of the ring and battling to the bitter end. Sometimes, though, no matter how great the buildup, no matter how talented the men inside the ring, things just don't pan out. Like . . .

THE 6 MATCHES THAT JUST DIDN'T LIVE UP TO THE HYPE

6. **The Rock vs. Goldberg:** Call it a case of "shoulda been." The Rock was the biggest star for WWE from 1999 until 2004, prior to beginning his full-time movie career. During that same time, Bill Goldberg was WCW's top draw. Utilizing the Reese's principle, these two great tastes should have blended perfectly together. Or at least done killer business together. Didn't happen. Though the match was first rumored to happen in time for *WrestleMania XIX*, the sides couldn't come to an agreement, and Goldberg's WWE debut didn't happen until after *WrestleMania* the next year. This effectively meant Goldberg was out of the public eye for two years, which may have made a difference in his drawing ability. More likely, though, the real

killer of the deal was WWE's insistence on giving big Bill a "personality," which they attempted to do via a "comedy" skit in which he had a blond wig atop his bald skull. Memo to any promoters fortunate enough to have a roster that includes Bill Goldberg: Bill Goldberg kills people. He does not do "comedy," especially stupid comedy like wearing a wig. You'd think this would be common sense, but apparently not, as the most successful wrestling company ever blew this one miserably.

5. **The *WrestleMania IV* WWF Title Tournament:** Make no mistake, the WWF crew was in a tough position when it was asked to follow up the legendary Andre-Hogan-fueled *WrestleMania III*. The company believed Hogan-Andre 2 wasn't enough of a draw on its own, so they booked Hogan to lose the title on free TV in a controversial manner, thus setting up a fourteen-man title tournament for the belt. Unfortunately, the tournament was long, drawn-out and, well . . . flat-out boring. The show ran almost four hours, which had fans looking for their snooze alarms.

4. **Matt Hardy vs. Edge:** In this age, when "smart" fans seem to know more about what happens behind the scenes than what goes on inside the ring itself, this was money. It was the oldest wrestling storyline there is: Edge, the heel, steals babyface Matt's girlfriend, Lita. The catch? It was real life. Lita, who had been with Matt for six years, really did sneak behind the poor guy's back with Edge, and, as you'd expect, all hell broke loose. Matt went online and told his side of the story, which WWE felt was unacceptable behavior. He was given notice, and it looked as though he would be getting the hell out of

Dodge. Instead, fans at WWE shows constantly chanted for him, to the point that the company really had little choice but to bring Matt back. And back he came, to a true hero's welcome. The match could not be avoided, and was thus set, with fans eagerly awaiting see Edge get his comeuppance. Instead, they saw Matt get pummeled, left beaten and bloody, in less than ten minutes. Matt never again regained that initial momentum, while Edge went on to become WWE's top heel and champion. Sometimes life just isn't fair. Ironically, life becomes even less fair when shortsighted promoters are involved.

3. **Brock Lesnar vs. Goldberg:** As noted above, Bill Goldberg's WWE career was everything his WCW career wasn't. While the usually idiotic WCW crew knew how to book big Bill (i.e., he never loses), WWE didn't (i.e., put a wig on his head). So, as his one-year contract was coming to a close, the company decided to feed him to one of its top stars, Brock Lesnar, at *WrestleMania*. Just one problem: Brock, burned out on the constant travel that was part of being a WWE star, was planning on leaving as well. Fans suddenly hated both men and proceeded to boo them throughout the bout. The match mercifully came to an end as Goldberg pinned him clean, which led to the only cheers in the match. Because, you see, the match was over. When fans cheer only when a match ends, that there's a bad sign.

2. **Warrior vs. Hogan 2:** Ah, our old friend Jim Hellwig joins us again, this time in a rematch against Hulk Hogan. The original *WrestleMania VI* bout, in front of over 60,000 screaming fans, saw Warrior take the title. It made him one of the very few who ever held a winning record over the mighty Hulkster. It seemed a rematch was inevitable, but the

WWF decided against it, and thus "inevitable" became nine years later, in WCW no less. The storyline to the match was so simple: Warrior was the one guy Hogan never got the better of. Indeed, each week all Warrior needed to do was come out and state this fact. Instead, Warrior began to play "mind games," which included appearing in a "magic mirror" to Hogan and then seducing Hogan's pal Ed Leslie and putting him into bondage. Believe it or not, it was actually *worse* than what that sentence would indicate, as the spectacular bout of nearly a decade earlier became a total farce, the highlight of which was Hogan attempting to throw fire at Warrior. Hogan couldn't get the paper to light, so he basically threw a piece of paper at Warrior, who sold this violent parchment-related offense and did the job. Warrior vanished shortly thereafter, never to return.

1. **Sting vs. Hulk Hogan:** The buildup for this match was, without question, the greatest in the history of World Championship Wrestling. In fact, it was so stellar that every person who has — or wants — a job in the business should be forced to study it. Sting vs. Hogan was the very definition of "dream match," one that had been on magazine covers for years before the two were even in the same company. Each man was the most popular performer in his respective company, and when the time to square off finally came, WCW head Eric Bischoff did something very smart: he made fans wait. And wait. And wait. For eighteen months, not only was the bout teased, but Sting himself virtually disappeared from in-ring competition. By the time the bout took place, fans were dying to see their hero finally shut up Hogan and his nWo cronies once and for all. And by all rights, there was no other way the match could have gone. But, this being WCW, of course it

did, becoming an overbooked mess, with Hogan pretty much beating the tar out of Sting before losing in a fluke decision. While the match drew the largest buyrate in the history of the company, it was also the beginning of the end, as Hogan quickly regained the title and fans became bored of the tired nWo formula. But, hey, that's a story for another book — one already written, in fact. (It's called *The Death of WCW*, and you should buy it immediately. Sheesh, with a cheap plug like that, you'd think one of us wrote it or something.)

As noted above, sometimes promoters have to deal with things outside their control. For instance, performers with giant egos who came up with . . .

THE TOP 4 EXCUSES FOR NOT DOING A JOB

4. He's Too Small: You've likely noticed that wrestling is a business of large, large men. These large men do not like losing to men smaller than themselves. They feel that by losing to smaller men, they somehow look weak. We would like to let these large men in on a little secret, one they might not know about. This whole wrestling thing? It's predetermined. You aren't really competing in an athletic contest. With this in mind, perhaps in the future we can avoid situations like the one the WWF faced in 1993 when Hulk Hogan was scheduled to drop the title to the up-and-coming Bret Hart. Hogan played the size card, thus killing the program dead. The Hulkster would actually be shown the door shortly after this, but not before dropping the WWF title on the way out. And to whom did he lose? The 550-pound-plus Yokozuna. Thankfully Yoko didn't also play this card, or he might still be champ, long after his passing.

3. I Think I'm Having a Heart Attack: There are a lot of folks who fancy themselves clever politicians in the wrestling world, but we'd put Kevin Nash near the top. Despite his lack of mobility and in-ring talent, the self-dubbed Big Sexy has had top-dollar gigs in the business for the past fifteen years, which is even more amazing when you consider how rarely he actually looked out for the well-being of the promotion he worked for. For instance, when he was employed by WCW during its hot period, he would quite often simply refuse to lose. Maybe he thought everyone was too small (and make no mistake, he used that one too). Whatever the reason, Nash often felt as though he was above lying on his back. To his credit, he'd often come up with creative reasons for why he couldn't lose — and why he couldn't compete at all. When WCW had its biggest PPV in company history, *Starrcade '97*, Nash was nowhere to be found. In the weeks leading up to the event, Nash was in a feud with the Giant. Since the Giant was actually larger than Nash, excuse No. 4 (above) didn't hold water. He was forced to come up with a new one, and it was a doozy. See, the day of the show, Nash was having "chest pains," and it looked like he might be having a heart attack. As Nash had been claiming for weeks that he had no intention of losing to the Giant, the only real heart attack might have resulted from him doing the job cleanly.

2. I Lost My Smile: During their time together in the WWF, Kevin Nash and Shawn Michaels were virtually inseparable. Michaels would impart his in-ring knowledge to Nash, who in turn apparently taught him the finest in backstage politics, something also passed on to fellow Clique members Scott Hall and Triple H. Michaels made a career of avoiding counting the lights, and this would easily be his most famous excuse. At *WrestleMania XII*, Michaels defeated Bret Hart for the WWF title. A year later, the plan was for Michaels to return the favor. He decided against doing this, as he was "diagnosed" with a "career-ending" knee injury, so he was unable to lose to Bret. Sadly, he came out before a nationwide audience, forfeiting the title and claiming he had "lost his smile" and therefore had to go away. A video package of Shawn's career played as a tearjerker song warbled in the background, pleading, "Tell me a lie/And say that you won't go." Sure enough, a few months after his knee was so badly injured, he was back, better than ever. Maybe he did tell us a lie.

1. **Those Were Actually Weights in My Son's Toy Box and I Didn't Notice:** Hey, remember Kevin Nash? No? What the hell's wrong with you? We just wrote about him in the last two items. Heck, we could have named this list "The Kevin Nash Memorial List of Worst Excuses Not to Do a Job." And yeah, we're well aware he is not, in fact, dead. Anyway, as we stated, he has a knack for having employment regardless of his reputation. Following a laughably bad run in WWE, it seemed he'd finally have to settle into retirement. This being professional wrestling, that would not be the case, as there's always a sucker promoter who's willing to overlook past transgressions in the hope of rekindling some long-lost fire, and this time it was TNA who decided to roll the dice. Not sure who came up with this, but the idea was that Nash would give a rub to the company's X-Division. For those unfamiliar with this subsection of the TNA roster, it would be comprised of high-flyers, most of whom are under six feet in height and under 200 pounds. Kevin Nash, we should point out, is around six-ten and in excess of 320 pounds.

The thought here was that the much larger Nash would come in, make fun of the lightweights, and then one of these small men would beat Nash, thus proving the old adage "It's not the size of the dog in the fight, but the size of the fight in the dog." What actually happened was indeed a dog analogy, but it was another old standby — "You can't teach an old dog new tricks." Nash originally agreed to lose, but then that loss got pushed back and back. Finally the time came for him to pay up, and wouldn't you know it, he got injured. See, the poor guy was moving his son's toy box and he hurked it up only to discover that it was much heavier than he thought: the toys in the chest had apparently been replaced by weights. You know, like dumbbells. Kinda like the dumbbells that fired Nash after this event . . . only to rehire him a scant six weeks later.

As we've watched wrestling over these past many years, we've seen every conceivable match. Tags, Triple Threats, Fatal Four-Ways, Royal Rumbles, Elimination Chambers, War Games . . . seen 'em all. And after all these bouts, we have but one question: what happened to just a plain ol' one-on-one, man-on-man, may-the-best-man-win match? Does every contest need some goofy stipulation? It seems bookers these days feel the need to overcomplicate things, generally to the benefit of no one. And to make our point, we give you . . .

THE 8 MOST NEEDLESSLY COMPLEX — OR JUST DOWNRIGHT STUPID — MATCHES IN WRESTLING HISTORY

8. **Inferno Match:** Remember back when you'd win a match by pinning a man's shoulders to the mat? Or making him submit? How lame is

that? You know what would really be interesting? If you won the match by setting your opponent on fire! Such an idea might sound like nothing short of stupid — and trust us, it is — but that did not stop the WWF from promoting such an encounter between Kane and the Undertaker in 1998, going so far as to place burners all the way around the ring. Thankfully, no one was seriously injured, and even more thankfully, the company put the kibosh on any future such matches shortly afterward. While the WWF may have nixed Inferno matches, WCW didn't, promoting their first-ever Human Torch match between Vampiro and Sting in 2000. That particular encounter featured such stupidity as "Sting" (actually a really badly disguised stuntman) being lit aflame and then jumping from about fifteen stories to the ground. It was as though Sting's thought process was, "Hmmm . . . I am on fire. What should I do? I know — jump off this balcony and plunge one hundred feet! The fall will put the fire out!"

7. **Punjabi Prison:** While 2006 wasn't a banner year for WWE, the company did debut one huge new piece of talent. And we emphasize the word *huge* and kinda sorta just mention the word *talent* in passing. For when the Great Khali hit the scene, we were completely astonished. Not since the heyday of Giant Gonzales had wrestling seen such a man lacking in even the basics of pro wrestling. It didn't matter, though, because his promos . . . man, his promos were great. You had absolutely no idea what the hell he was saying, of course, but they were a blast to listen to: he basically yelled something we believe was a primitive dialect of English. Thankfully, the crack *Smackdown* announce crew informed us that he was screaming about the Undertaker, and a feud for the ages was born. The Undertaker actu-

ally lost clean to Khali in their first encounter, setting up a natural rematch in which the Dead Man would hope to exact revenge. But this would not be just any old match, it would be one in which Khali (supposedly) excelled: the Punjabi Prison Match, a cage contest with giant bamboo shoots in the place of steel bars. Who knew Pier One made wrestling cages?

6. **The Great American Turkey Hunt:** Take it from us: any time a match is contested with something "on a pole," it sucks. We're not sure who came up with the original idea to have a pole match, but should we ever find out, we will hunt him down and shove a pole up his ass. And maybe a turkey, too. Bizarre segue? Yes, but one with a basis in actuality. You see, in the dying days of the American Wrestling Association, the company tried to spur interest by creating a series of bizarre stipulation matches, like football matches and Behind the 8-Ball Battle Royals. Sadly, this didn't involve grown men throwing billiard balls at each other. But the one stip that did live up to its name was the Great Turkey Hunt, in which Colonel DeBeers and a jobber by the name of Jake "the Milkman" Milliman dueled in an attempt to climb a pole and grab a turkey. Yes, a big, fat, uncooked turkey, just like you'd throw in the oven on the fourth Thursday of November. Amazingly, this did not revive the AWA, which collapsed shortly thereafter. Maybe if they'd used a live turkey . . .

5. **Doomsday Cage:** Over the past few years, the whole purpose of a cage match has been forever obliterated. See, a cage match used to be how main-event feuds were settled: two men truly hate each other to the point that they have to get in the cage and battle it out. The

key, of course, is that the cage offered the heel no chance to escape, nor to have his buddies run in. Keep this in mind the next time you see a cage match, be it a standard one, a Hell in the Cell or whatever variant someone comes up with next, because nine times out of ten, someone winds up running in or getting away. We digress. What we'd like to do is bring to light the single dumbest cage match in history: WCW's Doomsday Cage, which had three — count 'em, three — levels! Why, exactly, a cage needed three levels was never fully explained. And, to be fair, such contraptions had been built before. But those matches didn't feature Hulk Hogan and Randy Savage beating up Ric Flair, Arn Anderson, Meng, the Barbarian, Kevin Sullivan, Lex Luger, Zeus and The Ultimate Solution. Yes, those two guys beat eight other guys. Oh, and they just left the cage whenever they felt like it. Worst cage match ever.

4. **Chamber of Horrors:** Oh, wait, no it wasn't. There was another WCW caged catastrophe years earlier dubbed the Chamber of Horrors, which took place at *Halloween Havoc '91*. Two teams competed inside an extra-large cage that had been decorated for Halloween. Apparently by a class of third-graders. The object of the match wasn't to pin your opponent or make him cry uncle, but rather to trap your foe in an electric chair and throw a switch, presumably killing him. Comedy ensued, including the announcers talking in the middle of the bout about the need to pull the "fatal lever" into the on position to win the match. At which point, the camera zoomed in on said switch, which was, in fact, in the on position. Still, the ending of the encounter, in which Abdullah the Butcher shook about like a fish out of water, was the height o' hilarity. Too bad for WCW it wasn't meant to be funny. We don't think.

3. Junkyard Invitational: People said WCW was garbage in the late 1990s, and this was the match to prove it. Literally. A complete mess, the Junkyard Invitational was exactly as billed — a contest taking place in an honest-to-God garbage dump. Wrestlers hit each other with tires, locked their foes in the trunks of cars and attempted to crush one another into cubes. There would have been at least some comedy value, were it not for one factor: you couldn't see a damn thing. The lighting was so bad that the only way to follow the action was by listening to the commentators. You'd think if the company went through the hassle of spending a reported $100,000, they'd at least have put some of that money into lighting. On top of that, about half of the competitors wound up with legit injuries. Oh yeah, and there was no prior advertisement of the match, so they garnered zero additional buys by spending all that cash and hurting all those guys. Man, we loved WCW.

2. Dog Poo Match: We've kind of veered off the path of intricate matches to talk about just plain stupid ones. And no list of idiotic bouts could leave out this bout, in which the Rock and Davey Boy Smith attempted to throw each other into dog feces. Do you really need more description than that? We didn't think so.

1. King of the Mountain: Enough with the stupid matches, let's get back to something that makes you pay attention — pay attention to the point that you need to take notes. That's the way TNA likes it, after all. You see, the folks in charge of TNA apparently feel wrestling is too basic these days. So they make it more challenging, not only for competitors, but for those watching at home. For instance, in 2006 they had a Fight for the Right tournament that included a reverse battle royal. That's right, you had to climb from the floor over the top rope into the ring. See? It's different and complex. Sure, it makes no fucking sense, but hey, it's unique, dammit. And now, we present TNA's crown jewel: the King of the Mountain match. Now, try to follow the rules here. As Mike Tenay once said, "It's actually quite simple." We should note that he then spent ten minutes explaining just how simple it was, and when he was done, we were more confused than when he had started.

The match begins with five men, all of whom are "ineligible." For what, we will explain later. Anyway, to earn eligibility, a competitor must score a pinfall or submission. Now, if you get pinned or submit, you must go into a "penalty box," like in hockey. You will stay in there for two minutes, at which point you can come back out and attempt to become eligible. Oh yeah, eligibility . . . we should probably talk about that. See, you become eligible to take a title belt, which you must retrieve from a TNA official. Whoever is eligible can take the belt. Oh yeah, and find a ladder. And then climb the ladder and hang it above the ring. Oh, and if the belt is dropped, then the official gets it back. See, it really was quite simple. If you're a rocket scientist who moonlights as a nuclear physicist and does brain surgery in your spare time.

Is there any better feeling than finally scoring that big win, finally grasping the championship you've been hoping for all your life? If so, we hope you have something better to say than this . . .

THE SINGLE WORST VICTORY SPEECH IN WRESTLING HISTORY

1. Andre the Giant's Speech After Winning What? The thrill of victory. Whenever an athlete finally claims a championship he's chased for

years, often times he'll get on the microphone and say a few emo-
tionally charged words. When Andre the Giant claimed the WWF
World Heavyweight Championship from Hulk Hogan (with the help
of evil twin referee Earl Hebner and Ted DiBiase) on NBC's 1988 prime-
time special *The Main Event*, it meant that Andre, one of the biggest
stars in the history of the World Wrestling Federation, was finally the
top dog. "Mean" Gene Okerlund hopped in the ring, and Andre proceeded to give a victory speech that made Sly Stallone in *Rocky II*
seem like vintage Shakespeare. Andre's tear-jerking words: "This is no
surprise, I told you I would win the World World Tag Team
Championship." What the hell did he say? In his excitement, did he
suddenly forget the name of the company that had been paying him
all decade long, as well as what belt he was fighting for? While the
audience was pondering what he had just rattled off, Andre did what
he was paid to do by the Million Dollar Man, and that was to hand
the world title over to him. Andre did so by stating, "Now, I surrender
the World World Tag Team Championship to Ted DiBiase." And that
was that. Andre's lone moment as the man on the top of the mountain, mumbling and stumbling on live television about some fictitious
wrestling federation and his imaginary tag team partner. He may be
gone now, but to us, he'll always be the greatest World World Tag
Team Champion that ever lived.

But let's be realistic here for a moment. Wrestling isn't just about moves
or matches — it's entertainment. Matches are designed with different spots
in mind, sections of a match that are designed to achieve certain things.
For instance, you might want to turn the match's momentum from the

good guy to the bad guy. Or maybe you want to draw attention elsewhere, perhaps to a manager. Or maybe it's just time to make the folks in the seats laugh. If that's what you're looking for, look no further than . . .

THE 11 SPOTS THAT ARE GUARANTEED COMEDY

11. **Getting Your Balls Kicked:** Trust us, when you're looking for comedy, nothing beats a kick through the uprights. It's funny for guys, because they know how much it hurts. It's funny for women, because they're all wenches who want men to feel pain. (*Note from editor:* It would come as no shock to me if you guys never actually had a date.) Plus, anything with feet is generally comedy gold, so the equation "feet + testicles" must equal super comedy gold.

10. **Getting Your Balls Punched:** As funny as it is getting kicked down there, it's even better when there's a hand involved. See, because it's two guys, that means one of them is actually close to copping a feel on another dude's nutsack. Hee hee! Nutsack! This is funny!

9. **Getting Your Balls Uprooted by a Forearm Through the Legs From Behind:** A favorite amongst women in the wrestling community, this strategic maneuver takes place as the competitor is facing elsewhere. For instance, if we were in Detroit, a heel like, say, Randy Orton might be mouthing off about how horrible the Lions are. In comes a Lions-loving babyface from behind, and whammo! The Lions faithful won't be the only ones in pain!

8. **Getting Your Balls Ignored by Female Valets While Anticipating Fornication:** A bit of backstory here. There was a wrestler named

Meat . . . Hmm, that sounds like the start of a dirty limerick. But it's true! There was a wrestler named Meat, and he was managed by those evil and vindictive Pretty Mean Sisters. Not only were they vicious to those they didn't like, they were also cruel to their own man. They would tease that he'd get to live up to his name, but then they'd pull back and he'd get nothing, leaving the poor guy sexually frustrated. One time he even went to the ring with a boner. No doubt the women in the crowd found that wildly amusing. (*Note from editor:* I'm starting to think you guys have never even seen a woman.)

7. **Getting Your Balls Hit with a Singapore Cane:** As we've seen, it's comedy to get kicked or punched south of the border. But what's even funnier is when that pain is amplified, like if it were done with a baseball bat. While we've not seen that (though it has most assuredly been done), we have seen guys get their 'nads pummeled with a Singapore cane countless times. And we laugh and laugh and laugh every time we see it.

6. **Getting Your Balls Caught on the Top Rope:** This one's like Old Faithful — you see it on nearly every show. Wrestler A goes to the top rope, and Wrestler B catches him and shakes the ropes. And where does that leave Wrestler A? Crotched on the ropes. Now, if Wrestler B *really* wants to ratchet up the hilarity, he would proceed to grab the ropes and bounce poor Wrestler A up and down, with his testicles taking even more damage. It's comedy, we tells ya.

6. **Getting Your Balls Caught on the Barricade Outside the Ring:** This would be exactly as described above, but on the metal guardrail that keeps

THE WRESTLECRAP BOOK OF LISTS!

the fans from the action. On the plus side, metal is harder than a ring rope, so it's more painful. On the minus side, you can't exactly bounce the guy up and down. Too close to call which is funnier, and that's why both are ranked No. 6. And here you thought we had a typo.

5. Getting Your Balls Grabbed in a Claw Hold: Remember how we mentioned that it's funnier to get punched than kicked in your twig and berries? Well, let's take that logic a step further and state that it's far more humorous for a guy to just grab another dude by the curly q's and not let go. Many in the business have dubbed this move "the testicular claw," but we'd just say it's comedic genius.

4. Getting Your Balls Accidentally Hit by Your Tag Team Partner, Who Falls on Them in an Oral-Sex Position: This one requires quite a bit of planning and can only be accomplished in a tag bout, but trust us, it's well worth the setup. The first thing that needs to happen is for the heel opponent to be set up in the corner, as described below for Al Snow's bowling bit. His partner needs to be pummeled in front of him, until he is so out of it that he turns and falls face-first right into . . . wait for it . . . his partner's Rocky Mountain oysters! And it looks like he's blowing him! *Co-me-dy*, baby!

3. Getting Your Balls Hit by a Bowling Ball: This may sound completely absurd, and it is, but yes, it has happened in a wrestling ring — on more than one occasion, believe it or not. Actually, Al Snow used to do this maneuver all the time; he'd set his groggy opponent on the ground with his back to the turnbuckles, kick the guy's legs open and then attempt to pick up a 7-10 split. Sadly, Al would always fail, with the ball going right into the man's groinal area. Wait, did we write "Sadly"? We meant "Hilariously."

2. **Getting Your Balls Hit with a Chair . . . While They Have a Cinderblock on Top of Them:** Some of these are just starting to sound really stupid. Stupidly *funny*, that is! Especially if the thought of Tommy Dreamer's scrotum and its cargo being transformed into a pancake makes you giggle like a schoolgirl. And so it came to pass at ECW's *Hostile City Showdown* in 1996, as poor old Tommy got the cement/chair combo. Not sure whose idea this one was, but he's hardcore, all right — a hardcore idiot.

1. **Getting Your Balls Hooked Up to a Battery with Jumper Cables:** Okay, so Kane has Shane McMahon trapped and . . . Oh wait, we already covered that elsewhere in the book. Sorry.

And after reading that list . . . our balls are very thankful we're not pro wrestlers.

Can You Believe It?
Someone Bought This!

A successful wrestling company isn't just one that gets fans to attend events or tune in to its television shows. Sure, that crap is important, but there's more money to be made from the marks than just by gouging them at the ticket window. The most successful companies are those that get those fans to shell out the cash for merchandise. In fact, we dare say that WWE's greatest accomplishment is the creation of a loyal fanbase willing to shell out top dollar for any ridiculous item with a WWE logo slapped on, be that an action figure, video game or Diva snow globe.

And yes, WWE really has made — and sold — Diva snow globes. We got one as a Christmas present one year.

In fact, some of the stuff wrestling companies have sold over the years has been even more ridiculous than two plastic women wailing at each other with pillows inside a water-and-confetti-filled glass sphere. Take, for instance, the oldest staple in the business: the T-shirt. Certainly, it's no shame to have been tooling around in an Austin 3:16 shirt. We all had that one. But we have to question who the hell was enough of a doofus to purchase . . .

THE 7 ARTICLES OF WRESTLING CLOTHING WE'D NEVER BE CAUGHT DEAD IN

7. **1990 Captain Mike T-Shirt:** Not sure if you've picked it up yet by reading this book, but WCW often appeared to have been run by a bunch of monkeys. Although, to be fair, we dare say that Curious George may have done a better job than, say, Jim Herd. Anyway, buffoonery was the order of the day at the company in the early 1990s, especially in their marketing department. Now, to be fair, you could rightly argue that the wrestling end of things didn't give them much to work with at times. For instance, there was a storyline that saw evil Mike Rotundo turn babyface. Simple enough, right? Well, you see, Rotundo was Captain Mike at the time and he led the Varsity Club, a heel conglomerate comprising the likes of Kevin Sullivan and Rick Steiner. When the group split up and Rotundo became a good guy, he was still Captain Mike, but he was no longer the captain of a team, he was the captain of a yacht, complete with sailor hat. To commemorate this gloriously idiotic event, WCW released a shirt for the good Captain that featured a boat from which a giant Mike Rotundo head protruded. Would have made a good Transformer, but it made a dumb shirt. And come to think of it, it would have made a horrible Transformer, as we can't imagine Megatron quivering at the thought of a yacht that flipped to reveal Mike Rotundo's smiling kisser.

6. **1990 Steiner Brothers T-Shirt:** While Captain Mike was lame, the duo on this fine shirt was actually one of the company's hottest acts: Rick and Scott Steiner, a University of Michigan duo that was tearing up the tag ranks. The shirt didn't single out either man, but rather featured both Rick and Scott together. And when we say "together," we

PHOTO: MIKE LANO

Hmm . . . maybe a Siamese Twin version of these guys isn't so far-fetched after all.

mean as in they were joined at the hip. Those unfamiliar with wrestling no doubt thought the Steiner Brothers were, in fact, Siamese twins. No other shirt before or since has matched this level of creepiness.

Because, you see, as WCW got on in years, its shirts simply became more gooftastic. To wit . . .

5. 1999 WCW Bret Hart T-Shirt: As anyone who has followed wrestling for, say, ten seconds could tell you, Bret Hart is a proud Canadian, a hero in the Great White North in the way that many of our coveted football players are in America. To that end, the WWF created a legendary storyline in which Bret, who was a heel in America, was a hero in his native Canada. It was a great feud with an incredible dynamic; on any given week, Bret would be received very differently depending on where the show was taking place. And his final WWF match, in which he was screwed over in Montreal, may have been the single most talked about encounter in wrestling history. Montreal, you might recall, is in Canada. Where he was a national hero. Did we mention that yet? Anyway, that was his final match before coming to WCW. With this in mind, what kind of shirt did the company create for him? One with a killer photo of Bret, standing proud . . . in front of an American flag. God Bless WCW.

4. Kevin Nash Stovepipe Hat: Speaking of proud Americans, there is likely none prouder in the history of this great land than our sixteenth president, Abraham Lincoln. And what better way to honor him than by putting the equally legendary Kevin Nash under one of his trademark stovepipe hats? Sadly, even Big Sexy wasn't able to restore the stovepipe to the pinnacle of the fashion world. Which is unfortunate, as we were looking forward to WCW attempting to bring back other antiquated clothing items. We're thinking that DDP bow ties and Madusa Miceli bloomers would have been all the rage.

3. **Carlito Spit-or-Swallow Shirt:** We'd make up some zany nonsense about this shirt, but WWE.com in its infinite wisdom did it for us: "What is the meaning of Life? Who killed Kennedy? What came first, the chicken or the egg? These are all questions that we have been searching the answer to for many years. But one question stands out above all the rest, one question that psychologists, astrologists and philosophers have debated about for years . . . Do you Spit or Swallow?" Not dumb enough? We should probably mention that the shirt also featured the world's dumbest caricature: that of Carlito in apple form. *In apple form.* We can only long for the day when fans are given the opportunity to purchase a Carlito Appleseed shirt with the phrase "Want my seed?" splattered across the back.

2. **APA T-Shirt:** Prior to his rise to the top of WWE ranks as rich Texan/New Yorker JBL, John Layfield was saddled with several horrible gimmicks. One of these was as a member of the Undertaker's evil ministry, along with Ron Simmons. The duo were known as the Acolytes, and they were pretty much bottom-feeders on the WWF roster. Following the breakup of the Ministry, though, they were able to revise their characters and became beer-drinking thugs for hire as the Acolyte Protection Agency, or APA. And they actually became popular enough for the WWF to create a brand-new T-shirt for their fans to purchase. We believe, however, there must have been a miscommunication within the WWF marketing department as to what APA actually stood for, as we can't believe someone thought a shirt that read "APA: Always Pounding Ass" would actually be a big seller. Maybe they'd heard all the stories about Layfield torturing guys in the shower backstage or something.

1. **Smoking Gunns Giant Foam Cowboy Hat:** As you might suspect from their name, the Smoking Gunns were a cowboy tag team. They'd come to the ring hooting and hollering, and firing toy .45's in the air. Thrilling, no? To be fair, the team was obviously designed to get over with the younger set. Even with that in mind, we can't imagine any self-respecting four-year-old wanting to prance around in a giant foam neon cowboy hat. Which would have left only flaming rodeo clowns to purchase the item, a demographic that probably wasn't large enough to make this venture profitable.

Of course, selling shirts and foam hats is just one way a wrestling company can make money. There are tons of others, such as opening up a food stand and charging eight dollars for a basket of fries cut in the shapes of the letters W-W-E. Think we're crazy? That we're now just making stuff up? Then we implore you to visit . . .

THE TOP 5 WRESTLING-THEMED RESTAURANTS

5. **WWF New York:** When you think of the biggest money losers in WWE history, stuff like the XFL springs to mind. It might shock you to know, then, that the Times Square-based eatery/disaster known as WWF New York (later known as the World) was a huge money drain on the company as well, one of its biggest ever; the restaurant wound up losing almost $20 million for the company during its brief, four-year existence. And why was this the case? Well, the horrendous food might have had something to do with it. More than horribly over-priced horrible food, though, would have been the fact that it was located right in the middle of the most expensive land on the planet:

Times Square. Rent was outrageous, and worse yet, it required a long-term lease. In fact, when the company closed the establishment in March 2003, it came out just how long-term the lease was: it expired on October 31 of 2017. We doubt Vince had much of an appetite after taking such a bath on that dump.

This patron is all smiles now, but one greasy Mean Gene combo meal later and he'll be farting out the chorus to "Tutti Frutti" all day long.

4. **Mean Gene's Burgers:** For years, Gene Okerlund was known as the voice of wrestling. Whether it be his mild-mannered, ummm, manner, or the fact that he appeared to be a clone of the toilet-paper-squeezing Mr. Whipple, Mean Gene was almost as much a household name as Hulk Hogan. So why not try to make a buck by slapping some ground chuck on the grill and throwing it in a bag with his likeness? And thus Mean Gene Burgers were born. One can only hope

that somehow, someday, he will face off with Ronald McDonald, the Burger King and that Raggedy Ann-lookin' ho Wendy in a fatal four-way for burger-joint supremacy.

3. Hulk Hogan's Pastamania: Some have called Hulk Hogan the smartest man in wrestling, and now we understand why. In the mid-1990s, he decided to cash in on being the world's most famous wrestler by selling Spaghetti-O's to stupid kids at a ridiculous markup. That would be clever enough, but he was more Einstein than that, getting WCW to publicize the restaurant on early episodes of *Nitro*; in fact, the first-ever *Nitro* took place not at your standard arena, but at the Minneapolis Mall of America, not so coincidentally the home of Pastamania. Of course, none of this actually saved the eatery from its eventual demise, as apparently while kids may have been dumb enough to pay ten dollars for a bowl of Beefaroni, adults weren't.

2. WCW Nitro Grill: Ever wanted a Booker T-bone? How about Onion Rings of Saturn? Well, we have the place for you! During the heyday of WCW, executives decided that nothing would be better than to open a WCW restaurant right smack-dab in the heart of the Las Vegas strip. Located inside the popular Excalibur Hotel (you know, the one that looks like a big castle), the Nitro Grill should have been a stunning success. Sadly, this wasn't the case, as WCW's popularity bit the dust starting in 1999 and never recovered. Even had *Nitro* remained the most popular show on cable TV, the venture still would likely have failed, because the Excalibur featured something far more entertaining and barbaric than pro wrestling: the legendary Tournament of Kings, a show that not only feeds visitors, but also features "jousting, invading armies, dragons and fire wizards." Sorry, but not even a guy like Ric Flair could top a fire wizard. We don't even know what a fire wizard is, but we bet it's damn cool.

1. **Abdullah the Butcher's House of Ribs and Chinese Food:** Everyone loves barbeque ribs. Let's face it, if you don't like them, you're either a vegetarian or a communist. Maybe both. There's truly nothing quite as satisfying as gnawing meat right off the bone like a caveman, especially when said carcass is slathered in a hickory-smoked molasses concoction. And who better to serve it to you than a guy with a forehead with half-inch-deep crevices — no less than Abdullah the Butcher himself. One can only wonder if the forks used at the tables are those that the Madman from the Sudan formerly used on his opponents. Our only request: when handing out silverware, please don't produce it by reaching down into your tights. That just doesn't seem sanitary.

Abdullah hasn't cornered the market on wrestler-based celebrity tie-ins, though. Not by a long stretch. For years, wrestling personalities have attempted to use their likeness to sell all kinds of useless crap, some of which you might even see if you're up late enough and tuned to the local UHF station. Items like . . .

THE 4 GREATEST ITEMS WRESTLERS HAVE EVER ATTEMPTED TO PAWN OFF ON FANS — VIA THE INFOMERCIAL

4. **Would You Pay $30 for a Quarter?** Joey Styles may be known as the voice of Extreme Championship Wrestling (in both its original and new incarnations), but to us, he'll forever be the man who introduced the

world to the fine artistry of painted coins. Sometime between the death of the original ECW and its half-breed, inbred rebirth, Joey was apparently looking for work, which he found in an infomercial in which he attempted to sell viewers U.S. quarters. Yes, the same you'd use to pop into a Pepsi machine to score a Dr Pepper. But these weren't just any old quarters, oh no. These quarters were *hand-painted*. That's right — no longer was George Washington just a monotone, silvery impression. He now had skin tone, and his hair was white. And that eagle on the back? Multicolored feathers. (In fact, it looked more like a peacock.) And these quarters, hand-painted by the masters, which usually retail for twenty-five cents, could now be yours for the low, low cost of $29.95, no doubt payable in three easy instalments of $9.99.

3. **Jesse Ventura — Now with Slot-Car Racing Action:** Has any one man ever had a more diverse resumé than Jesse Ventura? Let's review all of Jesse's exploits, shall we? Navy Seal. Pro wrestler. Actor. Governor. Slot-car racer. Slot-car racer? Yep. In the fall of 1989, Jesse took to the "race track" to do his best NASCAR-ish Tom Cruise, as he starred in an infomercial disguised as a kid's afternoon special, one best described as *Jesse Ventura: Afternoons of Blunder*. Hired by Hasbro Toys to shill its new *Record Breakers: World of Speed* toy line of four-inch, battery-operated slot-racing cars, Ventura would pit his toy car against some ten-year-old brat's hoopty in a race that had all the excitement of a Coy and Vance Duke scrub episode of *Dukes of Hazzard*. If that wasn't enough fun for the kiddies, Ventura later provided in-your-face commentary of other geeks' races, in a special segment entitled "Jesse's Crash Bash," which featured "awe-inspiring" slow-motion wrecks and collisions of these tiny toy cars that ran on the awesome horsepower

of three — count 'em, *three* — AA batteries. Surprisingly, this show did nothing to boost the sales, as Hasbro quickly pulled the plug on the Record Breakers line. In retrospect, this nutty infomercial makes the WWF/Karate Fighters toy promotional tie-in of the mid-'90s seem like a Broadway revival of *The Karate Kid*.

2. **A Grill that Looks Just Like the George Foreman Grill, But Is Somehow a Million Times Better:** Pity poor Hulk Hogan. While he is arguably the most famous wrestler who ever lived, he simply doesn't have the best timing. Sadly, he missed out on the single largest money-making opportunity of his lifetime. For when the inventors of what would become the George Foreman Grill came up with their earth-shattering, fat-reducing creation (one that involved — now try to follow us here — a slanted grill so that the fat cooked off and slid away), they didn't want that old, bald, washed-up boxer; they wanted that old, bald, washed-up wrestler. Sadly, when they called him, he was at the grocery, and they called up Foreman instead. That's right, they didn't leave a message, or call his agent, or attempt to contact him on another day. They just assumed that if he was unable to take this specific call, this meant he was uninterested in their product. (Don't ask us for the details: they change every time Hogan tells the story.)

Having missed out on the grill, Hogan charged on undeterred and sold a mixer instead; the Thunder Mixer, to be precise. This mixer was so powerful that, according to the instructions, it could not be used to mix ice. It may shock you to learn that a mixer unable to crush ice failed miserably. Hulk contemplated this missed opportunity for years, before finally coming up with a solution: create the Hulk Hogan Grill. Now, this grill may have looked exactly like the Foreman Grill, but it was a million times better, and he explained how with a handy, dandy infomercial. And what was that advantage? Well, according to the Hulkster, his grill could also be used to make waffles. Do you hear that sound? It's the sound of 55 million George Foreman Grills being thrown in the dumpster!

1. **The Genius Meets the Gazelle:** While Hogan and Styles may have shilled to the best of their abilities, they were both rank amateurs in comparison to Lanny Poffo. Anyone who wants to sell something should watch this man in action, preferably hunting down a copy of the spots he did with Tony Little to sell the world the Gazelle, a walking/running/skiing/slipping-on-ice-and-attempting-not-to-fall-on-your-ass exercise contraption. For the infomercial, Lanny told the story of how, in a match with Andre the Giant, Andre lifted him up in a suplex that caused his toes to curl up in his boots. While other men would have visited a podiatrist to right his wayward foot digits, Lanny instead became introspective. "I've been alive for forty-seven years," the former poet laureate explained to those transfixed on his every word on their couches at home, "and a lot of my tomorrows are yesterdays." He further explained that he wanted to be the best he could for his remaining days and, to that end, he was searching out exercise equipment.

He found it as a friend was flipping channels, and there he was — the man, the myth, the legend: Tony Little himself. "I said, 'Whoa! There's Tony Little!'" (Before we continue, just imagine for one moment that you are at home looking for something to watch and a friend of yours said such a thing. Okay, we'll continue now.) "When I saw that machine, the first thing I said was, 'It's low-impact. It's gentle on the joints. And it's very easy on the credit card." (Okay, sorry . . . Imagine once again you're watching TV with a friend and he said, and we quote, "That is very easy on the credit card." Onward.) According to Tony, though, Lanny's biggest contribution wasn't his shilltastic abilities, but rather that he helped a lot of men understand the Gazelle wasn't just for the ladies. Lanny agreed, then went even further, stating, "The Gazelle has an identity crisis. It's exercise equipment, but it thinks it's playground equipment." We are now eagerly anticipating the Kangaroo, which appears to be a refurbished bouncy castle that ships with a DVD of Lanny doing flips as Tony yells at him, "Reach for the stars!"

Of course, not everyone has thirty or sixty minutes to hock their wares. Sometimes you only get thirty or sixty seconds. That's when it's important to really strut your stuff, like . . .

THE TOP 10 COMMERCIALS STARRING PRO WRESTLERS

10. **Match of the Century:** Hulk Hogan vs. ALF: There's just no nice way to word this. The folks behind this thirty-second spot were stoned out of their minds. How else would you explain Hulk Hogan and ALF — ALF! — appearing in the same commercial, plugging a discount-phone-call company. Before you file that libel lawsuit, consider the following. Within the span of thirty seconds, Hogan appears dressed up as Ebenezer Scrooge, writes poetry and then chats it up with the Alien Life Form whose primary sustenance was cats, which leads the Melmac native to proclaim they are two brothers from different mothers. Narcotics. Heavy, heavy-duty narcotics. We rest our case.

9. Triple H . . . You Gotta Bee Kidding Us: One of the most ludicrous commercials ever, not just wrestling-related but of all time, had to be Triple H's bit for the sports drink YJ Stinger. We'll try to explain it as best we can without you having to seek professional help. A group of teenagers are gathered around the television set watching Trips wrestle, when the wiseass kid of the bunch gets up, talks some smack to Hunter and spits some of his YJ Stinger drink at the TV. Following this, nothing short of a Troma Studios B-grade horror movie ensues. The mist of YJ Stinger that the kid spit out sadly doesn't hit the screen and electrocute him, but rather transforms itself into a swarm of attacking bees. Bees that, much like nearly every WWE employee, are under Hunter's control. The kid, obviously knowing there was a potential for more stings than the *Halloween Havoc 2000* pay-per-view, exits the house and hops on his skateboard in a desperate attempt to escape the bees. So the poor kid scoots a few blocks, and that's when the real nightmare begins; you see, Trips cannot only control bees, but also has the power to teleport. With one quick smirk, Triple H just taps his toes three times and he's transported out of the TV and onto the street. The kid would get away, then Hunter would just teleport right back to being on the kid's ass again. After toying with the brat for about half a mile, he finally teleports right in front of him and knocks the beeswax out of him. Given his bizarre, mutant-like powers, one has to wonder why Trips wasn't a lock to be cast in one of the Marvel Comics X-Men sequels. Ah well, he was probably too busy dipping his stinger into the boss's daughter's honeypot.

8. Jeff Jarrett for Tracfone: When one thinks of the giant growth that occurred in the cell-phone industry at the start of the new decade, one has to look back at how companies introduced themselves to curious new consumers ready to purchase a cell phone for the first time. T-Mobile bribed that Welsh wench, Catherine Zeta-Jones, to take a moment away from her career of lying down and spawning new Michael Douglas children, and hired her to be their spokes-woman. Cingular Wireless hooked up with Marvel Comics and Spider-Man during the promotion of Spidey's incredibly successful first film. The guys at Tracphone? Well, they went with a marketing idea that was arguably worse than the whole New Coke fiasco, hiring Jeff Jarrett as their commercial spokesman. Tracfone's strategy was to have callers prepay minutes before they could use the phone. Our question to the Tracfone folks: why would you hire a guy who can't sell pay-per-views to sell a pay-per-call phone?

PHOTO: TROY FERGUSON

"We're here to deliver this pizza — and kick your stinkin' teeth in!"

7. Demolition — Hold the Olives: "Here comes the Ax, and here comes the Smasher. The Demolition, walking . . . pizza-delivery guys?" When you think of all the greasy and sleazy pizza-delivery guys who have shown up at your doorstep, driving a rusty '72 Nova with no exhaust, supreme pizza in hand, did it ever occur to you that it could be worse? In 1990, it was. When a poor lady who had just ordered a pizza opened the door, she would find two face-painted men clad in black, screaming at her at the top of their lungs. It was Ax and Smash, and get this — they didn't even have any pizzas in their hands. In the commercial, they were sent door-to-door by the Pizza Hut corporation to promote Pizza Hut's new kiddie-themed, dine-in promotion entitled "Kid's Night." Apparently, the Pizza Hut employee taking orders on the phone misheard the lady when she ordered a "supreme with extra cheese" and instead sent something "supremely cheesy."

6. **Sergeant Slaughter for Diet Coke:** It was the mid-1980s when diet colas received their first giant advertising push, complete with lots of commercials featuring slim and fit models, often frolicking poolside with a refreshing, low-calorie, carbonated beverage in hand. When Diet Coke reintroduced itself with a brand-new NutraSweet-filled taste, the Coca-Cola company brought in attractive A-list female stars such as Whitney Houston and, later on down the road, Paula Abdul to do promotion via song-filled advertisements. With all that cash being thrown around, Coke would eventually have to become accountable for its spending budget and hire B-level talent for their commercials. Eventually that B-list became Z-list, as they went a penny-pinching step further, hiring Sergeant Slaughter for a Diet Coke commercial. In a thirty-second spot filled with various images and actors, it wasn't hard to miss the Sarge, as he sang Diet Coke's catchphrase of the time, "Just for the Taste of It." It marked the only time in recorded history when

an overweight, overchinned man was featured shilling a diet soft drink. And honestly, it wasn't a bad marketing idea. Here was a guy dressed in camouflage, with a huge beer gut sticking out, saying, "Hey, I'm fat. I don't care one bit about my physique or losing weight. I'm drinking this potentially harmful-to-my-body, aspartame-filled soft drink for only one reason: just for the taste of it."

5. **Paul Orndorff for Absorbine Jr.:** One of the first commercials from wrestling's big boom in popularity during the mid-80s featured one of Hulk Hogan's biggest rivals of the time, Paul "Mr. Wonderful" Orndorff. Seems Paul's muscles were a little sore from having to carry Mr. Bollea in matches, night in and night out, so he needed a little help recovering. He went to his medicine cabinet and what did he find? A giant stash of pills outlawed in most states? No, silly, he reached for the perfectly legal, over-the-counter, pain-relieving gel Absorbine Jr. No liver-damaging capsules needed here. Paul simply rubbed the ointment over his aching joints, and he was ready to bench-press the entire planet. And we mean that literally, as the commercial ended with Mr. Wonderful hoisting the planet Earth over his shoulders. Impressed? Considering that when Superstar Billy Graham was all 'roided up, he used to do the hula hoop with the ring of Saturn, we're not.

4. **Macho Man Snaps into a Slim Jim:** If you were a wrestling fan in the '90s, odds are you watched your fair share of Slim Jim television commercials featuring the Macho Man, Randy Savage. For years, Macho Man shilled his cowboy hat off for the company, whether he was ass-beating some chump inside a wrestling ring or adopting the more conventional method one would use to promote a greasy chicken

and beef by-product meat snack — interrupting a high school production of *Romeo and Juliet* and destroying the entire set with said
meat snacks in hand. With Macho Man displaying the mental com-
posure of the Son of Sam killer in these spots, did you ever wonder
why he was chosen? Because, believe it or not, he was more stable
than Slim Jims' original spokesman . . .

3. **Ultimate Warrior Snaps . . . Period:** Possessing an acting grace that
makes Randy Savage seem like the next Sir Laurence Olivier, Jim
Hellwig was initally chosen by the fine folks at Slim Jim as the man
to convince already-overweight wrestling fans to consume massive
amounts of monosodium-glutamate-filled beef sticks. However, his
first commercial from 1989 was missing only one thing . . . a public-
service-announcement narrator warning you of the hazards of con-
suming Slim Jims. The commercial starts with three kids sitting around
in a garage. Suddenly, the garage door is savagely smashed open by
none other than the Warryah himself. With Slim Jims in hand, and
all the style of an average neighborhood drug dealer hopped up on
cocaine, Warrior says to the kids, "Are you boys a bit bored?" Like
every young middle-school kid would, the three succumb to the peer
pressure. Well, maybe they might've been able to withstand it if
Warrior wasn't yelling in their faces, destroying their stereo equipment, throwing chairs around and intimidating them by ripping a
phonebook in half.

But something even more disturbing was about to take place. These
Slim Jims that Warrior was peddling seemed to be so stimulant-filled,
they would've set off the three-alarm of WWE's Wellness policy. The
first kid who took a bite, well, he might just as well have pulled a Jim

Belushi and ate a speedball-laced Slim Jim, 'cause with the first bite not even swallowed, he rocketed to the ceiling of the garage, only to come crashing down on the couch, semiconscious. Another kid tried one of Hellwig's treats and went on a "trip" so bad that his chair started spinning rapidly and he ended up with a giant 'fro. The third kid? Not sure, but we think he just straight-up overdosed and died, as the final shot showed all three kids in the now semi-destroyed garage, looking to be "knock, knock, knockin' on heaven's door." You know, we're not quite sure what the advertising and marketing agents were thinking back then, but I guess they thought abusing and scaring the living shit out of potential consumers was the way to go. After witnessing Savage destroy Juliet's castle, Demolition bitch out a poor housewife and Warrior kill three kids, we didn't think it could get any more brutal. But the folks at Post Cereal proved us wrong . . .

2. **Andre the Giant for Honeycomb:** When you consider all the villainous acts Andre the Giant committed in the late '80s, you're bound to think of his heel turn against Hulk Hogan, which led to him screwing Hogan out of his WWF title with the help of Ted DiBiase. However, these actions pale in comparison to the behavior of a savage man known only as "Andre the Honeycomb Junkie." In a commercial for everyone's favorite breakfast cereal shaped like a beehive, a group of kids, along with their robot sidekick (it was the '80s, *Star Wars* was still hot), were shown enjoying their bowls of Honeycomb from the safety and peacefulness of a tree house. Little did the sugar-addled kids know that the tree house would soon be under the attack from a sugar-jonesing giant. The look of horror on the faces of the little brats was priceless, as Andre, with a growl that sounded like it was dubbed in by

Frankenstein, reached through the treehouse window and, with the mindset of every rapist that ever walked the earth, took the cereal he wanted without one iota of permission from the kids. Despite having their Honeycomb stolen, the kids laughed and frolicked with the thieving Giant, who proceeded to use their teeter-totter as a launching device, and blasted their robot to the moon. How this made parents want to buy cereal is beyond us. We watched it and immediately went out and purchased handguns, in case we ever encountered any cereal-stealing, child-bullying, robot-abusing giants.

1. **WCW Roos:** When comparing the early WCW to the WWF of the late '80s, one thing is certain. Vince's marketing of his stars was a hundred times better than anything Ted Turner attempted. However, the fortunes down south appeared to be changing when some of the WCW stars were signed on by the Roos shoe company to be featured in commercials. What's that you say? You don't remember Roos tennis shoes? Of course not. You, like the rest of the Earth's population, were probably too busy shining up your stylish new pair of Nike Air Jordans to be even remotely interested in the ugly Roos shoe that the resident dorky-looking poindexter was wearing. After all, nothing is geekier than a shoe whose mascot is a freakin' kangaroo. The selling point of Roos, if you can call it that, was a secret pouch on the side you could put your stuff in. Imagine that, a shoe with a picture of a marsupial on it and a pouch to stash all your nerdy stuff, like your spare pencil erasers, twelve-sided Dungeons & Dragons die and officially licensed *Star Trek* "I Grok Spock" button. Enlisted to help sell the world's stupidest shoe was the world's stupidest wrestler, Rick Steiner. While Lex Luger and Sting also had their own Roos commercials, Steiner's spot was the most

memorable. With a bunch of dogs in tow, Steiner put the pair of Roos on both hands and started crawling down the sidewalk on all fours, barking at the other mutts. Let's do a quick review. Nike: Michael Jordan flying through the air with an awe-inducing slam dunk. Roos: Rick Steiner preparing to become Scrappy Doo's love bitch. With crappy shoe gimmicks and horrible marketing, is it any wonder the Roos shoe brand is now extinct?

In recent years, wrestling has hit upon a gold mine with the surge in popularity of the DVD. You want to know WWE's single greatest asset? It's not the roster of top stars; it's the massive tape library. In addition to the company's own history, it also holds the rights to every single match or program from WCW, ECW, World Class, AWA and pretty much every other company under the sun. That's how WWE has been able to churn out plenty of quality releases for everyone from Hulk Hogan to the late, great Brian Pillman. Sadly, not every release has come to fruition, as some were deemed too limited in appeal to ever make it to store shelves. Now, these are just rumored titles, but we can only imagine the impact of . . .

THE 7 GREATEST WRESTLING DVDS THAT NEVER HIT STORE SHELVES

7. *Van Hammer: Behind the Music:* One of wrestling's true pioneers, "Heavy Metal" Van Hammer is often dismissed as little more than a poser by fans. Was Mark Hildreth the lost fifth member of Van Halen? Or was he wrestling's answer to Milli Vanilli? Everything is explored in this tell-all documentary constructed by legendary filmmaker and rock enthusiast Marty DiBergi. From the dizzying heights of his debut, when he squashed Terrence Taylor in under forty seconds, to the

depths of darkness, when he was cast out of Raven's homoerotic Flock, this DVD has it all. Discover the real story behind his problems with Southern rocker J.T. Southern, the training regimen he followed to become the winner of the first-ever Jesse "the Body" Ventura arm wrestling championship and his true feelings about Ron Reese. Plus, for the very first time, he discusses Mick Foley's accusations regarding the comment he made about being a savior in WCW. Whaddya say — let's boogie!

6. *Hulk Hogan: Bald Be Not Proud:* He may be the most famous wrestler ever to walk the earth, but Terry Bollea isn't without shame. No amount of money and fame can overcome his greatest disgrace: his bald head. Over the years, Hogan has attempted several times to hide his shiny slaphead. Even when the world consisted of more Hulkamaniacs than not, in the late 1980s, the Hulkster couldn't overcome his follicle-driven embarrassment and attempted to cover up courtesy of a plastic helmet with a fist atop it. Later, when he had turned heel in WCW, he channeled the spirit of his *Three Ninjas: High Noon at Mega Mountain* character, Dave Dragon, and sported a truly awful blond wig. Neither of these head covers lasted long, and soon the Hulkster was back in the ring with head a-glowing. As if all this weren't enough, booker/inmate Vince Russo would later assault Hogan with a verbal barrage at *Bash at the Beach 2000*, calling Hogan a "big bald son of a bitch." Hogan was so filled with rage he promptly filed a lawsuit against both WCW and Russo himself. This DVD also addresses the long-rumored belief that the defense's main argument was, "But only like twelve people even bought that show." A must for every Hulkamaniac.

5. ***The Rise and Fall of GLOW:*** The Gorgeous Ladies of Wrestling are back in the spotlight with this exciting two-disc DVD set! GLOW was a true revolution in the world of professional wrestling; its unique and innovative television shows are directly responsible for the WWF Attitude era and the oeuvre of Vince Russo, as well as a precursor to the Ring of Honor promotion. Relive the tag team finesse of Hollywood & Vine, a duo who the *Wrestling Observer*'s Dave Meltzer said "will make everyone forget Manami Toyota and Akira Hokuto." Enjoy a full hour of bonus footage with Jackie Stallone, the very same woman *Pro Wrestling Torch*'s Wade Keller claimed had "better promos than Jim Cornette, Ric Flair and Roddy Piper . . . combined." All this and much, *much* more!

4. ***The World's Strongest Man: A Retrospective:*** Mark Henry. Ken Patera. Ted Arcidi. The names may change, but the fact remains that wrestling has long been filled with "the World's Strongest Men." While these men were rarely technicians inside the ring, few could compete with their mighty might. With this in mind, for the first time ever, WWE releases a disc that contains no wrestling whatsoever. In its absence, you get countless feats of strength, including, yet not limited to, coin-bending, phone-book tearing and men becoming human tow trucks by pulling cars with only chains and their bare hands. Plus four straight hours of bench-pressing! Order today, and get a bonus disc of Doug Furnas and Bill Kazmaier in a tug of war. This DVD is Vince McMahon's personal favorite and is sure to be yours as well.

3. ***Sex, Drugs, Rock & Roll . . . and Oh So Many Firings: The Marty Jannetty Story:*** He is the man known to wrestling fans as "the other Rocker."

While Shawn Michaels went on to headline *WrestleManias*, Marty Jannetty's life was never the same following the incident in which his longtime friend and partner superkicked him in the jaw and sent him through Brutus Beefcake's barbershop window. What was going through Marty's head on that fateful day? Aside from shards of glass, that is. Did he believe Shawn would go on to such greatness? Did he believe his new Rockers tandem with Al Snow could revive his career? And who exactly is he blowing to get hired again and again by WWE after being fired again and again by WWE? All this, plus a world exclusive: Marty's career highlights set to music in a remake of "Alone Again . . . Naturally" by Wham!'s Andrew Ridgeley.

2. ***A Dudley Family History:*** Even the most casual wrestling fan knows of the exploits of the infamous Dudley Boyz, brother's Ray and Devon. Those more in the know are aware of the exploits of Brother Runt (formerly Spike). But how many know of the other Dudleys who have long since been forgotten? We open the family photo album and look not just at its most famous three members, but the entire clan. What happened to Sign Guy Dudley? How about Chubby Dudley? Was Big Dick really aptly named? And to what tribe did Dances with Dudley belong? Most important, what kind of crack whore of a mother did these poor kids grow up with? Plus, Brother Runt openly discusses the drug issues that earned him the nickname Little Spike Dudley (LSD). It's a story that will bring you tears of joy one moment and tears of sadness the next. A true heartwarmer that is not to be missed.

1. ***Andre the Giant — Farting in Elevators:*** Although wrestling fans know of Andre's exploits inside the ring, they may not know of his slapsticky

antics outside it. Amazingly, not all of them involved him being drunk and flipping over cars. Following in the footsteps of such ground-breakers as Allen Funt's *Candid Camera*, WWE Home Video brings you hidden-camera footage that was thought to have been long lost. You'll laugh out loud at the Eighth Wonder's hijinx as he does the fish dance, stomps grapes to make wine, and drops his trousers to the amazement of onlookers baffled by the size of his enormous schwanstucker. And no documentary of Andre's soft side would be complete without his favorite trick: he stands in an elevator with Bobby Heenan, breaks monster wind and then asks the elevator's other patrons how "that little girl could fart so loud." It's a laugh-a-minute riot!

When you step back and think about it, it's not really fair that WWE stands to make so much money on footage of its past performers. Those who are no longer with the company have to come up with other ways to support themselves, be it working indie shows or finding other employment. The advent of eBay has certainly helped some wrestlers, as workers have often made top dollar on props that were just sitting around in their closets. Be it Tammy Sytch's breast implants or a pair of Iron Sheik's curly toed boots, you just never know what you might find online. Which is why we log on daily, in hopes of finding one of . . .

THE 5 WRESTLING ITEMS NEVER OFFERED ON EBAY THAT YOU'D GIVE YOUR KIDNEY FOR

5. **Sid Vicious's Self-Defense Squeegee:** One of pro wrestling's most humorous stories is that of the time Sid Vicious engaged in a bar fight with a man about 100 pounds and six inches his junior, one

Brian Pillman. Upon getting his rear handed to him by the Flyin' one, an embarrassed Sid ran out of the bar, only to return brandishing the ultimate revenge weapon — a squeegee from a gas station. Screw putting a gun in your bedside drawer — you'll sleep more soundly at night with the knowledge that any potential burglar to your homestead will be facing a lethal squeegee.

4. **Miss Elizabeth's Skirt from *SummerSlam* '88:** Before the days of generic Divas prancing around with dental floss crammed up their tuchas, there was only one woman who had the hearts of every hormone-overloaded male wrestling fan — Miss Elizabeth. And what '80s pre-pubescent kid could forget Liz's lone moment of PG-style stripping at the inaugural *SummerSlam*, when she ripped off her skirt and did her best skank-ho street walk, in an attempt to distract Andre the Giant and Ted DiBiase. Her actions worked, as her men Hulk Hogan and Randy "Macho Man" Savage popped up from certain defeat and toppled the drooling Megabucks. Simultaneously, I'm sure other Hulkamaniacs "popped up" as well. Imagine being the proud owner of Liz's skirt from that evening and popping up anytime you want, in the comfort of your own jerkatorium.

3. **Koko B. Ware's Stuffed Frankie:** When Koko B. Ware's longtime parrot mascot, Frankie, perished in a house fire in 2003, a downcast Koko didn't rush out to buy a replacement bird. You try buying one of those exotic birds on an honest indie performer's salary. Most indie guys are lucky if they can afford a two-piece with biscuit from KFC. No, Koko did the next best thing: he took off for the local taxidermist and had his companion stuffed. We await the day Koko decides

to flip us this bird on eBay, hopefully with an autographed copy of his mega-smash hit record, *Piledriver*.

2. **Robert Gibson's Glass Eye:** In the 1980s, no tag team was hotter than the Rock 'n' Roll Express. And speaking of hot, remember the days of Robert Gibson coming to the rescue of Ricky Morton with that oh-so-inspiring "hot tag"? That Robert, he had such a gleam in his eye. Probably because he had just waxed it and shined it up before his match. In this fast-paced day and age of PlayStations, Xboxes, and Wiis, imagine the thrill of seeing your youngster unwrap Gibson's glass eye this Christmas. Your little one would probably toss the video games in the trash and quickly take up marbles, schooling all the neighborhood kiddies with his new rock 'n' rolling eyeball marble, thus giving new meaning to kids using the playground insult "You can't see me!"

1. **Jose Lothario's Prosthetic Leg:** Where would Shawn Michaels' career have been without the teachings of one Mr. Jose Lothario? He wouldn't have a leg to stand on. Literally. Such was the case back in the day when Sid Vicious ripped off poor Jose's prosthetic leg and attempted to beat Shawn with it. We abhor such violence and long for the day when the leg finds its way up for auction. Just imagine all the day-to-day uses for it. You say you've got a worn-out window that just won't stay open during the summer? Don't let yourself be a potential victim of heat stroke; just prop Jose's leg in the windowsill and ensure you'll receive enough cool breeze to survive until the fall months. Got a pesky horsefly that is too big to be killed by the average flyswatter? Stop that awful pest's buzzing with a swift swing of the "Super Sock's" plastic limb. Or maybe you

could fashion it with a light bulb and shade and have the wrestling version of *A Christmas Story* sitting in your front window. That trophy is a leg up on all others.

Conversely, there are also items you kind of wish never had been offered. This is especially true if you are a parent with a child who loves watching action inside the squared circle. Because let's face it — today's wrestling isn't the same type of family entertainment that geezers like the authors of this book grew up watching. Don't believe us? Then check out . . .

THE 4 PIECES OF WRESTLING MEMORABILIA OFFERED UP FOR AUCTION ON WWE.COM THAT YOU DON'T WANT YOUR KID TO HAVE

4. **Candice Michelle's Wet 'n' Wild Used Bucket:** Allow us to quote from the actual listing on this site, if we may: "When Torrie Wilson and Candice Michelle compete in a Wet 'n' Wild match, it's something that nobody wants to miss. We had a chance to catch up with Candice after the match and get her to sign the bucket that she used in the match. This is the exact bucket that was used in her match on the 6/12/06 episode of *Raw*. Place your bid today on this hot item that was used to cool off two of the hottest Divas in the WWE." Damn is that lame. Here's what we would have had for a description: "When Torrie Wilson and Candice Michelle compete in a Wet 'n' Wild match, it's something you probably want to miss. After all, there's a big world of porn out there on the Internet, and instead of watching two women spray each other with water, in vain hopes of seeing a slightly less obscured nipple, you could watch full-on penetration with just a few keystrokes. To that end, you'd probably want a bucket to catch all

your bodily excretions. Place your bid today on this item that can do just that." Wait a minute . . . WWE got someone to pay $269? For a *bucket*? Never mind.

3. **Trish Moppy:** In his prime in the late 1990s, Perry Saturn was quite the wrestler. However, in May of 2001, during a preliminary match with a guy by the name of Mike Bell, Saturn went loco following a missed spot and began to legitimately beat the crap out of his job-berly opponent. Officials were not pleased, and decided if Saturn wanted to go insane, they'd let him do just that by giving him the worn-out "crazy man" gimmick. To his credit, Saturn just rolled with the punches, blathering out nonsense like "Doggies eat applesauce to save the ozone layer. You're welcome!" If that weren't sufficient for a stay at Bellevue, he soon began talking to a mop, a mop appropriately enough named Moppy. Soon he started a love affair with Moppy, and the two became an item. Sadly, his ex-girlfriend (and non-mop, although she was almost as skinny as the pole that held Moppy's head aloft) Terri decided to join forces with the nefarious Raven, and the pair was able to mopnap Moppy and toss her into a woodchipper. Just when it seemed Saturn would never recover, Trish Stratus gave him a new mop, with a face that looked just like her own. Parents, take note — stuff like this is why you need to NetNanny WWE.com right off your kids' computers. You never know when they might spot a mop with Trish's head on it, and you'd wind up with a $202.50 WWE.com purchase on your MasterCard.

2. **Diva Bras and Panties:** You'll note we didn't name any particular Diva's bras and/or panties here. Because let's face it, if you're buying them,

you're not purchasing them for your girlfriend or grandma to wear. They're not presents. They're not something you're going to hang on the wall. If we may, let us be blunt: you're buying them as a jerk rag. In fact, we're shocked that WWE doesn't do some kind of deal with Jergens to include a free sample bottle of lotion in the package. Honestly, we know exactly what is going on here: you're buying them, groping them and rubbing them on your genitals, all the while saying, "Oh yeah, Mickie . . . these were on your boobies! Let me lift your tail and be your little love stallion!" Oh, and if you bought a piece of Diva lingerie and even think of denying this, come on . . . just preferably not on us.

1. **The Katie Vick Cheerleader Outfit:** The saga of Katie Vick, in which Kane was accused of having a necrophiliac relationship with a deceased cheerleader, was easily the most idiotic storyline in the history of professional wrestling. In fact, it was one of those things that made you uneasy to even *admit* you were a wrestling fan. Want something even more bothersome? How about the fact that WWE would later offer up for auction the outfit the mannequin wore? Not only would you get the skirt, the top and the tube socks, but even the pom-poms were included. Oh, yeah . . . for all you perverts that bought item No. 2 listed above? Sho' nuff, this little ensemble came with Katie's bra and no fewer than four sets of panties. Let us recap here — it came with a bra and panties that a mannequin wore in a necrophilia wrestling skit. Whoever bought this crap is without question the sickest, dirtiest, filthiest, scummiest, most mentally damaged individuals in the history of man. The guys who bought this crap are. . . .

Two anonymous WrestleCrap authors and everyone's favorite dead, cheerleading mannequin, Katie Vick.

Kind of makes you want to drop this book and go wash your hands, no?

9

And So It Comes to This: The 25 Worst Characters in Wrestling History

We started this book with a chapter on characters, and we end it with another. But unlike every other chapter in this literary classic, this has but one list. Rest assured, however, it's the big one.

When you run a Web site that fancies itself the foremost authority on the very worst of pro wrestling, and you write a book with the word *WrestleCrap* in the title, you get asked the same freaking question over and over and over again: What the hell is wrong with you, you nerd?

Oh, and you also get this one: What was the single worst gimmick you've ever seen?

And we're damn sick of answering it.

So here, today, finally, in print, we answer that question. In fact, we have compiled not just the single worst — but the twenty-five worst — characters ever, just so we will never, ever have to answer that stupid question again. Here goes.

25. George Ringo: When one thinks of the world's most famous rock 'n' roll quartet, the Beatles, probably the furthest thing from one's mind is violence. That is, unless your name was Bob Sabre, a veteran grappler from Chicago who, in the 1960s, adopted a moppy-looking Beatles haircut, picked up a six-string guitar and was off to start his own "British Invasion" — in AWA wrestling rings — as George Ringo, the Wrestling Beatle. What was Bob thinking? Was he tripping on too much "Lucy in the Sky with Diamonds"? To be fair, it wasn't poor Bob's fault; we have to blame Dick the Bruiser for this one, as he came up with the gimmick when he should have just "let it be." Ahem. Thankfully, before Verne Gagne had a chance to jump on the Beatles bandwagon, becoming John Paul and staging a nude protest with Yoko Oh No (played by any hairy, annoying AWA woman wrestler of the time), Ringo had become enhancement talent and stepped away from the ring a few years later.

24. **The Candyman:** Poor Brad Armstrong. One of the most gifted wrestlers of our generation, he was plagued throughout his career with a terminal case of "gimickitis," a virus the likes of which had previously only been diagnosed flowing through the bloodstream of Ed Leslie. Besides portraying bad stoner rip-offs of his brother, goofy masked tagalong of the Fabulous Freebirds, a Spider-Man wannabe and Master P's "keepin' it real gangsta" BA, there was this sweet morsel of a gimmick from 1990. Brad, dressed in candy-cane-striped tights, was stuck with the gimmick of being a "kinder, gentler pedophile." On his way to the ring, a happy-go-lucky Brad waved to everybody, flashed his pearly whites and tossed candy out to the youngsters in the crowd. Yes, you read that right. In a booking discussion with Ole Anderson and various other people trying to devise a character for the returning Armstrong, the best idea any of those schmucks could come up with was, "I don't know what the fuck to do with him. Have him throw candy to the

kids." Unfortunately, this gimmick didn't last long enough for the Candyman to get his own talk-show segment, which we have no doubt would have been entitled "Talking to Strangers."

23. **The Artist Formerly Known as Prince Iaukea:** Unquestionably one of the greatest and most eccentric musical acts of our generation was the legendary Prince. What child of the '80s doesn't remember his big, chart-topping hits like "1999," "Let's Go Crazy" and "When Doves Cry"? But somewhere along the way, Prince's popularity declined, and after becoming disenchanted with his record company and the music business in general, he changed his name to a symbol and declared himself "the artist formerly known as Prince." A few years later in WCW, a disenchanted ex-WCW Television champion Prince Iaukea and new WCW writer Vince Russo decided to steal Prince's entire gimmick, note for note, in a worldwide global wrestling trek that can best be described as the Prince Iaukea: When Crowds Cry Spring/Summer Tour '00. Iaukea did the imitation to the proverbial T, wearing the same bizarre hats, striking lewd poses and displaying a love for all things purple. Along for the ride in Iaukea's crappy red Corvette was Sharmell Sullivan, who went by the name Paisley in homage to Prince's Paisley Park recording studio. WCW had hoped for a *Purple Rain*-like success, but what they got in return was more like *Under the Cherry Moon*, Prince's second movie, which you have probably never even heard of. Despite a brief run with the WCW Cruiserweight title, Iaukea's "purple reign" would best be described by some trendy music magazine as a "no-hit blunder."

22. **Blackblood:** Billy Jack Haynes. Just reading that name makes us want to kidnap the nearest wrestling midget, dress him as a leprechaun —

oh, wait, we forgot: most wrestling midgets actually come predressed as leprechauns and travel up to the Pacific Northwest, where they can spend the days frolicking in the fields, picking four-leaf clovers and getting drunk off of Mickey's Malt Liquor. That's the kind of Irish spirit Oregon's Billy Jack Haynes used to bring to the wrestling world. In 1991, though, he decided to piss in our box of Lucky Charms when he did the Irish equivalent of Hulk Hogan taking off the yellow and red and joining the nWo — he moved from Oregon to a little town in France and traded in his trademark black hat with yellow trim for an executioner's hood and a battle ax. Yes, a battle ax, which brings up a point we've always wondered about. Why do some guys carry weapons like axes and chainsaws to the ring? We've heard of "one fall to a finish" matches, but we've yet to encounter a single "one amputee to a finish" stipulation. WCW, not wanting Blackblood to be responsible for their having a three-limbed gimp as its world champion, quickly gave Blackblood an ax of his own — the ax of termination.

21. **Bastion Booger:** Mike Shaw was never one of the more handsome men in wrestling. In fact, his stints as Makkun Singh, Norman the Lunatic and Trucker Norm were gross enough to make most female wrestling fans sterile. But Shaw saved his worst for last. Actually, we should say that the WWF saved Shaw's worst for last, having him become Bastion Booger. No subtlety on display here; he was pretty much exactly what you would imagine when you hear the name "Bastion Booger" — a fat, slovenly pig of a man who liked to fart and burp and generally be the world's biggest slob. They even went so far as to create an outfit for Shaw in which his massive back fat was squeezed together to make a hump. He worked as a heel, which,

believe it or not, was probably the wrong move. Keep in mind that during the early-1990s period in which Booger slimed WWF rings, the company still primarily catered to a children's audience. As Shaw himself put it in an interview with *Slam! Wrestling*, "Think they could have gone to a comical character with it, almost like the Norman character. Because kids liked screaming Booger, it was almost like they were swearing and getting away with it." Amazingly, Bastion Booger was actually better than the original idea for Shaw, which was to be a gargoyle from the sewers. Maybe kids screaming "Booger!" wouldn't have been so bad after all.

20. **Repo Man:** On principle, the idea of a wrestler who repossesses objects isn't that bad. After all, there's nothing scarier than missing a few payments on your car and having some 300-pound guy who looks like he was a stuntman in the movie *Deliverance* come to your neighborhood in the middle of the night and peel out of the driveway in your new Lexus. When said repo man walks, talks and dresses like some B-level villain from *Scooby Doo*, mixed with a dash of Frank Gorshin's *Batman* villain, the Riddler, well, out the window goes all potential for getting over. The man behind the Repo Man's Lone Ranger-style mask was longtime veteran grappler Barry Darsow, most notable for his run as Smash of the WWF championship tag team Demolition. To be fair, Darsow, when given any goofy character (and he had tons of them, such as Stewart Pain, evil golfer), played the part to the hilt. No matter how dumb the idea was, he made it fun to watch because he just went so completely over the top you couldn't take your eyes off the train wreck. In the case of the Repo Man, said locomotive catastrophe took the form of a series of

vignettes in which he would repossess stuff from deadbeats, even if they were just a day late on their payments. Probably the greatest of these segments had him repossessing a kid's bicycle. He walked up, basically told the child, "Look over there," and then hopped on it and rode it away. He himself would also ride off into the sunset just a year or so later, no doubt on a twelve-year-old's Schwinn.

19. **KISS Demon:** KISS cofounder and businessman extraordinaire Gene Simmons is a master at making the almighty dollar. Whether it is the marketing of KISS condoms, KISS French ticklers, KISS caskets or KISS garden fertilizer, consisting of factory-processed particles of Gene's own feces (trust us, he will have it for sale someday), the man is a businessman's businessman. So it should come as no surprise that when Eric Bischoff was blowing Ted Turner's money left and right during WCW's heyday, Gene took up the offer to make a buck off of a licensed KISS wrestler. We can only imagine the origin of this idea, with Eric throwing down some Jack Daniels and playing air guitar to "Detroit Rock City" and thinking, "Whoa . . . a KISS wrestler would totally kick ass!" Okay, the idea probably didn't come about in a drunken stupor. But it would have been a good excuse. By the time Eric had recovered from his '70s-flashback moment, it was too late. KISS had already done a guest appearance on *Nitro*, playing some songs for a crowd that was more accustomed to the Limp Bizkit-style rap-rock of the time. The ratings for the segment were not good, and the company was rumored to have thrown anywhere from a quarter- to a half-million out the window.

The worst was yet to come, however, as the band had also licensed a wrestler to the company, and thus the KISS Demon, portrayed originally by Brian Adams, debuted arising from his slumber in a Gene

Simmons-style coffin. Seeing the reaction from the crowd, the company put the idea on the shelf for six months. But the contract with the band stated that the Demon was to be a main-eventer, and Simmons wouldn't let it lie. So back came the Demon, this time portrayed by Dale Torborg, who engaged in such riveting angles as feuding with Norman Smiley, because the screamin' one had messed around with the Demon's coffin. Come to think of it, that may have been a deleted scene from *KISS Meets the Phantom of the Park*.

18. **Papa Shango:** In wrestling the viewer is often required to suspend disbelief. However, when Charles Wright took to the ring in his guise as Papa Shango, a demented voodoo worshipper, you were required not only to suspend disbelief, but to take it around the side of the building and bash its skull in with a tire iron. Papa Shango was everything you'd want in a wrestling voodoo man: big hat, furry coat adorned with skulls, white face paint and billows of smoke. Lots and lots and lots of smoke. And mirrors, too, we should probably add. You see, a large part of the Shango character was the black magic he employed, spells that caused a jobber's hand to catch on fire and black goo to ooze from his head. One time Papa Shango even made the Ultimate Warrior vomit on-screen. And here we thought he was just watching a replay of one of his own matches. Wright would eventually ditch Shango and become something even more magical: an honest-to-God wrestling pimp, the hemp-smoking Godfather, complete with hos — a huge hit for the WWF during its peak late-1990s run.

17. **Outback Jack:** The mid-1980s saw a huge boom in the U.S. for all things Australian, due in large part to the mainstream success of Paul

Hogan in *Crocodile Dundee* and the vegemite-sandwich-fueled tunes of Men at Work. So it should come as little shock that the WWF attempted to hop aboard the Aussie Express with a character from the land down under, one Outback Jack. Portrayed by a legit Aussie by the name of Peter Stilsbury, Jack was introduced to fans in a never-ending series of television vignettes in which he roamed his native land hanging out with Aborigines and drinking beer with cows. No joke — one skit actually showed him in a bar with a bovine, downing some Foster's. You'd think a guy who got liquored up with Elsie would get over huge, but you'd be wrong: the Aussie fad left as quickly as it came, and Jack went back to his homeland of Humpty Doo.

16. **Who:** In a world where celebrities are often enticed to make cameos in the ring, we're almost wishing that our No. 16 entry chronicled a wrestling appearance from Pete Townsend and Roger Daltrey. Sadly, it doesn't. Instead, the masked character Who (Jim Neidhart) was a play on the old "Who's on first?" bit made famous by Abbott and Costello. Basically, the pair are talking about a baseball game in which a man named "Who" is playing first base. Hilarity ensues when the two bicker for twenty-five minutes as to what the guy's name really is. Like this:

Costello: Who's on first?

Abbott: Yes.

Costello: I mean the fellow's name.

Abbott: Who.

Costello: The guy on first.

Abbott: Who.

Costello: The first baseman.

Abbott: Who.

Costello: The guy playing—

Abbott: Who is on first!

Sound funny? No, wait, scratch that. Sound like a good idea to base a wrestling character on? No, of course not. That got old just typing it. Now imagine listening to it on WWF TV for four weeks straight. Now don't, because even those guys got sick of it, and it was mercifully killed very quickly.

15. **Duke Droese:** Hailing from Mount Trashmore, here's "more trash" from the WWF's creative department, this time in the form of Duke "the Dumpster" Droese. He was a wrestling garbageman. He would bring a trash can to the ring and yell, "It's time to take out the trash!" Indeed it is, need we really say more? Next!

14. **Isaac Yankem, DDS:** Now, we might've been able to buy into the idea of a wrestling garbageman; those guys tend to be big and bulky, while possessing a little toughness to keep tossing that stinky garbage around week after week. But a wrestling dentist? One who comes down to the ring to the annoying sounds of a dentist's drill as his theme music? It appears someone in creative must've been inhaling too much nitrous oxide. Nevertheless, in the summer of 1995, Jerry "the King" Lawler enlisted the help of his favorite dentist, Dr. I. Yankem (played by Glen "Kane" Jacobs), to help him in his feud against Bret Hart. The reasoning behind these guys forming a partnership? A week or two earlier, Hart had bested Lawler in a "Kiss My Foot" match, which saw the Hitman shove the King's foot right into his own mouth. This caused Lawler all sorts of dental damage, and so the King visited

his dentist and discovered him to be an evil man who loved to make people scream. Why, exactly, Lawler chose a dentist who liked to cause pain is anyone's guess. Why, exactly, the WWF thought this would make for good television is also anyone's guess.

13. **Super Duper Mario:** If you ever wondered if silly gimmicks were the sole property of WCW and the WWF, oh no. No no no no no, a thousand times no. Stupid stuff like this exists in every wrestling promotion on the planet, no matter how large or small it might be, no matter where it's located. With this in mind, does it shock anyone that Donkey Kong's nemesis Super Mario graced rings? Wait, scratch that. It wasn't Super Mario — it was Super *Duper* Mario, a competitor in the old International Championship Wrestling. And he looked exactly like you would hope a guy named Super Duper Mario would look, with the hat, the overalls and the little hammer, just in case any flaming barrels might happen to come rolling his way in the midst of a match. This stinker of a gimmick also had a stinker of an ending, as the guy behind ICW, Tony Atlas, thought it would be funny to have the poor guy defecate in the ring and thus never be heard from again. Sorry, Mario, but our toilet paper is in another castle.

12. **Dink the Clown:** One term that could aptly describe all the antics that go on in the world of professional wrestling would be *circus*. In 1993, fans shuddered when the WWF actually became part circus, with the introduction of Doink the Clown. Honestly, the idea of a wrestling clown has about as much potential for disaster as an alcoholic tightrope walker, but unbelievably the WWF — and more precisely, Doink's alter ego, Matt Borne — made it work. You see, Doink was not just any

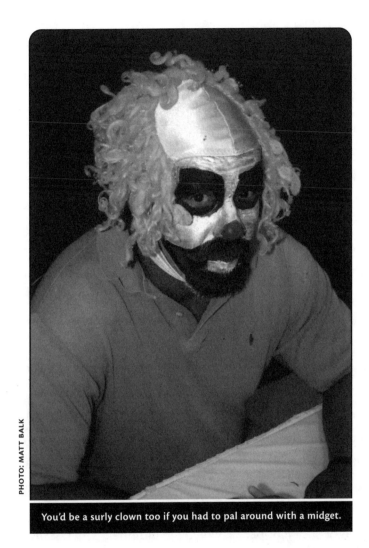

PHOTO: MATT BALK

You'd be a surly clown too if you had to pal around with a midget.

clown, no siree. He was an *evil* clown, who came down to the ring with demonic, circus-themed music that would make Freddy Krueger wake up screaming for Mommy. Ever the crowd-pleaser, Doink always took time to pop balloons in kid's faces (with a lit cigar, no less) or throw water or other wet and slimy substances on people. And it got mega-heat on the clown. Among Vince McMahon's greatest successes, we'd have to include this — successfully getting a wrestling clown over was the equivalent of turning feces into filet mignon. However, Doink met the same fate as every great heel before or after him: the bookers decided to take all the pops he got as a heel and repackage him as a babyface, in an attempt to get Doink even more over.

Note to promoters — unless your wrestler's name is Steve Austin or Roddy Piper, don't attempt this number too frequently, as most times it fails. Especially if the face turn entails the wrestler hooking up with a midget clone of himself. And thus we got Dink, the smiling, happy, waving-to-the-crowd Mini-Me clone of Doink. And it sucked. Sucked sucked sucked sucked sucked. All the wind was immediately taken from Doink's sails, and the impossible idea of a wrestling clown being hot popped just like a balloon snuffed out by a cigar.

11. T.L. Hopper: You want to know why the WWF was on the verge of going bankrupt in the mid-'90s? Some may say bad business ideas, and even worse booking. We've got better reasoning. Vince McMahon, Pat Patterson and everyone else at WWF Headquarters were obviously abducted by aliens in the middle of the night and replaced by thoughtless pod people, à la *Invasion of the Body Snatchers*. That is our sanest explanation for why in the brown hell they ever introduced the character of T.L. Hopper, a wrestling plumber. *A wrestling plumber.* Obviously the WWF's business at the time was going down the shitter, but a fictional plumber was not going to help unclog the dark and murky situation they had fallen into.

10. Mantaur: Half-man. Half-bull. All shit. This was apparently the formula in 1995 when the WWF introduced the world to Mantaur, a

400-pound beast managed by Jim Cornette. And what an outfit his protegé had, featuring not only painted horns on his head, but a giant bull head that looked for all the world like something you'd see at Disney World. Honest to God, you could look into his mouth and see the poor guy's eyes. And what did Mantaur do once his head-gear was removed? Well, according to wikipedia.com, "Mantaur's arsenal included charging, mauling and mooing at his opponents." Apparently in the mid-90s WWF, a moo was an offensive weapon. Which sadly defeated no opponent.

9. Yeti: When compiling this Top 25 list of all-time worst gimmicks, we ran into a slight problem — what to do about the Dungeon of Doom? Ah yes, arguably every member would've been worthy of inclusion in this countdown, taking up half the spots in the process. Therefore, we're going to limit them and take an Oscar-like approach to who gets the glory of being the worst of the worst. Ed Leslie's schizophrenic portrayal of a living pair of black-and-white Zubaz known as the Zodiac? The original man-eating leprechaun, Braun? The caked-in-flour, screaming-like-banshees leader of the bunch, King Curtis? The Shark, who claimed his eating habits consisted of dining on Hulkamaniacs? While antics such as looking like a bipolar idiot, screaming like a temper-tantrum-throwing baby and straight-up cannibalism were all good enough to get us to change the channel to *Monday Night Raw*, the distinction of being the worst of the worst must go to one man, and one man only. Accepting the award for the Dungeon of Doom is . . . Yeti. Truly fitting for this group, Yeti was a mythical creature who made his debut by breaking out of a giant block of ice. Yes, a block of ice. It gets better. What emerged appeared to be the world's largest mummy, a seven-foot guy draped from head to toe in toilet paper. He proceeded to shamble down to the ring, where fellow heel the Giant had Hulk Hogan trapped in a bear hug. Deciding to "help out," he snuck behind the Hulkster and began what can only be described as dry-humping the poor guy's ass. So, while all the other goofs in the Dungeon were just that — goofs — none had the combination of ice/toilet paper/anal-raping action the Yeti embodied.

8. **Giant Gonzales:** There was, on the television screens and in our hearts, only one true giant of professional wrestling. Andre the Giant was the first larger-than-life behemoth most of us saw wrestle, and the rest that have come since — even those who were actually taller than Andre in his prime — have fallen way short of his achievements. Andre overcame the inability to put on five-star technical master-pieces due to his massive size by having the charm to woo a crowd and keep them entertained in a simple, yet enjoyable, manner. And what of the seven-foot-plus big men since then? Well, quite frankly they've almost all sucked. And at No. 8 is the worst of the worst, Giant Gonzales. The poster boy for horrid wrestling giants, Gonzales was no different than any other giant shoved down our throats since the '90s. Most could barely speak English, and all lumbered around the ring with an arsenal of moves outnumbered by the colors of the rainbow. Could the seven-foot-seven Gonzales compensate for that with an uncanny ability to dazzle a crowd? Put it this way: if mosquitoes relied on sucking charisma to survive, they would die an instantaneous death upon biting our oversized buddy. To their credit, most bookers can recognize a lack of charisma and attempt to disguise it with an eye-catching outfit. Look at the other personality-

impaired giants of the era. The Yeti had his coat of 1,119 rolls of Charmin. Giant Silva and Kurrgan rocked their hippie-dippy Oddity tie-dyes. Gonzales's previous character in WCW, El Gigante, walked around with tin foil on his head that looked like it was salvaged from

PHOTO: JEFF COHEN

That is one giant, GIANT ass.

a Jiffy Pop container Dusty Rhodes had just consumed, making it the only time in history a Jiffy Pop product failed to register a pop.

As much an eyesore as these three colossal wardrobe disasters were, they all paled in comparison to the horror that was Giant Gonzales: Naked Bigfoot Exhibitionist. Yes, from the minds that allowed you to see a wrestling plumber's ass crack came the naked wrestling sasquatch. Wearing tights that featured airbrushed muscles, Gonzales seemed like he was practically naked, save for a few patches of fake fur sewn onto his forearms, shoulders and crotch. Amazingly, though, his bare ass was left . . . well, bare. Seriously, they had the guy out there before the crowd with a backside outfitted with an airbrushed ass. Not sure about anyone else, but seeing that gave us the uncomfortable feeling of being forced to stare into the boy's high school locker room during showers. So the next time you're bored to tears by the Great Khali, just be grateful that, unlike Gonzales, he's wearing pants and not making a literal ass out of himself.

7. **Shockmaster:** When some gimmicks are introduced, you pretty much know they are destined to fall on their face — as in the case of the Shockmaster. Literally. Pity poor Fred Ottman. The man who had previously been cast with the awful role of being a human boat (Tugboat) no doubt thought his fortunes were turning as he entered WCW and was positioned to be a key babyface alongside such top stars as Sting and Davey Boy Smith. Instead, he gave us the most infamous blunder in wrestling history. On a live *Clash of the Champions* broadcast, Ottman was set to make his grand debut. The outfit was questionable: a sleeveless leather trench coat, acid-washed jeans and a *Star Wars* Stormtrooper mask painted powder blue, complete with glitter. Think

gay *Urban Cowboy* meets *Return of the Jedi*, and that's pretty much the deal. That would have been a tough sell to the crowd. He never even got the chance, however. In a scene that has since become an Internet download favorite, Ottman burst through a fake wall . . . and fell flat on his face, tumbling to the ground like a broken Weeble. Even commentator Jesse Ventura couldn't keep a straight face, letting loose with "What an entrance by the Shockmaster!" before laughing for five straight minutes. To its credit, WCW realized the folly of its ways and repacked Ottman as lovable Uncle Fred, whose gimmick was that he was clumsy. Shockingly (pun fully intended), this didn't get over, either.

6. **Saba Simba:** Our No. 6 entry is proof positive that there are actually eleven commandments in the Bible. Sure there are the usual ten suspects, but you should also add this one — "Thou shall not piss Vince McMahon off and then come begging for your job back later." Otherwise, your destiny may end up like that of Tony Atlas. Possessing one of the greatest builds in the history of the sport, Atlas was well-deserving of his nickname "Mr. U.S.A." But like Sergeant Slaughter and Jimmy "Superfly" Snuka before him, Atlas found himself on the outs with the WWF, right as it began its rise in mainstream popularity. After toiling in the indies and battling various personal issues, Atlas showed back up in the WWF in 1990. And what an idea the company had for him: he was to become Saba Simba, the backstory being that he had rediscovered his African roots. Or maybe *Roots*, as in the television show; Simba would appear to crowds barefoot and hopping around as though dancing on hot coals. With his giant spear and shield, he looked for all the world like an extra from a Johnny Weissmuller *Tarzan* flick. After seeing Saba Simba do his "dancing on

hot coals" bit, we're left wondering — hey, Tony, is collecting unemployment checks really that bad?

5. **Beaver Cleavage:** The vaunted Attitude era was built, in many ways, on a level of crudity never before seen in wrestling. You had guys flipping the bird, women nearly naked in the ring and guys telling each other to "suck it." It was a time that saw pro wrestling evolve from the Hulk Hogan superhero era of the '80s to programming content in the late '90s that gave *Cinemax After Dark* a run for its money in terms of sleaziness. With such groundbreaking material flowing amongst the bookers, the WWF inexplicably showed the kind of booking stupidity that got them into the near-death hole they were in before the likes of "Stone Cold" Steve Austin and D-Generation X revived them. Going retro in wrestling usually means bringing someone or something back that was popular from a decade earlier. Leave it to Vince Russo to go ultra-retro, by going back not just one decade, but several, when it came time to create a brand-new star: Harry "Beaver" Cleavage. Introduced via retro black-and-white-television style, sexual innuendo-filled vignettes that featured his "mother," Mrs. Cleavage (with highlights such as Mrs. Cleavage wiping Beaver's messy face after a meal, saying, "Nobody likes a sloppy Beaver"), it would prove to be the first new gimmick to fail during the WWF's resurgence. After only one wrestling appearance on *Raw* after weeks of hype, the ex-Headbanger Chaz publicly dropped the gimmick in a backstage skit, stating point-blank that it just wasn't working. He went back to wrestling under his real name and brought his "mother," real-life girlfriend Marianna Komlos, along for the ride. Following this revamping, the duo did little of note, short of a fantastically taste-

less angle in which Marianna falsely accused Chaz of physical abuse. And no, shockingly, they did not re-rename him "Beat-her Cleavage."

4. **Black Scorpion:** When Sting captured his first WCW World Heavyweight Championship from Ric Flair at WCW's *Great American Bash '90*, it signaled the dawn of a new era for the rasslin' business down south. WCW began to steer away from the previous decade of Flair's technical dominance, heading toward building the company around a Hulk Hogan/Superman-like babyface character to lead them into the the '90s. In turning to the young, face-painted surfer dude, they hoped to increase pay-per-view buys, as well as drive up toy and T-shirt sales in the youth demographic. After feuding on and off with Flair for the better part of two years, head booker Ole Anderson needed to provide Sting with an equally fresh and vibrant opponent if he was to match the popularity of the WWF champion at that time, the Ultimate Warrior. One slight problem: Ole didn't have a single person for Sting to face in a long series of matches. In a perfect world, or in the wettest dry dream a wrestling booker could have, Ole would acquire the services of the current WWF champion Warrior and bring him in to face Sting in an epic clash. Ah, a man can dream, can't he? Nothing wrong with that, right? Well, it is wrong when you decide to make that dream a reality. Again, Ole did this despite the fact the Warrior was under contract to the WWF. Not really knowing who would play the character, Ole went ahead and introduced the world to the Black Scorpion, a mysterious figure claiming to be from Sting's past, with a hope that by the time the Scorpion was revealed, he could get the Warrior to join WCW to take the role. It was a plan that made as much sense as a losing NFL team like the Detroit Lions or Houston Texans changing

their entire playbook around in the preseason, just in case Peyton Manning's multimillion-dollar contract suddenly became null and void, and he wanted to jump on a sinking ship of a football team. That scenario would never happen in a million years. Likewise, the Warrior stayed with the WWF, and WCW was back where it started: with no clue who would portray the Scorpion, or where to take the angle, which had already been playing out on television for weeks, with Ole himself portraying the mysterious figure quite literally shrouded in darkness, cutting voicebox-enhanced promos that made zero sense. At this point, Ole chose to turn the Scorpion into a rent-a-magician. Literally. The company hired a magician to perform a series of skits. The Scorpion's black-magic repertoire included such mystic feats as turning "wrestling fans" (actually plants) into tigers and grabbing female stagehands and teleporting across the arena with them. When he was done abducting female employees, David Cop-a-feel was ready for his grand finale: the main event of *Starrcade '90*, in which he would duel with the Stinger in a title vs. mask encounter. And what an entrance he had planned for the folks, arriving at the arena via a spaceship. So now he was apparently an astronaut in addition to being a magician. To be fair, said "spaceship" was a prop you might see in a grade-school production of *E.T.*, so perhaps he was an art teacher in addition to being a magician. With no one else to turn to, WCW had Ric Flair go under the guise of the Scorpion that night, ultimately losing and unmasking to Sting, and then doing the only magic trick the Black Scorpion ever did right — disappearing off of the face of the earth.

3. **Ding Dongs:** In the summer of 1989, WCW executive Jim Herd came up with a brilliant idea: create a Saturday-morning cartoon-like tag

team that all the young kids would fall in love with. After all, wrestling fans vary in age and, at that point, WCW was still making the transition from the traditional ways of the NWA and grasping the concept of "sports entertainment." With the bulk of the roster appealing to your basic old-school wrestling fans, why not give little Jimmy a more juvenile-friendly wrestler he can cheer on when he goes to the matches with his older siblings? On paper, Herd wanted a team to amuse the kids. In reality, he got a team whose gimmick could've doubled as a baby-crib jungle gym. A baby-crib jungle gym that couldn't even keep a toddler amused. Yes, direct from Bellville, U.S.A., Jim Herd presents the masked tag team of the Ding Dongs. Clad in the most awful, bright fluorescent orange head-to-toe spandex this side of *Sesame Street*, the Ding Dongs made their national television debut at *Clash of the Champions VII: Guts and Glory.* But they didn't make their debut alone, oh no. Not only did they have illustrated bells sewn onto their suits, they wore bracelets made of bells as well. Not enough? Okay, how about the duo bringing a giant bell — on a stand no less — to the ring. And throughout the entire match, whichever man was outside the ring would ring the bell constantly. The culprits behind this abomination? Longtime jobber Jim Evans played the role of Ding and, Lord knows, we can't forget about his partner in crime, Richard Sartain, who was cast as Dong. Yes, his name was Dong. Out of all the names one could christen a supposed kiddie-themed wrestler, this has to be the all-time worst. And the saddest part? The original idea was for the team to be a pair of Quasimodo wrestlers, with humpbacks. See, that way they could never be pinned, as they'd always have one shoulder off the mat. Maybe a guy named Dong wasn't so bad after all.

2. **Gobbledy Gooker:** While all the previous gimmicks listed have been bad, at least they all had one thing in common — they were human beings. Our top two, though, weren't. One of the most infamous ideas of all time, the Gobbledy Gooker was a bird that hatched out of a giant egg at the *1990 Survivor Series*. Yes, the WWF had a turkey hatch out of an egg in the name of wrestling. Upon incubation, he hopped out of the egg and into the ring, dancing a funky jig with "Mean" Gene Okerlund. The chorus of boos that rained down on Gene and the Gooker was not enough to keep him off television, as the Gookmeister returned for the next few weeks, appearing in promos, culminating with a guest spot on WWF's *All American Wrestling*. Thankfully, the WWF sent the Gooker to some anonymous pen — hopefully a filthy, non-PETA-approved one — only letting him out one more time, for the *WrestleMania XVII* Gimmick Battle Royal.

The Gooker was obviously a horrible idea with even worse execution, but we're not going to sit here and chat about how stupid and unbelievable it was having a turkey hatch out of an egg. But we would like to take a moment and contemplate the egg itself. Let's assume that it is a normal, everyday occurrence for humungous, ten-foot-by-ten-foot prehistoric eggs to just randomly be laid in today's modern society. Forget about Vince having us actually believe a turkey with human legs hatched in a wrestling arena. Vince, please explain to us just who or what supposedly laid that egg. The only rational explanation for the birth of the Gobbledy Gooker is that somewhere out there, there is a Mama Gooker. Judging by the fact that the Gobbledy Gooker was about six feet tall at birth, she's got to be pushing fifty feet tall. And she's probably really pissed off at the wrestling world for the years of abuse her offspring has taken in print and on the

Internet. Please, Vince, wherever you've got the fifty-foot Gooker currently locked up, keep her shackled tight. The last thing we need is her escaping and going on a nationwide rampage, crushing this book's two authors flat, taking a five-star dump on Dave Meltzer's house, and culminating her shenanigans by grabbing TNA's president Dixie Carter, and scaling the WWE Headquarters building in Stamford, Connecticut. And, Vince, if the fifty-foot Gooker doesn't exist, well, we've just written the bulk of the script for WWE Films' first Godzilla/King Kong-style smash-'em-up monster movie.

1. **Red Rooster:** After all the lists in this book, after all the silliness and lunacy, here we are at No. 1, the single worst gimmick in pro wrestling history. It could be argued that any of the previous twenty-four characters could have the right to be called the very worst of the worst. We had characters who tripped, ones who poofed smoke and one with the potential to be arrested for public indecency. But here's one who actually could be found guilty of murder in a federal court. A character idea so bad, it did everything short of embalming the wrestler portraying it and stuffing him into a pine box. Sure the '80s were full of crazy characters, but it was a great time period for finding a good, no-nonsense technical grappler, maintaining that '60s/'70s work ethic in a flashier decade. One such man was Paul W. Taylor III or, as you might know him by his ring name, Terry Taylor.

Or by his career killer's name, the Red Rooster.

Rising to prominence in Bill Watts' Mid-South/UWF territory, Taylor was pegged by many as a potential successor to Ric Flair's throne as the world's greatest technical wrestler. Not only were his movements in the ring clean and crisp, but he also possessed good looks that made female fans swoon. If ever there was a wrestler to come forth who had limitless potential, it was Terry Taylor. And early in his career, he made the most of it. He picked up countless regional belts, eventually reaching the pinnacle of success, the one company that everyone in the business aspires to work for: the World Wrestling Federation.

Little did he know that his dream would become the single worst nightmare in pro wrestling history.

In 1988, a storyline began in which legendary manager Bobby "the Brain" Heenan claimed he was so smart he could make anyone a world champion. He didn't need someone to be seven feet tall, he didn't need someone who could bench-press a Volvo. He just needed someone — anyone — who had tights and the physical ability to get in the ring. And so he hunted down and found just such a schmo, a guy with limited speed, limited size and limited ability: Terry Taylor. In fact, Heenan said Taylor was actually nothing more than his "Little Red Rooster."

What should have been nothing more than a one-off one-liner somehow stuck, and soon enough the name Terry Taylor was gone from WWF television, with commentators openly referring to him as the Red Rooster. The storyline went that Heenan would constantly badger the Rooster, who eventually got fed up and attacked Heenan, which led to a match between the two at *WrestleMania V*. Logic would dictate that the erstwhile Taylor would pummel Heenan, then prove he was not a chicken, but an actual, honest-to-God wrestler, and revert to his original ring name.

But as we've seen throughout this book, logic rarely applies in pro wrestling, and such was the case here. He soon spiked his hair, sprayed it red and came to the ring with music that began with a loud cock-a-doodle-doo. Not only that, but he began to do what we can only describe as "pecking" as he walked to the ring. In an on-air debate with Heenan, he told the world he would embrace being a rooster, and never, ever wanted to be known as Terry Taylor again. Little did he know how prophetic those words would be.

As a babyface, the Red Rooster failed to get over. To be fair, he did get a hell of a reaction when he came to the ring. Unfortunately, that reaction was universal — and loud — laughter. And that mockery was something from which his promising career never recovered.

He went to other places. He changed names. He changed his look. It didn't matter. To fans, he would forever be known as the Red Rooster. His career, which looked to have no limit just a couple of years before, was done.

And that's why the Red Rooster is the single worst character of all time.

Still, we can't help but marvel that the worst two characters in wrestling history were a guy dressed up as a turkey and a guy dressed up as a chicken.

You know what?

Pro wrestling *is* dumb.

But that's why we love it.